A Guidebook of Statistical Software
for the
Social and Behavioral Sciences

N. Clayton Silver
University of Nevada, Las Vegas

James B. Hittner
College of Charleston

D1379544

Allyn and Bacon
Boston · London · Toronto · Sydney · Tokyo · Singapore

Between the time Website information is gathered and then published, it is not unusual for some sites to have closed. Also, the transcription of URLs can result in unintended typographical errors. The publisher would appreciate notification where these occur so that they may be corrected in subsequent editions. Thank you.

Copyright © 1998 by Allyn & Bacon
A Viacom Company
160 Gould Street
Needham Heights, MA 02194

Internet: www.abacon.com
America Online: keyword: College Online

ISBN 0-205-20063-X

Printed in the United States of America

10 9 8 7 6 5 4 3 2 1   01 00 99 98 97

TABLE OF CONTENTS

PREFACE

Because standard statistical packages (e.g., SAS, SPSS, SYSTAT) do not account for every possible research situation, this book was designed to aid those researchers who have statistical problems that these packages do not handle at this time. Our purpose in compiling this book was to provide researchers and data analysts with a compendium of statistical software programs along with the information necessary to obtain the programs. Our book does not represent a tutorial on data analytic procedures nor does it offer a collection of statistical algorithms. Instead, our aim has been to supplement existing texts and statistical resources by providing a sourcebook of statistical software programs. Many of the programs mentioned in this volume augment the standard statistical packages, are peer reviewed in the scientific literature, and are available for either no charge or for a nominal fee. Furthermore, many of these programs include documentation, worked examples, and the actual listing to aid in their friendliness to users. In addition, a sizeable number of the programs are fully executable on a stand alone basis (e.g., a FORTRAN compiler is not needed for many of the "FORTRAN" programs). Therefore, you do not need to be a quantitative psychologist, nor do you need to be proficient in computer programming to use these programs. To facilitate user friendliness of this volume, the programs are listed alphabetically by statistical procedure. Furthermore, we have included both author and key word indices. The key word index should be particularly useful as it allows the reader to cross-reference statistical procedures (e.g., correlation and power). Although the number of entries in this book are by no means exhaustive, we tried to include the most recent versions of programs and those programs that are also integrative of previous programs. Hence, in order to accommodate as many programs as possible, we decided to exclude earlier versions. Moreover, we have attempted to contact the authors to make sure that our information is as up to date as possible. The authors of this book, however, make no claims concerning the feasibility or accuracy of each program mentioned. Yet we believe that acquisition of these programs can only provide your university or organization with the most current tools necessary for data analysis. We sincerely hope that you will find this book helpful in your research or teaching activities.

Acknowledgments

The authors would like to acknowledge Priscilla Levasseur of the College of Charleston and Monica Centeno, Joseph Daluz, Alanna Fowler, Michele Sheremeta, and Kenneth Tubilleja of the University of Nevada, Las Vegas for their help in gathering information for this book. Finally, the authors would also like to thank David C. Howell, University of Vermont, Roger E. Kirk, Baylor University, and Bruce Rind, Temple University, for their constructive comments and service as reviewers.

N. Clayton Silver
University of Nevada, Las Vegas

James B. Hittner
College of Charleston

ADAPTIVE TESTING - BAYESIAN

Title: ALPHATAB: A Lookup Table for Bayesian
Computerized Adaptive Testing

Author: Ralph De Ayala and W.R. Koch

Source: *Applied Psychological Measurement*, 1985, *9*, 326.

Description: This program uses Jensema's (1974) alpha statistic
to calculate Bayesian estimates of ability based on item responses.
A three-way lookup table (ability level by standard error of
estimate by items) is then generated. The only user input consists
of the test items.

Program Name: ALPHATAB

Language: TURBO PASCAL 2.0

Compatibility: IBM PC's and compatibles

Memory Requirements: 512K

Cost of Program: $5 (if you do not send a diskette)

How to obtain a copy of the program:

Send a formatted 3.5" diskette and
a self-addressed, stamped mailer to:

Dr. William R. Koch
Educational Psychology Department
University of Texas at Austin
Austin, TX 78712
e-mail: b.koch@mail.utexas.edu

AGREEMENT

Title: A Generalized Agreement Measure

Author: Kenneth J. Berry and Paul W. Mielke, Jr.

Source: *Educational and Psychological Measurement*, 1990,
          50, 123-125.

Description: The subroutine extends kappa (a measure of
agreement) to multiple judges with any level of measurement. The
output consists of the generalized measure of agreement and its
associated probability value. The user inputs the number of objects
being rated (from 2 to 20), the number of judges (from 2 to 10), the
number of responses (from 1 to 5), and the data. The dimensions
may be changed.

Program Name: AGREE (subroutine)

Language: FORTRAN 77

Compatibility: IBM and UNIX mainframes, IBM PC's and
          compatibles

Memory Requirements: None Specified

Cost of Program: No Charge

How to obtain a copy of the program:

The authors prefer to e-mail the program,
however, you may send a formatted 3.5"
diskette and a self-addressed, stamped mailer to:

Dr. Kenneth J. Berry
Department of Sociology
Colorado State University
Fort Collins, CO 80523
e-mail: berry@lamar.colostate.edu

ALGEBRA CONCEPTS

Title: Algebra Concepts: Volume One

Author: Warren Gamas

Source: *Journal of Computers in Mathematics and Science Teaching,* 1990, *9*, 95-98.

Description: This program is a computer-based learning system that allows individuals to study the following topics: variables and expressions, real numbers, building and solving equations, polynomials, and factoring polynomials. Includes an equation for plotting utility that allows up to x^3 terms and their coefficients to be plotted.

Program Name: Algebra Concepts

Language: BASIC

Compatibility: Versions are available for Macintosh, Apple, and IBM/IBM compatible machines

Memory Requirements: None Specified

Cost of Program: $59.95 for a single computer
$109.95 for a 5-pack
$159.95 for a 10-pack
$359.95 for a 30-pack

How to obtain a copy of the program:

Send a written request and payment to:

Ventura Educational Systems
P.O. Box 425
Grover Beach, CA 93483-0425
e-mail: ventura ES @ aol.com
Phone: 1-800-336-1022

ANALYSIS OF VARIANCE

Title: ONEWAY: A BASIC Program for Computing
ANOVA From Group Summary Statistics

Author: Joseph S. Rossi

Source: *Behavior Research Methods, Instruments, & Computers,*
1988, *20,* 347-348.

Description: This program computes a one-way ANOVA using
summary statistics (e.g., means and standard deviations).
Moreover, the degrees of freedom, measures of effect size
(Cohen's *d*, omega-squared, eta-squared, eta) and a modified *t*
value (Howell, 1982) that is robust to heteroscedasticity are output.

Program Name: ONEWAY

Language: GWBASIC

Compatibility: IBM PC's and compatibles

Memory Requirements: 128K

Cost of Program: No Charge

How to obtain a copy of the program:

Send a formatted 3.5" diskette and
a self addressed, stamped mailer to:

Dr. Joseph S. Rossi
Cancer Prevention Research Center
University of Rhode Island
2 Chafee Rd.
Kingston, RI 02881
e-mail: kzp101@uriacc.uri.edu

ANALYSIS OF VARIANCE - TEACHING

Title: ANOVAGEN: A Data Generation and Analysis of Variance Program for Use in Statistics Courses

Author: Leslie J. Cake and Roy C. Hostetter

Source: *Teaching of Psychology,* 1992, *19,* 185-188.

Description: This program allows the user to generate data sets for six designs (one-, two-, and three-factor between subjects, one- and two-within subjects, and a one-between, one-within mixed design) by providing the number of levels for each variable and their means and standard deviations.   Data are then produced for each student which includes their name, descriptive text, and condition labels, for example. The instructor output includes the ANOVA summary table along with the intermediate steps (e.g., totals and squared totals). Examples of the input and output (both for student and instructor) are found in the article.

Program Name: ANOVAGEN

Language: Microsoft BASIC

Compatibility: IBM PC's and compatibles which use either GW-BASIC or BASICA

Memory Requirements: None Specified

Cost of Program: No Charge

How to obtain a copy of the program:

Send a formatted 3.5" diskette and
a self-addressed, stamped mailer to:

Dr. Leslie Cake or Dr. Roy Hostetter
Department of Psychology
Sir Wilfred Grenfell College
University Drive
Corner Brook, New Foundland
Canada
A2H 6P9
e-mail: lcake@beothuk.swgc.mun.ca
e-mail: rhostett@beothuk.swgc.mun.ca

ANALYSIS OF VARIANCE - TEACHING

Title: A Computer Program That Demonstrates the Difference
Between Main Effects and Interactions

Author: Michael J. Strube and Miriam D. Goldstein

Source: *Teaching of Psychology,* 1995, *22,* 207-208.

Description: This program first provides a description of main
effects and interaction to the student. Practice problems are
provided that illustrate all significant and nonsignificant main
effect and interaction combinations for a 2 x 2 design. Using a
graphical approach, the student varies the height of the bars and
when the student is satisfied with this difference (e.g., a significant
A effect), an ANOVA is conducted. The program provides
feedback as to how to create the desired effect. Finally, a self-test
is provided concerning main effect and interaction interpretation.

Program Name: None Specified

Language: QuickBASIC

Compatibility: IBM PC's and compatibles

Memory Requirements: 32K

Cost of Program: No Charge

How to obtain a copy of the program:

Send a formatted 3.5" diskette and
a self-addressed, stamped mailer to:

Dr. Michael J. Strube
Department of Psychology
Box 1125
Washington University
St. Louis, MO 63130
e-mail: mjstrube@artsci.wustl.edu

ANALYSIS OF VARIANCE - TEACHING

Title: ANOVA Multimedia: A Program for Teaching
ANOVA Designs

Author: Jeffrey Lee Rasmussen

Source: *Teaching of Psychology,* 1996, *23,* 55-56.

Description: This interactive multimedia program provides the user with a tutorial of 10 different ANOVA designs. In particular, there are two examples each of a one-way independent groups design (IGD), a two-way IGD, a subjects x trials repeated measures design (RMD), a subjects by condition by trials RMD, and a subjects/A x B mixed groups design. For each selected design, students are asked to (a) indicate whether an IGD or RMD exists, (b) identify the relevant sources of variance, and (c) indicate the correct degrees of freedom.

Program Name: ANOVA Multimedia

Language: IconAuthor (AimTech Corporation, 1993)

Compatibility: Windows 3.1 or higher on IBM PC's and
compatibles

Memory Requirements: The CD-ROM occupies over 40MB.
The program works for an equivalent
computer using 16MB RAM, 424 MB
hard disk, and 2MB graphics card.

Cost of Program: Variable (ranges from $100 or $150 to over
$1000 depending on the number of requests)

How to obtain a copy of the program:

Although the program is free, the cost of the CD-ROM is based on the number of requests. Few requests range from $100 to $150, whereas if they are mass produced, a single master would cost about $1000 and $2 per disk. For more information, contact:

Dr. Jeffrey Lee Rasmussen
Department of Psychology
Purdue School of Science at Indianapolis
402 North Blackford Street
Indianapolis, IN   46202-3275
e-mail: irhf100@indyvax.iupui.edu

ANALYSIS OF VARIANCE - TEACHING

Title: Demonstrating the Consequences of Violations of Assumptions in Between-Subjects Analysis of Variance

Author: Roberto Refinetti

Source: *Teaching of Psychology,* 1996, *23,* 51-54.

Description: This program demonstrates the consequences of violating the assumption of homoscedasticity in ANOVA using various types of distributions. Hence, using this simulation, the student can determine the robustness of the test. Moreover, this demonstration can be used for equal and unequal sample sizes in order to determine the effect on Type I error.

Program Name: DEMO

Language: Quick BASIC

Compatibility: IBM PC's and compatibles

Memory Requirements: 640K RAM and 10MB hard drive

Cost of Program: No Charge

How to obtain a copy of the program:

Send a formatted 3.5" diskette and
a self-addressed, stamped mailer to:

Dr. Roberto Refinetti
Department of Psychology
College of William & Mary
Williamsburg, VA 23187
e-mail: refine@mail.wm.edu

ANALYSIS OF VARIANCE - TEACHING

Title: ANOVA/TT: Analysis of Variance Teaching Template for Lotus 1-2-3

Author: Max Vercruyssen and James C. Edwards

Source: *Behavior Research Methods, Instruments, & Computers,* 1988, *20,* 349-354.

Description: This program computes an ANOVA (between groups, repeated measures, or mixed designs) and a summary table is provided along with graphs of the interaction. Subsequent tests such as the Tukey WSD are also provided. Limitations to the program include having data for up to 16 observations per cell and equal sample sizes. An example of the output is provided in the article.

Program Name: ANOVA/TT

Language: None Specified

Compatibility: IBM PC's and compatibles; used with Lotus 1-2-3

Memory Requirements: 384K memory and 5.25" floppy disk drive

Cost of Program: $20

How to obtain a copy of the program:

Send a written request and payment to:

Dr. Max Vercruyssen
Department of Psychology
University of Hawaii at Manoa
Honolulu, HI 96822
e-mail: vercruys@hawaii.edu

APPROXIMATE RANDOMIZATION TESTS

Title: SAS Procedures for Approximate Randomization Tests

Author: Ru San Chen and William P. Dunlap

Source: *Behavior Research Methods, Instruments, & Computers,*
1993, *25,* 406-409.

Description: Approximate randomization tests are used when the traditional parametric statistical assumptions of normality and heterogeneity of variance are not met. This program computes the test of the equality of two (or more) means and tests for the significance of a correlation. Onghena and May (1995) in *Behavior Research Methods, Instruments, & Computers* (pages 408-411) have provided modifications to the algorithms of Chen and Dunlap.

Program Name: None Specified

Language: SAS

Compatibility: None Specifed

Memory Requirements: None Specified

Cost of Program: No Charge

How to obtain a copy of the program:

Send a formatted 3.5" diskette and
a self-addressed, stamped mailer to:

Dr. William P. Dunlap
Department of Psychology
Tulane University
New Orleans, LA 70118
e-mail: dunlap@mailhost.tcs.tulane.edu

ASSOCIATION COEFFICIENTS

Title: A Turbo Pascal Program for the Computation of Scale-Dependent Association Coefficients

Author: Stef Decoene

Source: *Behavior Research Methods, Instruments, & Computers,* 1996, *28,* 126-130.

Description: This program computes association coefficients for absolute, ratio, log-ratio, additive, interval, log-interval, ordinal, and nominal scales for nominal, ordinal, or interval variables using formulae by Zegers (1986) and Stine (1989). The input consists of an ASCII file in which the number of judges and number of objects to be judged are contained in no larger than a 100 x 100 matrix. Association coefficients can be obtained for uniform (50 x 50) and nonuniform (e.g., 100 x 50) matrices.

Program Name: SDAC

Language: Turbo Pascal Version 6

Compatibility: IBM PC's and compatibles

Memory Requirements: 640K minimum

Cost of Program: $30

How to obtain a copy of the program:

Send a written request and payment to:

Dr. Stef Decoene
Department of Psychology
Centrum Mathematische Psychologie
Tiensestraat 102
3000 Leuven Belgium
e-mail: stef.decoene@psy.kuleuven.ac.be

ASSOCIATION MEASURES

Title: Program for Computing Measures of Association in Two-Way Contingency Tables

Author: James Arbuckle

Source: *Behavior Research Methods & Instrumentation*, 1979, *11*, 403.

Description: This program computes several measures of association for two-way contingency tables. Two of the measures, namely an estimated product-moment correlation based on the polychoric series (Lancaster & Hamdan, 1964) and a maximum likelihood estimate of the product-moment correlation (Tallis, 1962) yield tetrachoric correlation coefficients that are applicable when the tabled data result from polychotomizing ordinally- or continuously-scaled variables. The program also outputs additional measures of association including Pearson's chi-square test of independence, Pearson's coefficient of contingency, and Tschuprow's coefficient of association.

Program Name: None Specified

Language: FORTRAN IV

Compatibility: Can be modified to run on any system capable of supporting the FORTRAN language.

Memory Requirements: A minimum of 28K is recommended

Cost of Program: No Charge

How to obtain a copy of the program:

The program listing with documentation and sample input and output can be obtained by contacting:

Dr. James Arbuckle
Department of Psychology
Temple University
Philadelphia, PA 19122
e-mail: arbuckle@astro.ocis.temple.edu

ASSOCIATION MEASURES

Title: A Measure of Association for Nominal Independent Variables

Author: Kenneth J. Berry and Paul W. Mielke, Jr.

Source: *Educational and Psychological Measurement*, 1992, *52*, 895-898.

Description: Two subroutines compute a permutation test of significance for the association between a nominal independent variable and a dependent variable that is either nominal, ordinal, or interval. The input consists of the names of the input and output data files, the numbers of dimensions, categories, and sample size in each category.

Program Name: ASSOC

Language: FORTRAN 77

Compatibility: IBM and UNIX mainframes, IBM PC's and compatibles

Memory Requirements: None Specified

Cost of Program: No Charge

How to obtain a copy of the program:

The authors prefer to e-mail the program, however, you may send a formatted 3.5" diskette and a self-addressed, stamped mailer to:

Dr. Kenneth J. Berry
Department of Sociology
Colorado State University
Fort Collins, CO 80523
e-mail: berry@lamar.colostate.edu

AVERAGING

Title: An Excel Macro for Transformed and Weighted Averaging

Author: Stanley A. Klein

Source: *Behavior Research Methods, Instruments, & Computers,* 1992, *24,* 90-96.

Description: This program averages data in a number of different ways from an Excel spreadsheet. These processes include a weighted average in order to decrease the influence of outliers, providing power or log transformations (other transformations are possible), and a heterogeneity factor. The output includes the average, standard error, and chi-square goodness-of-fit test, and plots of the data. The macro program listing is found in Figure 3 in the article.

Program Name: None Specified

Language: EXCEL (macro)

Compatibility: IBM PC's and compatibles and Macintosh

Memory Requirements: None Specified

Cost of Program: No Charge

How to obtain a copy of the program:

Mention whether you want either an IBM or Macintosh version.

Send a formatted 3.5" diskette and a self-addressed, stamped mailer to:

Dr. Stanley A. Klein
School of Optometry
University of California
Berkeley, CA 94720
email: klein@garnet.berkeley.edu

BAYES ESTIMATES

Title: A Program for Monotonizing Two Empirical Bayes Estimators in Binomial and Hypergeometric Data Distributions

Author: Miao-Hsiang Lin, Chao A. Hsiung, and Chin-Fu Hsiao

Source: *Psychometrika*, 1994, *59*, 423-424.

Description: This program computes monotonized versions of two empirical approximate Bayes estimators (one for the binomial distribution and one for the hypergeometric distribution) which are useful for determining the expected value of a probability distribution function associated with a series of domain test score items. Input consists of the examinees' test score data, the number of test items, and the number of domain items. Output includes the test score values, their associated relative frequency counts, and the nonmonotonized and monotonized Bayes estimators under the binomial and hypergeometric distributions.

Program Name: None Specified

Language: FORTRAN

Compatibility: VAX/VMS mainframes, IBM PC's and compatibles

Memory Requirements: None Specified

Cost of Program: No Charge

How to obtain a copy of the program:

Send a formatted 3.5" diskette and a self-addressed, stamped mailer to:

Dr. Miao-Hsiang Lin
Institute of Statistical Science
Academia Sinica
Taipei, 11529
Taiwan, R. O. C.

BINOMIAL MIXTURES

Title: BINOMIX: A BASIC Program for Maximum Likelihood Analyses of Finite and Beta-Binomial Mixture Distributions

Author: Edgar Erdfelder

Source: *Behavior Research Methods, Instruments, & Computers,* 1993, *25,* 416-418.

Description: This interactive program outputs a histogram of the sample data along with absolute and relative observed frequencies. For the finite-binomial mixture, parameter and conditional probability estimates, observed and expected frequencies for the Y variable, standardized residuals, Pearson and likelihood-ratio goodness-of-fit statistics and their probabilities are provided. For the beta-binomial mixture, parameter estimates, observed and expected frequencies, standardized residuals, Pearson and likelihood-ratio statistics with their probabilities, mean and variance estimates of X (and conditional means and variances of X for a specified number of successes), and plots of the estimated beta-mixture density function are given.

Program Name: BINOMIX 5.0

Language: BASIC

Compatibility: IBM PC's and compatibles

Memory Requirements: 640K

Cost of Program: No Charge

How to obtain a copy of the program:

Send a formatted 3.5" diskette and
a self-addressed, stamped mailer to:

Dr. Edgar Erdfelder
Psychologisches Institut der Universität Bonn
Römerstraße 164
D-53117
Bonn, Germany
e-mail: erdfelder@uni-bonn.de

BIVARIATE NORMAL SCORES

Title: Generating Correlated Bivariate Random Normal
Standard Scores in QuickBASIC

Author: George M. Alliger

Source: *Educational and Psychological Measurement*, 1992,
52, 107-108.

Description: The program generates bivariate random normal
scores with a specified intercorrelation. The utility of this program
is found in Monte Carlo simulations. The input consists of sample
size (an initial N up to 2000, however, it is modifiable) and the
correlation. The output consists of the correlated z-scores, the
correlation, and the means and standard deviations.

Program Name: None Specified

Language: QuickBASIC

Compatibility: None Specified

Memory Requirements: None Specified

Cost of Program: No Charge

How to obtain a copy of the program:

Send a formatted 3.5" diskette and
a self-addressed, stamped mailer to:

Dr. George M. Alliger
Department of Psychology
State University of New York at Albany
Albany, NY 12222
e-mail:gmago@cnsibm.albany.edu

BONFERRONI PROCEDURE

Title: A SAS Macro Program for Applications of Five
Bonferroni Type Methods

Author: Jianmin Li, Weiming Luh, Stephen Olejnik

Source: *Applied Psychological Measurement,* 1992,
16, 364.

Description: The program computes the overall alpha level, the
ordered probability values, the adjusted alpha levels for each
comparison, and the number of rejections for the original
Bonferroni procedure and four modifications to this method.
The input consists of the number of probability values tested, a
specified Type I error rate, and the type of Bonferroni procedure to
be used.

Program Name: None Specified

Language: SAS

Compatibility: None Specified

Memory Requirements: None Specified

Cost of Program: No Charge

How to obtain a copy of the program:

Send a formatted 3.5" diskette and
a self-addressed, stamped mailer to:

Dr. Jianmin Li
Department of Educational Psychology
University of Georgia
Athens, GA 30602

BOOTSTRAPPING

Title: SIMSTAT: Bootstrap Computer Simulation and Statistical Program for IBM Personal Computers

Author: Normand Péladeau and Yves Lacouture

Source: *Behavior Research Methods, Instruments, & Computers,* 1993, *25,* 410-413.

Description: Bootstrapping uses the sample data similar to that of the population data. A large number of samples of the original sampling are drawn with replacement. A value of the estimated statistic is computed from each resampling. This menu driven program uses bootstrap procedures for determining the sampling distribution of the mean, median, standard deviation, variance, standard error, skewness, and kurtosis of a particular variable. Moreover, over 20 statistics may be bootstrapped. The program accommodates up to 30,000 cases and 500 variables for up to 20,000 iterations. The input may include files in ASCII, Lotus 1-2-3, SPSS/PC, dBaseIII and IV, or data entered from the keyboard.

Program Name: SIMSTAT

Language: FORTRAN 77

Compatibility: IBM PC's and compatibles

Memory Requirements: 400K RAM, MS-DOS 2.0 (or higher)

Cost of Program: $5

How to obtain a copy of the program:

For $55 (a registered version), a manual, technical support, and updates are provided. Otherwise, for a nonregistered (shareware) version, send a formatted MS-DOS 3.5" diskette, a self-addressed, stamped mailer, and payment to:

Dr. Normand Péladeau
5000 Adam Street
Montreal, QC
Canada H1V 1W5
e-mail: peladeau@psysoc.login.qc.ca

BOX-COX TRANSFORMATION

Title: Box_Cox: A Program for Computing the Box-Cox Transformations and Resulting Residual Sums of Squares

Author: William N. Dudley and Gary J. Lautenschlager

Source: *Applied Psychological Measurement,* 1990, *14,* 102.

Description: The program computes the Box-Cox transformation and the sum of squared residuals for potential utility in correcting nonlinearity and heterogeneity of variance in regression models. The program may be used for data containing up to 300 subjects.

Program Name: BOX_COX

Language: Turbo Pascal 5.5

Compatibility: IBM PC's and compatibles (DOS 2.0 or higher)

Memory Requirements: None Specified

Cost of Program: No Charge

How to obtain a copy of the program:

Send a formatted 3.5" diskette and a self-addressed, stamped mailer to:

Dr. Gary J. Lautenschlager
Department of Psychology
University of Georgia
Athens, GA 30602-3013
e-mail: garylaut@uga.cc.uga.edu

CALCULUS - TEACHING STATISTICS

Title: Introduction of Differential Calculus Into the Elementary Statistics Curriculum: Can Computers Help?

Author: David J. Krus and Kun-Hsia J. Li

Source: *Educational and Psychological Measurement*, 1992, *52*, 87-91.

Description: This instructional program illustrates the basics of differential calculus for augmenting the understanding of the criterion of least squares.

Program Name: None Specified

Language: None Specified

Compatibility: Intel's iAPX 88/186/286/386/486 and MS-DOS operating systems

Memory Requirements: None Specified

Cost of Program: No Charge

How to obtain a copy of the program:

Send a formatted 3.5" diskette and a self-addressed, stamped mailer to:

Dr. David J. Krus
Educational Psychology Department
Arizona State University
Tempe, AZ 85287-0611

CANONICAL ANALYSIS

Title: XCANON: A BASIC Program for Canonical Analysis of Contingency Tables

Author: Richard F. Haase

Source: *Applied Psychological Measurement,* 1989, *13,* 300.

Description: Because chi-square analysis of contingency tables is simply a specific type of canonical correlation used on two sets of coded dummy variables, the program outputs Pillai's Trace, Cramer's *V,* the chi-square test with the appropriate significance level, eigenvalues, intermediate matrices, and normalized and scaled canonical weights for both classification variable categories. The input consists of sample size, contingency table dimensions, and cell frequencies. The program handles up to a 20 x 20 matrix.

Program Name: XCANON

Language: BASICA, GW BASIC, CP/M 80 BASIC

Compatibility: IBM PC's and compatibles

Memory Requirements: 6K for the code

Cost of Program: No Charge

How to obtain a copy of the program:

Indicate whether you want the BASICA, GWBASIC, or CP/M 80 BASIC versions.

Send a formatted 5.25" diskette and a self-addressed, stamped mailer to:

Dr. Richard F. Haase
Department of Counseling Psychology
ED220
State University of New York at Albany
Albany, NY 12222

CANONICAL CORRELATION

Title: Structure, Redundancy, and Measures of Association
Statistics for a Canonical Correlation Analysis

Author: Holly Hollingsworth

Source: *Educational and Psychological Measurement,* 1981,
41, 217-218.

Description: This program computes the structure correlations,
the redundancy index, and amount of variance accounted for by
each canonical variate. The input consists of a correlation matrix,
the matrix of the canonical variate coefficients, and the first
canonical correlation.

Program Name: CANBAK

Language: BASIC

Compatibility: None Specified

Memory Requirements: None Specified

Cost of Program: No Charge

How to obtain a copy of the program:

Send a blank 3.5" diskette and a
self-addressed, stamped mailer to:

Dr. Holly Hollingsworth
Director of Academic Computing
Saint Louis University
221 N. Grand Blvd.
St. Louis, MO 63103

CANONICAL CORRELATION

Title: CANPOW: A Program That Estimates Effect or Sample Sizes Required for Canonical Correlation Analysis

Author: Bruce Thompson

Source: *Educational and Psychological Measurement*, 1988, *48*, 693-696.

Description: The program outputs the effect or sample sizes (expected or actual) coupled with the chi-square statistics and plots of a chi-square x effect size (or sample size). Moreover, "g" and "s" functions (Sexton et al., 1988) are also provided to illustrate how differences in the squared canonical correlations may affect the overall effect size. The input includes the effect size which can be specified in terms of lambda or a series of squared canonical correlations.

Program Name: CANPOW

Language: BASIC

Compatibility: None Specified

Memory Requirements: None Specified

Cost of Program: No Charge

How to obtain a copy of the program:

Send a formatted 3.5" diskette and
a self-addressed, stamped mailer to:

Dr. Bruce Thompson
Department of Educational Psychology
Texas A & M University
College Station, TX 77843
e-mail: e100bt@tamvm1.tamu.edu

CANONICAL CORRELATION

Title: CANBAK: A Program Which Performs Stepwise Canonical Correlation Analysis

Author: Bruce Thompson

Source: *Educational and Psychological Measurement,* 1982, *42,* 849-851.

Description: This program computes the canonical function, structure, squared structure index, adequacy, redundancy, and communality coefficients for each step of the analysis. The input consists of a correlation matrix and a specification of variable set sizes.

Program Name: CANBAK

Language: FORTRAN

Compatibility: None Specified

Memory Requirements: None Specified

Cost of Program: No Charge

How to obtain a copy of the program:

Send a formatted 3.5" diskette and a self-addressed, stamped mailer to:

Dr. Bruce Thompson
Department of Educational Psychology
Texas A & M University
College Station, TX 77843-4225
e-mail: e100bt@tamvm1.tamu.edu

CATEGORICAL DATA ANALYSIS

Title: A Computer Program for Ordered Categorical Data Analysis

Author: Michael J. Glencross

Source: *Behavior Research Methods & Instrumentation,* 1981, *13,* 695.

Description: This program first calculates the mean and standard deviation of subjects' responses to each item contained on a given Likert-type or semantic differential rating scale. Second, the program calculates Whitney's (1978) t statistic for each item and an estimate of the frequency (or probability) with which each item response occurs. Whitney's test is useful as a means of gauging the degree of item response agreement among subjects. Input includes the number of respondents, the number of items, and the number of item response alternatives. Output includes a respondent by item response matrix, Whitney's t statistic for each item, and the associated probability level for each t statistic. The program can accommodate a maximum of 150 items and seven item response alternatives. Dr. Glencross has updated the aforementioned program and this information will now be provided.

Program Name: QUEST

Language: QBASIC (FORTRAN and SAS versions too)

Compatibility: Mainframe systems that use FORTRAN or SAS, IBM PC's and compatibles

Memory Requirements: Less than 1 MB

Cost of Program: No Charge

How to obtain a copy of the program:

Send a formatted 3.5" diskette and a self-addressed, stamped mailer to:

Dr. Michael J. Glencross
Department of Mathematics and Science Education
University of Transkei
Private Bag X1, Unitra
UMTATA
South Africa 5117
e-mail: glencross@getafix.utr.ac.za

CATEGORICAL DATA ANALYSIS

Title: Exact Probabilities for First-Order and Second-Order Interactions in 2 x 2 x 2 Contingency Tables

Author: Paul W. Mielke, Jr. and Kenneth J. Berry

Source: *Educational and Psychological Measurement,* 1996, *56,* 843-847.

Description: This program computes exact probabilities for the three first-order and one second-order interactions of a 2 x 2 x 2 contingency table with fixed marginals. The input is composed of each of the eight observed cell frequencies. The output is composed of the observed cell frequencies and the exact probabilities for the first- and second-order interactions. An example is provided in the article.

Program Name: E1222

Language: FORTRAN 77

Compatibility: IBM and UNIX mainframes, IBM PC's and compatibles

Memory Requirements: None Specified

Cost of Program: No Charge

How to obtain a copy of the program:

The authors prefer to e-mail the program, however, you may send a formatted 3.5" diskette and a self-addressed, stamped mailer to:

Dr. Kenneth J. Berry
Department of Sociology
Colorado State University
Fort Collins, CO 80523
e-mail: berry@lamar.colostate.edu

CATEGORICAL DATA ANALYSIS

Title: Contingency Table Testing for Categorical Data: SAS
Implementation

Author: Lynn M. Veatch and Larry P. Gonzalez

Source: *Behavior Research Methods, Instruments, & Computers,*
1995, *27,* 404-407.

Description: This program analyzes a 2 x *k* contingency table
using Fisher's fourfold-table test for variables with two categories,
Fisher's contingency table test for variables with more than two
categories, and the contingency table test for ordered categories.
Examples demonstrating the utility of these tests are provided in
the article.

Program Name: Contingency Table Tests for Ordered
Categories

Language: SAS

Compatibility: Any system that uses SAS

Memory Requirements: None Specified

Cost of Program: No Charge

How to obtain a copy of the program:

Send either a 3.5" or 5.25" formatted diskette
and a self-addressed, stamped mailer to:

Dr. Larry P. Gonzalez
Department of Psychiatry and Behavioral Sciences
University of Oklahoma Health Sciences Center
Research Building
Room 308
P.O. Box 26901
Oklahoma City, OK 73190-3000
e-mail: larry-gonzalez@uokhsc.edu

CATEGORIZED DATA - NORMALITY

Title: A Program for Testing Categorized Data for Normality

Author: George M. Alliger

Source: *Educational and Psychological Measurement*, 1988, *48*, 711-712.

Description: This program computes the Kolmogorov-Smirnov test and z-tests for skew and kurtosis when examining categorized data for normality. Applications for this program might include examining the normality of test scores or rating distributions. The program will accommodate up to 25 categories.

Program Name: None Specified

Language: BASIC

Compatibility: IBM PC's and compatibles

Memory Requirements: None Specified

Cost of Program: No Charge

How to obtain a copy of the program:

Send an MS-DOS formatted 5.25" diskette and a self-addressed returnable mailer to:

Dr. George M. Alliger
Department of Psychology
State University of New York
1400 Washington Ave.
Albany, NY 12222
e-mail:gmago@cnsibm.albany.edu

CENTRAL TENDENCY

Title: Wanted -- Central Tendency and Variability of Test
Norm Tables: How to Recover Them

Author: David J. Krus and Kun-Hsia T. Liang

Source: *Educational and Psychological Measurement,* 1984,
44, 123-129.

Description: This subroutine estimates means and standard
deviations from the tabled values of standard test scores. The input
consists of the mean and standard deviation of the standard
distribution and the raw-standard score pairs. The subroutine is
provided on page 127 and an application of the algorithm is given
in the article.

Program Name: SLEUTH (subroutine)

Language: FORTRAN

Compatibility: None Specified

Memory Requirements: None Specified

Cost of Program: No Charge

How to obtain a copy of the program:

Send a blank 3.5" diskette and a
self-addressed, stamped mailer to:

Dr. David J. Krus
Educational Psychology Department
Arizona State University
Tempe, AZ 85287

CHI-SQUARE

Title: EXACON: A FORTRAN 77 Program for the Exact
Analysis of Single Cells in a Contingency Table

Author: Lars R. Bergman and Bassam El-Khouri

Source: *Educational and Psychological Measurement*, 1987,
47, 155-161.

Description: This program produces a two-way contingency table
with the observed and expected frequencies, the chi-square
component for the cell, one-tailed probabilities for the complete
independence and fixed marginals models, the overall chi-square,
the contingency coefficient, and sample size. The data may be
entered either by a file or from the terminal.

Program Name: EXACON

Language: FORTRAN 77

Compatibility: Prime Computers, however, it is easily
modifiable to any system that supports
FORTRAN

Memory Requirements: None Specified

Cost of Program: No Charge

How to obtain a copy of the program:

Send a formatted 3.5" diskette and
a self-addressed, stamped mailer to:

Dr. Lars R. Bergman
Department of Ophthalmology
Karolinska Institute
St. Erik's Eye Hospital
Stockholm, Sweden

CHI-SQUARE

Title: R by C Chi-Square Analyses With Small Expected Cell Frequencies

Author: Kenneth J. Berry and Paul W. Mielke, Jr.

Source: *Educational and Psychological Measurement*, 1986, *46*, 169-173.

Description: The subroutine provides a nonasymptotic chi-square algorithm for use with extremely disproportionate marginal totals or small expected cell frequencies. The output contains the adjusted chi-square statistic, its mean, variance, and skewness, and the probability value.

Program Name: CHI2 (subroutine)

Language: FORTRAN 77

Compatibility: IBM and UNIX mainframes, IBM PC's and compatibles

Memory Requirements: None Specified

Cost of Program: No Charge

How to obtain a copy of the program:

The author prefers to e-mail the program, however, you may send a formatted 3.5" diskette and a self-addressed, stamped mailer to:

Dr. Kenneth J. Berry
Department of Sociology
Colorado State University
Fort Collins, CO 80523
e-mail: berry@lamar.colostate.edu

CHI-SQUARE

Title: A FORTRAN IV Computer Program for Partitioning
Chi-Square Contingency Tables

Author: Ted K. Konnerth and William P. Dunlap

Source: *Behavior Research Methods & Instrumentation,*
1976, *8,* 412.

Description: This interactive program outputs the observed and
expected frequencies, percentages by rows and columns, the r x c
chi-square, the degrees of freedom, probability value, and
Cramer's *V* coefficient. The Bresnahan and Shapiro (1966)
breakdown of larger contingency tables into individual 2 x 2 tables
along with the probability for each table is also provided. The
input consists of entering the row and column frequencies, labels
for the rows and columns, and the row and column contrast vectors
for the subsequent orthogonal breakdown.

Program Name: CHI

Language: FORTRAN

Compatibility: IBM mainframes, IBM PC's and compatibles

Memory Requirements: None Specified

Cost of Program: No Charge

How to obtain a copy of the program:

Send a formatted 3.5" diskette and
a self-addressed, stamped mailer to:

Dr. William P. Dunlap
Department of Psychology
Tulane University
New Orleans, LA 70118
e-mail: dunlap@mailhost.tcs.tulane.edu

CHI-SQUARE

Title: High Precision Chi-Square and Normal Curve Integration

Author: D. Louis Wood

Source: *Behavior Research Methods, Instruments, & Computers,* 1985, *17,* 429-431.

Description: This program computes the chi-square and normal curve areas. For the chi-square program, the input includes the degrees of freedom. The program also provides the normal curve area over a particular range (e.g., between z = -.5 and .3). A listing of the program is available on pages 430-431. The program must be run in double precision. The author is willing to furnish GWBASICA upon request.

Program Name: CHSQINT.BAS

Language: GWBASICA

Compatibility: IBM PC's and compatibles

Memory Requirements: 1 MB

Cost of Program: No Charge

How to obtain a copy of the program:

Send either a 3.5" or 5.25" formatted diskette and a self-addressed, stamped mailer to:

Dr. D. Louis Wood
University of Arkansas at Little Rock
2801 South University
Little Rock, AK 72204

CHI-SQUARE - GOODNESS-OF-FIT

Title: Nonasymptotic Goodness-of-Fit Tests for Categorical Data

Author: Kenneth J. Berry and Paul W. Mielke, Jr.

Source: *Educational and Psychological Measurement*, 1994, *54*, 676-679.

Description: A subroutine (GOF) computes two goodness-of-fit statistics using the methodology supplied by Mielke and Berry (1988) for categorical frequencies. An example of the utility of this program is provided in the article. The user inputs the number of categories, observed cell frequencies, and expected cell probabilities. The output includes the two goodness-of-fit tests, their probability values, and summary statistics.

Program Name: GOF (subroutine)

Language: FORTRAN 77

Compatibility: IBM and UNIX mainframes, IBM PC's and compatibles

Memory Requirements: None Specified

Cost of Program: No Charge

How to obtain a copy of the program:

The authors prefer to e-mail the program, however, you may send a formatted 3.5" diskette and a self-addressed, stamped mailer to:

Dr. Kenneth J. Berry
Department of Sociology
Colorado State University
Fort Collins, CO 80523
e-mail: berry@lamar.colostate.edu

CHI-SQUARE - INDEPENDENCE

Title: Analyzing Independence in R-Way Contingency Tables

Author: Kenneth J. Berry and Paul W. Mielke, Jr.

Source: *Educational and Psychological Measurement*, 1989, *49*, 605-607.

Description: The subroutine (RWAY) computes a Pearson chi-squared statistic and a modified chi-squared statistic with their corresponding probability values for testing independence in r-way contingency tables. The user inputs the number of dimensions, number of categories within each dimension, and the observed frequencies.

Program Name: RWAY (subroutine)

Language: FORTRAN 77

Compatibility: IBM and UNIX mainframes, IBM PC's and compatibles

Memory Requirements: None Specified

Cost of Program: No Charge

How to obtain a copy of the program:

The authors prefer to e-mail the program, however, you may send a formatted 3.5" diskette and a self-addressed, stamped mailer to:

Dr. Kenneth J. Berry
Department of Sociology
Colorado State University
Fort Collins, CO 80523
e-mail: berry@lamar.colostate.edu

CIRCULAR DATA ANALYSIS

Title: Two-Sample and Multisample Testing of Circular Data

Author: Jerrold H. Zar

Source: *Behavior Research Methods & Instrumentation,* 1976, *8,* 329-330.

Description: This program calculates the mean and angular deviation for any number of samples containing circular data (e.g., compass direction, clock time). The significance of the mean is assessed via Rayleigh's test and the null hypothesis that all mean angles are the same is evaluated using the Watson and Williams test. Input may be in the form of degrees, radians, sectors, or times of day. Output includes the two aforementioned tests and their associated probability values, the mean angle in both angles and radians, and the angular deviations in both angles and radians.

Program Name: None Specified

Language: FORTRAN IV

Compatibility: IBM mainframes

Memory Requirements: None Specified

Cost of Program: No Charge

How to obtain a copy of the program:

The program listing with documentation may be obtained by contacting:

Dr. Jerrold H. Zar
c/o Graduate School
205A Provost
Northern Illinois University
DeKalb, IL 60115
e-mail: t80jhz1@wpo.cso.niu.edu

CIRCULAR DISTRIBUTIONS

Title: A FORTRAN IV Program for Rao's Test of
Uniformity in Circular Distributions

Author: Paul V. Hamilton

Source: *Behavior Research Methods & Instrumentation,*
1976, 8, 467.

Description: This program implements Rao's test of uniformity
for circularly distributed data. Rao's procedure provides a powerful
test of uniformity not only under unimodal conditions, but also
when the data are characterized by bimodal or multimodal
distributions. The input consists of data values in the form of
degrees, radians, or units of time. The output includes the mean arc
length and the U statistic which is used for testing the hypothesis
that the sample distribution derived from a uniform population.
Dr. Hamilton has a new SAS macro program that not only
performs Rao's test, but Rayleigh's test and the V-test as well.

Program Name: None Specified

Language: SAS

Compatibility: None Specified

Memory Requirements: None Specified

Cost of Program: No Charge

How to obtain a copy of the program:

The program listing with documentation
may be obtained by contacting:

Dr. Paul V. Hamilton
Department of Biology
Lewis Science Center
University of Central Arkansas
Conway, Arkansas 72035
e-mail: paulh@cc1.uca.edu

CIRCULAR STATISTICS

Title: Apple II Programs in Circular Statistics

Author: Eric Le Bourg and Guy Beugnon

Source: *Behavior Research Methods, Instruments, & Computers,*
          1985, *17,* 141.

Description: This program, which can be used for animal
orientation or biological rhythm data, computes Rayleigh's test, the
V-test, Rao's Spacing Test, Watson's U2 Test, Moore's Test,
Circular-Circular correlation (e.g., directional flight and time of
day), and a Circular-Linear correlation (directional flight and
amount of rain). Brief explanations of these tests are provided in
the article.

Program Name: CHAIN

Language: Applesoft BASIC

Compatibility: Apple IIe, II+, IIc, DOS 3.3 system. Can be
               converted for use on a Macintosh.

Memory Requirements: 48K

Cost of Program: No Charge

How to obtain a copy of the program:

Send two 5.25" diskettes and a
self-addressed, stamped mailer to:

Dr. Eric Le Bourg
Laboratoire d' Ethologie et de Psychologie Animale
U.M.R. C.N.R.S. 5550
Université Paul Sabatier
118 route de Narbonne
F-31062 Toulouse cédex
France
e-mail: lebourg@cict.fr

CLASSIFICATION ANALYSIS

Title: A BASIC Program for Classification Analysis Using Proportional and Maximum Chance Estimates of Prior Probabilities

Author: Robert S. Schlottmann

Source: *Behavior Research Methods, Instruments, & Computers,* 1989, *21,* 625-636.

Description: In order to determine, for example, if the predicted group corresponds to the actual group in a classification scheme (e.g., diagnostic groups), this program computes the total number of cases, the number of hits, and the percent correct classification. Moreover, using the proportional chance criterion, the total-group chance frequency of hits, the hit rate, and z statistic are provided. The chance frequency of hits and z statistics are also given for each group. Using the maximum chance criterion, the percent of cases appropriately classified and the z statistic are provided.   Finally, statistics for improvement over chance (overall and for each group) are given.   The input consists of providing the number and names of the groups and the number of cases in a particular group that were predicted to be in a certain group.

Program Name: CLASS version 1.0

Language: BASIC

Compatibility: IBM PC's and compatibles

Memory Requirements: 256K

Cost of Program: No Charge

How to obtain a copy of the program:

Send a formatted 3.5" diskette and a self-addressed, stamped mailer to:

Dr. Robert S. Schlottmann
Department of Psychology
Oklahoma State University
Stillwater, OK 74078
e-mail: bobsch@osuvms.bitnet
          bobsch@vms.ucc.okstate.edu

CLUSTER ANALYSIS - HIERARCHICAL

Title: Hierarchical Clustering Algorithms With Influence
           Detection

Author: Richard Cheng and Glenn W. Milligan

Source: *Educational and Psychological Measurement*, 1995,
           55, 237-244.

Description: The program identifies specific data points that
might affect a cluster analysis using the Hubert and Arabie (1985)
measure of internal influence combined with nine hierarchical
clustering procedures. These procedures are the single link,
complete link, group average, weighted average, centroid, medium,
Ward's minimum variance, and two beta-flexible procedures by
Lance and Williams (1967) and Belbin, Faith, and Milligan (1992).
The program allows up to 30 variables and 200 data points. A
documentation file is provided. The output consists of either a
hierarchical tree or an icicle plot, cluster centroids at specified
hierarchical levels, measure of internal influence, and other output
statistics. A partial listing is provided in the article.

Program Name: None Specified

Language: FORTRAN 77

Compatibility: IBM PC's and compatibles with DOS version
                 3.3 or later. Need at least an Intel 486 or Pentium
                 processor

Memory Requirements: Requires 640K of RAM and
                       4MB of extended memory

Cost of Program: No charge if in U.S. $20 in check or money
                   order from U.S. bank if outside of U.S. If
                   outside U.S., author will provide diskette,
                   mailing envelope, and international postage.

How to obtain a copy of the program:

Send a formatted 3.5" diskette and
a self-addressed, stamped mailer to:

Dr. Richard Cheng
7967 Hightree Drive
Westerville, OH 43081

CLUSTER ANALYSIS - HIERARCHICAL

Title: APPLECOR: An Apple II Implementation of
Hierarchical Clustering Analysis Using the CONCOR
Algorithm

Author: Andrew R. Gilpin

Source: *Behavior Research Methods, Instruments, & Computers,*
1985, *17,* 140.

Description: This program uses the CONCOR algorithm
developed by Breiger, Boorman, and Arabie (1975) for outputting
a dendrogram that sections off each cluster. The input consists of
the upper half of a correlation matrix.

Program Name: APPLECOR

Language: Applesoft BASIC

Compatibility: Apple Microcomputers

Memory Requirements: 16K RAM (at least)

Cost of Program: $2

How to obtain a copy of the program:

Send a blank 3.5" diskette and payment to:

Dr. Andrew R. Gilpin
Department of Psychology
University of Northern Iowa
Cedar Falls, IA 50614
e-mail: gilpin@uni.edu

CLUSTER ANALYSIS - HIERARCHICAL

Title: A Hierarchical Grouping Analysis Program for the IBM
Personal Computer

Author: C. Michael Levy

Source: *Behavior Research Methods, Instruments, & Computers,*
1985, *17, 577.*

Description: This program provides hierarchical grouping
analysis similar to the Watkins and Kush (1985) program. This
program also provides on-line instructions.

Program Name: None Specified

Language: BASIC

Compatibility: IBM PC's and compatibles

Memory Requirements: 64K memory

Cost of Program: No Charge

How to obtain a copy of the program:

Send a formatted 5.25" diskette and
a self-addressed, stamped mailer to:

Dr. C. Michael Levy
114 Psychology Building
University of Florida
Gainesville, FL 32611

CLUSTER ANALYSIS - HIERARCHICAL

Title: An Apple Computer Program for Hierarchical Grouping Analysis

Author: Marley W. Watkins and Joseph C. Kush

Source: *Behavior Research Methods, Instruments, & Computers,* 1985, *17,* 576.

Description: This program creates homogeneous groups via hierarchical grouping analysis (a multivariate technique for aiding in the classification of subjects which facilitates understanding of the relationships among subjects and variables). The program's limits are 90 subjects and 20 variables. A list of variables, cluster membership identifications, group combinations, and error terms for each grouping are output.

Program Name: HGROUP90N

Language: Applesoft BASIC

Compatibility: Apple II microcomputers

Memory Requirements: 1 MG

Cost of Program: $6 in USA; $8 outside of USA

How to obtain a copy of the program:

Send a 5.25" diskette, a self-addressed stamped mailer, and payment to:

Dr. Joseph C. Kush
Department of Counseling, Psychology, and Special Education
Room 410B Canevine Hall
600 Forbes Avenue
Duquesne University
Pittsburgh, PA 15282
e-mail: kush@duq2.cc.duq.edu

CLUSTER ANALYSIS - K-MEANS

Title: K-Means Clustering Methods With Influence Detection

Author: Richard Cheng and Glenn W. Milligan

Source: *Educational and Psychological Measurement*, 1996, *56*, 833-838.

Description: K-means clustering is a nonhierarchical approach that attempts to formulate a hierarchical tree. The Jancey (1966) and Forgy (1965) K-means procedures are provided in the program. The data file is in ASCII (the default consists of up to 30 variables, 550 data points , and 40 clusters). The input also consists of the selection of the clustering method, starting configuration, number of clusters, and name and format of the data file.   The output is composed of a summary of the input information, iterative history, membership list of each cluster, point-biserial statistics, and internal influential measures (in which the clustering assignments would change if these data points were removed from the analysis).

Program Name: None Specified

Language: FORTRAN 77 (some Mircoway NDP FORTRAN-specific routines). If recompiling this program for a different system, these routines may be commented in the source code.

Compatibility: IBM PC's and compatibles with DOS version 3.3 or later. Need at least an Intel 486 or Pentium processor

Memory Requirements: 640K of RAM and 4MB of memory

Cost of Program: No charge if in U.S. If outside U.S., $20 in check or money order from U.S. bank. Moreover, author will provide diskette, mailing envelope, and international postage.

How to obtain a copy of the program:

Send a formatted 3.5" diskette and a self-addressed, stamped mailer to:

Dr. Richard Cheng
7967 Hightree Drive
Westerville, OH 43081

CLUSTER SIMILARITY

Title: Microcomputer Programs for the Rand Index of Cluster Similarity

Author: Ralph Mason Dreger

Source: *Educational and Psychological Measurement,* 1986, *46,* 655-661.

Description: This program computes the Rand (1971) index of cluster similarity. A high index (e.g., above .70) would indicate cluster similarity. This index is related closely to Cohen's kappa and has some disadvantages (e.g., Milligan & Schilling, 1985). According to the author, however, the simplicity and interpretability of this index are distinct advantages.

Program Name: RAND/BAS - for smaller data sets
RAND2/BAS- for larger data sets
RAND3/BAS- for larger numbers of clusters
RAND4/BAS- allows storage of data

Language: GWBASIC

Compatibility: IBM PC's and compatibles

Memory Requirements: 1K

Cost of Program: No Charge

How to obtain a copy of the program:

Send either a formatted 3.5" or 5.25" diskette
and a self-addressed, stamped mailer to:

Dr. Ralph Mason Dreger
Department of Psychology
Louisiana State University
Baton Rouge, LA 70803
e-mail:rdreger266@aol.com

COCHRAN'S Q

Title: Nonasymptotic Probability Values for Cochran's Q Statistic: A FORTRAN 77 Program

Author: Kenneth J. Berry and Paul W. Mielke, Jr.

Source: *Perceptual and Motor Skills*, 1996, *82*, 303-306.

Description: For situations in which a small number of subjects each provide responses to a small number of treatment conditions and each response is classified in a binary fashion (e.g., correct/incorrect), this program (a) calculates the mean, variance, and skewness of Cochran's Q test for the equality of matched proportions under the nonasymptotic null distribution, (b) calculates the nonasymptotic equivalent of Cochran's Q, and (c) calculates a standardized z statistic and associated probability level to evaluate the significance of Q.

Program Name: QTEST

Language: FORTRAN 77

Compatibility: IBM PC's and compatibles

Memory Requirements: None Specified

Cost of Program: No Charge

How to obtain a copy of the program:

The authors prefer to e-mail the program, however, you may send a formatted 3.5" diskette and a self-addressed, stamped mailer to:

Dr. Kenneth J. Berry
Department of Sociology
Colorado State University
Fort Collins, CO 80523
e-mail: berry@lamar.colostate.edu

COEFFICIENT ALPHA

Title: ALPHATST: Testing for Differences in Values of Coefficient Alpha

Author: Gary J. Lautenschlager

Source: *Applied Psychological Measurement,* 1989, *13,* 284.

Description: The program outputs the chi-square statistic and probability value for examining the differences in coefficient alpha values using equations shown in Feldt et al (1987). The input includes sample sizes, number of items for each test, and sample coefficient alphas (a correlation matrix among test scores is also needed if this test is being used within the same sample) .

Program Name: ALPHATST

Language: FORTRAN 77

Compatibility: Any mainframe or IBM PC's and compatibles with a FORTRAN compiler.

Memory Requirements: 640K

Cost of Program: No Charge

How to obtain a copy of the program:

Send a formatted 3.5" diskette and a self-addressed, stamped mailer to:

Dr. Gary J. Lautenschlager
Department of Psychology
University of Georgia
Athens, GA 30602-3013
e-mail: garylaut@uga.cc.uga.edu

COEFFICIENT ALPHA

Title: ALPHAMAX: A Program That Maximizes Coefficient Alpha by Selective Item Deletion

Author: Bruce Thompson

Source: *Educational and Psychological Measurement,* 1990, *50,* 585-589.

Description: The program can be used in selecting a subset of items for maximizing coefficient alpha in test development. The input consists of a data file of scored item responses. The output consists of summary statistics (e.g., mean, standard deviations, coefficient alpha) for the total set. Using a bootstrap type approach, an optimal item subset is produced and the coefficient alpha is given at each step (i.e., for each item deleted). An example of the output and utility of the program is provided in the article.

Program Name: ALPHAMAX

Language: None Specified

Compatibility: None Specified

Memory Requirements: None Specified

Cost of Program: No Charge

How to obtain a copy of the program:

Send a written request to:

Dr. Bruce Thompson
Department of Educational Psychology
Texas A & M University
College Station, TX 77843
e-mail: e100bt@tamvm1.tamu.edu

COEFFICIENT OF CONCORDANCE

Title: A BASIC Program for Computing the Coefficient of Concordance, r_c

Author: Stephen W. Hebbler

Source: *Educational and Psychological Measurement*, 1989, *49*, 615-618.

Description: This program can be used for determining the degree of agreement between factors across studies or samples. The input consists of a data file in which an item x factor matrix is created for each study and the entries are the factor loadings. The output consists of a coefficient of concordance matrix (from 0 to 1) and the higher the value, the greater the agreement. Illustrations of the input and output are provided in the article. The program accommodates up to 51 factors.

Program Name: None Specified

Language: Microsoft BASIC

Compatibility: IBM PC's and compatibles

Memory Requirements: None Specified

Cost of Program: No Charge

How to obtain a copy of the program:

Send a formatted 3.5" diskette and
a self-addressed, stamped mailer to:

Dr. Stephen W. Hebbler
Evaluation and Assessment Laboratory
Department of Education
University of Alabama
203 Carmichael Hall
P.O. Box 870231
Tuscaloosa, AL 35487
e-mail: shebbler@ua1vm.ua.edu

COEFFICIENT OF VARIATION

Title: A Program to Test Equality of Two or More
Coefficients of Variation

Author: Andrew R. Gilpin

Source: *Behavior Research Methods, Instruments, & Computers,*
1993, *25,* 65-66.

Description: The coefficient of variation (standard deviation over the mean) examines variations across groups that have either different means or have measurements in different units.   This program computes the Doornbos and Dijkstra (1983) and Bennett-Shafer-Sullivan (1986) chi-square approximations, degrees of freedom and significance levels, and the coefficient of variation for each group along with the corresponding means and standard deviations. The input consists of the number of groups, the sample size for each group, and the raw scores (or means and standard deviations) for each group.

Program Name: COEFVAR

Language: QuickBASIC (version 4.5)

Compatibility: IBM PC's and compatibles

Memory Requirements: None Specified

Cost of Program: $5

How to obtain a copy of the program:

Send a written request and payment to:

Dr. Andrew R. Gilpin
Department of Psychology
University of Northern Iowa
Cedar Falls, IA 50614-0505
e-mail: gilpin@uni.edu

COHORT ANALYSIS

Title: A Simple Computer Program for Generating Person-Time Data in Cohort Studies Involving Time-Related Factors

Author: Neil Pearce and Harvey Checkoway

Source: *American Journal of Epidemiology,* 1987, *125,* 1085-1091.

Description: As an alternative to the proportional hazards method of analyzing person-time cohort data, this program summarizes raw data in a form that can be analyzed via Poisson regression analysis to generate various summary rate ratio estimates which in turn are adjusted for one or more potential confounders. The Poisson regression approach simplifies the interpretation of interactions and facilitates the modeling of disease rates. A strength of the program is that rather than generating a single record for each person, separate records for each person-year of data are calculated.

Program Name: None Specified

Language: SAS

Compatibility: IBM PC's and compatibles

Memory Requirements: None Specified

Cost of Program: No Charge

How to obtain a copy of the program:

A listing of the SAS program is contained in the source article.

For additional information, contact:

Dr. Neil Pearce
Wellington Asthma Research Group (WARG)
Department of Medicine
Wellington School of Medicine
P.O. Box 7343
Wellington
New Zealand
e-mail: neil@wnmeds.ac.nz

COMPARISONS - ANCOVA

Title: A BASIC Computer Program for Calculating Simultaneous Pairwise Comparisons in Analysis of Covariance

Author: Stephen Powers and Patricia B. Jones

Source: *Educational and Psychological Measurement*, 1986, *46*, 637-638.

Description: This program computes all pairwise comparisons of adjusted means in an analysis of covariance via the Tukey-Kramer procedure. The input consists of the covariate means, the adjusted means, sample size, mean square error from the one-way ANCOVA, and the critical value at the .05 level from the Studentized range distribution.

Program Name: None Specified

Language: BASIC

Compatibility: IBM PC's and compatibles

Memory Requirements: None Specified

Cost of Program: No Charge

How to obtain a copy of the program:

Send a formatted 3.5" diskette and a self-addressed, stamped mailer to:

Dr. Stephen Powers
Legal and Research Services
Tucson Unified School District
P.O. Box 40400
Tucson, AZ 85717

COMPARISONS - CORRELATIONS

Title: Spjøtvoll-Stoline-Like Pairwise Comparisons Among Independent Product-Moment Correlations

Author: Richard H. Williams

Source: *Educational and Psychological Measurement*, 1992, *52*, 119-121.

Description: Computes multiple comparisons of independent correlations using the Levy (1977) procedure. The user inputs the significance level, number (up to 10) and magnitude of correlations, and sample size. The output consists of the studentized q values and a comparison of that value to the critical values at the .05 and .01 alpha levels. The program also accommodates unequal sample sizes.

Program Name: TUKCOR.BAS

Language: QuickBASIC

Compatibility: IBM PC's and compatibles

Memory Requirements: 512K

Cost of Program: No Charge

How to obtain a copy of the program:

Send a formatted 3.5" diskette and
a self-addressed, stamped mailer to:

Dr. Richard H. Williams
Department of Educational and Psychological Studies
P.O. Box 248065
University of Miami
Coral Gables, FL 33124
e-mail: rwilliams@umiami.1r.miami.edu

COMPARISONS - CORRELATIONS

Title: Computing Pairwise Comparisons Among Correlations With the SAS System

Author: Richard H. Williams and William G. LeBlanc

Source: *Educational and Psychological Measurement*, 1995, *55*, 448-451.

Description: Computes multiple pairwise comparisons of independent correlations using procedures explained by Levy (1975, 1976, 1977). The user inputs the familywise alpha level, an identification value for each correlation, sample size, and the correlation itself. The output consists of the identification value, the sample sizes, and the Studentized q values with the probability values for each comparison. Sample output is provided in the article. Up to ten independent samples may be used.

Program Name: TUKCOR

Language: SAS

Compatibility: Runs on SAS versions 5.18 to 6.08 for any computer with SAS capabilities

Memory Requirements: None Specified

Cost of Program: No Charge

How to obtain a copy of the program:

Send a formatted 3.5" diskette and
a self-addressed, stamped mailer to:

Dr. William G. LeBlanc
Information Resources
University of Miami
P.O. Box 248011
Coral Gables, FL 33124
e-mail: bleblanc@umiamivm.1r.miami.edu
from gopher: gopher://asg1.1r.miami.edu/academic spt grp/papers/

COMPARISONS - CORRELATIONS

Title: Many-One Comparisons Among Correlations

Author: Richard H. Williams and William G. LeBlanc

Source: *Educational and Psychological Measurement*, 1995, *55*, 452-455.

Description: Computes many-one comparisons of independent correlations using procedures explained by Levy (1975, 1976, 1977) similar to Dunnett's test. The user inputs the familywise alpha level, an identification value for each correlation, and the correlation itself. The output consists of the identification value, the common sample size, the Fisher r to z transformations, standard errors, and the z value and associated probability level for each comparison. Sample output is provided in the article. Limitations to the program are that there must be equal sample sizes and no more than ten independent samples may be used.

Program Name: DUNNCOR

Language: SAS

Compatibility: Runs on SAS versions 5.18 to 6.08 for any computer with SAS capabilities

Memory Requirements: None Specified

Cost of Program: No Charge

How to obtain a copy of the program:

Send a formatted 3.5" diskette and
a self-addressed, stamped mailer to:

Dr. William G. LeBlanc
Information Resources
University of Miami
P.O. Box 248011
Coral Gables, FL 33124
e-mail: bleblanc@umiamivm.1r.miami.edu
from gopher: gopher://asg1.1r.miami.edu/academic spt grp/papers/

COMPARISONS - MEANS

Title: Approximate Degrees of Freedom Tests: A Unified Perspective on Testing for Mean Equality

Author: Lisa M. Lix and H. J. Keselman

Source: *Psychological Bulletin*, 1995, *117*, 547-560.

Description: This program computes an approximate degrees of freedom test for examining the differences among means for between- and within-subjects designs (including subsequent comparisons) when homoscedasticity has been violated. The program is available in the article on pages 559 and 560.

Program Name: WJGLM

Language: SAS/IML (version 6)

Compatibility: Any computer that uses SAS

Memory Requirements: None Specified

Cost of Program: No Charge

How to obtain a copy of the program:

For further information, contact:

Dr. H. J. Keselman
Department of Psychology
University of Manitoba
Winnipeg, Manitoba
Canada
R3T 2N2
e-mail: kesel@ccm.umanitoba.ca

COMPARISONS - MEANS

Title: SHAFHC: A FORTRAN Implementation of Shaffer's Multiple Comparison Procedure with HC Enhancement

Author: Jeffrey Lee Rasmussen

Source: *Psychometrika*, 1991, *56*, 153-154.

Description: This program performs Shaffer's (1986) rank-ordering multiple comparison procedures with the option of using the Holland and Copenhaver modification as a means of increasing power (provided that the positive orthant dependence assumption is met). Input includes the overall alpha level, the number of groups, and the number of probabilities (i.e., number of hypotheses tested). For each hypothesis, the program queries the user for the obtained probability value and the group numbers to be compared. Output consists of the Shaffer probability values and the significance level associated with each hypothesis.

Program Name: SHAFHC

Language: FORTRAN 77

Compatibility: With slight modifications, the program should run on any computer capable of supporting FORTRAN

Memory Requirements: None Specified

Cost of Program: Check with author for current pricing information

How to obtain a copy of the program:

Send a written request and payment to:

Dr. Jeffrey Lee Rasmussen
Department of Psychology
Purdue School of Science at Indianapolis
402 North Blackford Street
Indianapolis, IN 46202-3275
e-mail: irhf100@indyvax.iupui.edu

COMPARISONS - MEANS

Title: ANCOM: A BASIC Program for Analytical Comparisons Among Means

Author: Neil R. Shapiro and Robert A. Rosellini

Source: *Behavior Research Methods & Instrumentation,* 1980, *12*, 633.

Description: This program performs single degree of freedom contrasts among group means. The user inputs the group sample sizes, the group means, and a maximum of 10 contrasts (coefficient sets) for each variable. The program can accommodate unequal group sample sizes and can handle designs with up to four independent variables. Output includes the coefficient set for each variable and the mean square value for each specified contrast.

Program Name: ANCOM

Language: TRS-80 Level II BASIC

Compatibility: IBM PC's and compatibles

Memory Requirements: 16K

Cost of Program: $2 (unless you send diskette and mailer - then no charge)

How to obtain a copy of the program:

Send either a 3.5" or 5.25" diskette and a self-addressed, stamped mailer to:

Dr. Robert A. Rosellini
Computer Science Department
SUNY at Albany
1400 Washington Avenue
Albany, NY 12222-1000
e-mail: rar93@cnsunix.albany.edu

COMPARISONS - PROPORTIONS

Title: Computing Many-One Comparisons Among Independent Sample Proportions With the SAS System

Author: William G. LeBlanc and Richard H. Williams

Source: *Educational and Psychological Measurement*, 1995, *55*, 799-803.

Description: Computes many-one comparisons of independent proportions using procedures explained by Levy (1975, 1976, 1977) similar to Dunnett's test. The user inputs the familywise alpha level, the common sample size, an identification value for each proportion (control and experimental groups), and the proportion itself. The output consists of the sample size, the alpha rate, sample proportions, and z score and probability level for each comparison. Sample output is provided in the article. Limitations include equal sample sizes in the cells and the program only accommodates up to ten independent proportions.

Program Name: DUNNPROP

Language: SAS

Compatibility: Runs on SAS versions 5.18 to 6.08 for any computer with SAS capabilities

Memory Requirements: None Specified

Cost of Program: No Charge

How to obtain a copy of the program:

Send a formatted 3.5" diskette and
a self-addressed, stamped mailer to:

Dr. William G. LeBlanc
Information Resources
University of Miami
P.O. Box 248011
Coral Gables, FL 33124
e-mail: bleblanc@umiamivm.1r.miami.edu
from gopher: gopher://asg1.1r.miami.edu/academic spt grp/papers/

COMPARISONS - PROPORTIONS

Title: Multiple Comparisons Among k Independent Binomial
Samples

Author: Richard H. Williams

Source: *Educational and Psychological Measurement*, 1992,
52, 103-105.

Description: Computes multiple comparisons of proportions
using procedures explained by Marascuilo (1966). The user inputs
the familywise alpha level, sample size, and the sample
proportions. The output consists of the chi-square statistic testing
the null hypothesis that all population proportions are equivalent,
the critical value, and whether the null hypothesis was rejected or
not. If the omnibus test is significant, then the user provides
coefficients for contrasts and the subsequent chi-square value is
given along with whether it is significant or not. The program tests
up to eight proportions and can be used for testing trends via
orthogonal polynomials.

Program Name: MULTBIN.BAS

Language: QuickBASIC

Compatibility: IBM PC's and compatibles

Memory Requirements: 512K

Cost of Program: No Charge

How to obtain a copy of the program:

Send a formatted 3.5" diskette and
a self-addressed, stamped mailer to:

Dr. Richard H. Williams
Department of Educational and Psychological Studies
P.O. Box 248065
University of Miami
Coral Gables, FL 33124
e-mail: rwilliams@umiami.1r.miami.edu

COMPARISONS - PROPORTIONS

Title: Dunnett-Like Comparisons Among Proportions

Author: Richard H. Williams

Source: *Educational and Psychological Measurement*, 1992,
              52, 595-597.

Description: Computes multiple comparisons of proportions using procedures explained by Levy (1975). In this case, the control group's proportion is compared to each experimental group's proportion. The user interactively inputs the number and magnitude of proportions, sample size (must be equal n), and significance level. The output consists of the z-statistic for each Dunnett-like comparison, the critical value associated with each comparison, and a statement concerning statistical significance.

Program Name: DUNNPROP.BAS

Language: QuickBASIC (version 4.5)

Compatibility: IBM PC's and compatibles

Memory Requirements: 512K

Cost of Program: No Charge

How to obtain a copy of the program:

Send a formatted 3.5" diskette and
a self-addressed, stamped mailer to:

Dr. Richard H. Williams
Department of Educational and Psychological Studies
P.O. Box 248065
University of Miami
Coral Gables, FL 33124
e-mail: rwilliams@umiami.1r.miami.edu

COMPARISONS - PROPORTIONS

Title: Tukey-Like Comparisons Among Proportions

Author: Richard H. Williams

Source: *Educational and Psychological Measurement*, 1992,
              52, 913-914.

Description: Computes Tukey-type comparisons of independent
proportions using procedures explained by Levy (1977). The user
interactively inputs the magnitude of proportions, sample sizes,
and significance level. The output consists of the studentized q
values and the significant differences between proportions are
illustrated by an asterisk. The program allows up to 10 proportions
to be inputted.

Program Name: TUKPROP.BAS

Language: QuickBASIC (version 4.5)

Compatibility: IBM PC's and compatibles

Memory Requirements: 512K

Cost of Program: No Charge

How to obtain a copy of the program:

Send a formatted 3.5" diskette and
a self-addressed, stamped mailer to:

Dr. Richard H. Williams
Department of Educational and Psychological Studies
P.O. Box 248065
University of Miami
Coral Gables, FL 33124
e-mail: rwilliams@umiami.1r.miami.edu

COMPARISONS - VARIANCES

Title: An SAS Program for Pairwise Comparisons Among Variances

Author: William G. LeBlanc and Richard H. Williams

Source: *Educational and Psychological Measurement*, 1995, *55*, 795-798.

Description: Computes multiple comparisons of independent variances using procedures explained by Levy (1975, 1976, 1977). The user inputs the familywise alpha level and an identification value, the sample variance and the sample size for each independent sample (up to 10). The output consists of the identification values, sample sizes, sample variances, q values and the appropriate critical values. Sample output is provided in the article.

Program Name: TUKVAR

Language: SAS

Compatibility: Runs on SAS versions 5.18 to 6.08 for any computer with SAS capabilities

Memory Requirements: 512K

Cost of Program: No Charge

How to obtain a copy of the program:

Send a formatted 3.5" diskette and a self-addressed, stamped mailer to:

Dr. William G. LeBlanc
Information Resources
University of Miami
P.O. Box 248011
Coral Gables, FL 33124
e-mail: bleblanc@umiamivm.1r.miami.edu
from gopher: gopher://asg.1r.miami.edu/academic spt grp/papers/

CONFIDENCE INTERVALS

Title: Confidence Intervals and Standard Errors for Ratios of Normal Variables

Author: William P. Dunlap and N. Clayton Silver

Source: *Behavior Research Methods, Instruments, & Computers,* 1986, *18,* 469-471.

Description: This program computes the confidence intervals and standard errors for the ratio of normal variables via Fieller's theorem (Fieller, 1932). For example, if a pharmacological researcher was interested in evaluating the therapeutic safety ratio which is the ratio of the lethal dose (lethal for 50% of the subjects) to effective dose (effective for 50% of the subjects), then it could be assumed that both the distributions of lethal and effective doses approximate normality. Hence, these confidence intervals could be used in significance testing or as a descriptive statistic. A listing of the program is contained on page 471.

Program Name: FIEL

Language: FORTRAN

Compatibility: DEC-2060, IBM 3050, and IBM PC's and compatibles

Memory Requirements: None Specified

Cost of Program: No Charge

How to obtain a copy of the program:

Send a formatted 3.5" diskette and a self-addressed, stamped mailer to:

Dr. William P. Dunlap
Department of Psychology
Tulane University
New Orleans, LA 70118
e-mail: dunlap@mailhost.tcs.tulane.edu

CONFIDENCE INTERVALS

Title: Simultaneous Tests and Confidence Intervals

Author: Kevin E. O'Grady

Source: *Behavior Research Methods, Instruments, & Computers,* 1986, *18*, 325-326.

Description: In order to examine certain linear combinations of parameters that might have contributed to rejection of the null hypothesis, this program outputs the input matrices, canonical correlations, and Roy's greatest characteristic root test. Moreover, sums of squares, mean squares, *F*, and the partial squared multiple correlation for each univariate test are output. Finally, the upper and lower bounds of the confidence interval along with the standard error are output. Input consists of the error (and predictor) sums of squares and cross products matrix, or the error (and predictor) variance-covariance matrix, parameter estimates matrix, and contrast coefficient matrix. A parameter card containing the number of predictors, and number of contrast coefficient matrices is also input.

Program Name: None Specified

Language: FORTRAN IV

Compatibility: UNIVAC 1100/92

Memory Requirements: 53K Memory

Cost of Program: No Charge

How to obtain a copy of the program:

Send a formatted 3.5" diskette and a self-addressed, stamped mailer to:

Dr. Kevin E. O'Grady
Department of Psychology
University of Maryland
College Park, MD 20742

CONFIDENCE INTERVAL - KAPPA

Title: Confidence Interval of the Kappa Coefficient by
Bootstrap Resampling

Author: James Lee and K.P. Fung

Source: *Psychiatry Research,* 1993, *49,* 97-98.

Description: This program generates confidence intervals for the
kappa coefficient via bootstrap resampling (Efron & Tibshirani,
1986). Kappas and confidence intervals can be calculated for
dichotomous outcomes, nominal outcomes with three or more
categories, and ordinal outcomes with three or more categories.
The program also assesses for potential patterns of disagreement
via a McNemar-like test for off-diagonal sum symmetry and a
goodness of fit test for off-diagonal individual-cell symmetry.
Dr. Lee has published about 30 programs covering a wide variety
of statistical procedures. These programs (written in BASIC
and/or SAS) can be obtained for $10 (for postage and handling)
and two 3.5" diskettes.

Program Name: KAPCI.EXE

Language: Microsoft QuickBASIC

Compatibility: IBM PC's and compatibles

Memory Requirements: 50K

Cost of Program: No Charge

How to obtain a copy of the program:

Send a formatted 3.5" diskette and
a self-addressed, stamped mailer to:

Dr. James Lee
Epidemiology Program
Cancer Research Center of Hawaii
University of Hawaii
1236 Lauhala Street, Suite 407
Honolulu, HI 96813
e-mail: jamesl@crch.hawaii.edu

CONFIDENCE INTERVAL - MEDIAN

Title:　　An APL Function for Computing Distribution-Free Confidence Limits on the Median of a Population

Author:　Luc Wouters

Source:　*Behavior Research Methods & Instrumentation*, 1978, *11*, 401.

Description:　This function, which is used in conjunction with a descriptive statistics program, generates a confidence interval for a median value. Using formulae developed by Owen (1962), the function first calculates the binomial sum for the sign test and then solves for the value of A, which represents the critical value of the sign test or the smallest value lying within the confidence interval. Input includes the sample size and desired probability level. Output includes the value of A and its associated one-tailed probability level, the sample size, and the 100% confidence interval on the population median from the Ath largest to the (1+N-A)th largest value.

Program Name:　SCRITIC

Language:　VSAPL

Compatibility:　IBM mainframes

Memory Requirements:　None Specified

Cost of Program:　No Charge

How to obtain a copy of the program:

The program listing and test data may be obtained by contacting:

Dr. Luc Wouters
Open University Heerlen
P.O. Box 2960
6401 DL Heerlen
Netherlands

CONFIDENCE INTERVAL - PROPORTION

Title: Exact Confidence Limits for Proportions

Author: Kenneth J. Berry, Paul W. Mielke, Jr., and
Steven G. Helmricks

Source: *Educational and Psychological Measurement*, 1988,
48, 713-716.

Description: This subroutine computes exact confidence
intervals for proportions (number of successes in a finite
population) using the procedure developed by Buonaccorsi (1987).
The user inputs the size of the population, the size of the random
sample used, the number of instances in the sample possessing a
particular characteristic (e.g., number of successes), and alpha.

Program Name: CONFID (subroutine)

Language: FORTRAN 77

Compatibility: IBM and UNIX mainframes, IBM PC's and
compatibles

Memory Requirements: None Specified

Cost of Program: No Charge

How to obtain a copy of the program:

The authors prefer to e-mail the program,
however, you may send a formatted 3.5"
diskette and a self-addressed, stamped mailer to:

Dr. Kenneth J. Berry
Department of Sociology
Colorado State University
Fort Collins, CO 80523
e-mail: berry@lamar.colostate.edu

CONFIDENCE INTERVAL - PROPORTION

Title: QuickBASIC Program for Exact and Mid-P Confidence Intervals for a Binomial Proportion

Author: Terry Fagan

Source: *Computers in Biology and Medicine,* 1996, *26,* 263-267.

Description: This program computes exact confidence intervals for binomial proportions by iteratively performing the continued fraction for the incomplete beta function. This algorithm eventually converges on an upper and lower bound (i.e., confidence interval) for the true probability of N or more successes occurring out of NN trials.

Program Name: None Specified

Language: QuickBASIC

Compatibility: IBM PC's and compatibles

Memory Requirements: None Specified

Cost of Program: No Charge

How to obtain a copy of the program:

Send a formatted 3.5" diskette and
a self-addressed, stamped mailer to:

Dr. Terry Fagan
MICU/CCU
VAMC Wilkes-Barre
1111 East End Blvd.
Wilkes Barre, PA 18711

CONFIGURAL FREQUENCY ANALYSIS

Title: A Computer Program to Define Types by Configural Frequency Analysis

Author: John D. Morris

Source: *Behavior Research Methods & Instrumentation,* 1976, *8*, 311.

Description: This program performs configural frequency analysis (CFA) which is a nonparametric method that identifies modal types of subjects based on their scores on profiles of dichotomous variables. In identifying types, the occurrences of particular profiles are compared against what would be expected from the independent marginal variable frequencies. The types are tested for statistical significance and the resulting probability values are Bonferroni-corrected to control for experiment-wise error rate. Input includes the number of subjects, variables, and types to be tested, and the desired overall experimental error rate. Output includes the observed and expected frequencies, and tests of significance for each a priori specified type.

Program Name: None Specified

Language: FORTRAN IV

Compatibility: Designed for use on CDC CYBER and IBM mainframe systems

Memory Requirements: None Specified

Cost of Program: No Charge

How to obtain a copy of the program:

The program listing with documentation, and sample input and output, may be obtained by contacting:

Dr. John D. Morris
Department of Education
Florida Atlantic University
Boca Raton, FL 33431

CONJOINT MEASUREMENT

Title: CONJNT: Program for Solving Finite Conjoint Additivity

Author: Robert F. Morse and Hoben Thomas

Source: *Applied Psychological Measurement*, 1981, *5*, 202.

Description: This program implements Sherman's (1977) algorithm to determine whether any orders within a two-factor data set are conjointly additive. In analysis of variance language, the program assesses whether two-way interaction terms are real or whether they are artifactual. If the interactions are artifactual, then one concludes that a uniquely additive solution (i.e., main effects only model) best fits the data. The primary input consists of a data matrix, and output includes the rank order matrix and a set of vectors. By linearly combining the vectors, users can obtain the scale values that produce an additive solution.

Program Name: CONJNT

Language: PL/I and APL

Compatibility: Designed for use on systems that support the PL/I or APL language.

Memory Requirements: None Specified

Cost of Program: No Charge

How to obtain a copy of the program:

Send a written request to:

Dr. Hoben Thomas
Department of Psychology
513 Bruce V. Moore Building
The Pennsylvania State University
University Park, PA 16802
e-mail: hxt@psu.edu

CONJOINT MEASUREMENT

Title: CPCJM: A Set of Programs for Checking Polynomial Conjoint Measurement and Additivity Axioms of Three-Dimensional Matrices

Author: James R. Ullrich and Ronald E. Wilson

Source: *Applied Psychological Measurement,* 1990, *14*, 433.

Description: The program integrates a number of polynomial conjoint measurement tests (e.g., Krantz & Tversky, 1971) for independence, joint dependence, double and distributive cancellations for up to three-dimensional matrices. Tests for additivity (e.g., Sherman, 1977) are also provided.

Program Name: PCJM, CPCJM

Language: FORTRAN (PCJM) and Turbo C 5.0 (CPCJM)

Compatibility: UNIX mainframes, IBM PC's and compatibles

Memory Requirements: None Specified

Cost of Program: No Charge

How to obtain a copy of the program:

Send either a formatted 3.5" or 5.25" diskette and a self-addressed, stamped mailer to:

Dr. James Ullrich
Computer Science Department
University of Montana
Missoula, MT 59812
e-mail: ullrich@selway.umt.edu

CONTRAST ANALYSIS

Title: Contrast Analysis in Repeated Measures Analysis of Variance Designs: A SAS Implementation

Author: John F. Walsh

Source: *Educational and Psychological Measurement,* 1991, *51,* 655-658.

Description: This program allows users to generate their own contrasts following a statistically significant interaction in an ANOVA using the PROC GLM procedure in SAS.

Program Name: CNTRSTRM.SAS

Language: SAS

Compatibility: Any system that implements SAS

Memory Requirements: None Specified

Cost of Program: No Charge

How to obtain a copy of the program:

Send a formatted 3.5" diskette and
a self-addressed, stamped mailer to:

Dr. John F. Walsh
Department of Psychology
Fordham University
441 East Fordham Road
Bronx, NY 10458-5198
e-mail:aowalsh@murray.fordham.edu

CORRECTION FOR ATTENUATION

Title: ATTENU8: Correcting a Correlation Matrix for Degree of Attenuation

Author: Gary J. Lautenschlager

Source: *Applied Psychological Measurement,* 1989, *13,* 104.

Description: The program outputs a correlation matrix written in an ASCII file with the lower-triangle corrected for attenuation. This program also provides a procedure (different from the standard correction for attenuation formula) that might be more efficient when larger numbers of correlations are used. The input is simply composed of reliability estimates and a correlation matrix. Utility for this program may be seen in test construction, structural equation modeling, and multitrait-multimethod designs.

Program Name: ATTENU8

Language: FORTRAN 77

Compatibility: Any mainframe or IBM PC's and compatibles with a FORTRAN compiler

Memory Requirements: 640K

Cost of Program: No Charge

How to obtain a copy of the program:

Send a formatted 3.5" diskette and a self-addressed, stamped mailer to:

Dr. Gary J. Lautenschlager
Department of Psychology
University of Georgia
Athens, GA 30602-3013
e-mail: garylaut@uga.cc.uga.edu

CORRECTION FOR SHRINKAGE

Title: SHRINKR: A Program for Computing Estimates of R^2 in the Population and Formula Cross-Validation R^2

Author: Gary J. Lautenschlager

Source: *Applied Psychological Measurement,* 1987, *11*, 433.

Description: This program computes various shrinkage estimates of the squared population multiple correlation coefficient and various estimates of the squared multiple correlation coefficient used for cross-validation purposes. The input includes the sample squared multiple correlation, sample size, and number of predictors.

Program Name: SHRINKR

Language: FORTRAN 77

Compatibility: Any mainframe or IBM PC's and compatibles with a FORTRAN compiler

Memory Requirements: 640K

Cost of Program: No Charge

How to obtain a copy of the program:

Send a 3.5" formatted diskette and a self-addressed, stamped mailer to:

Dr. Gary J. Lautenschlager
Department of Psychology
University of Georgia
Athens, GA 30602-3013
e-mail: garylaut@uga.cc.uga.edu

CORRELATION

Title: A Computer Program for Correlating Pairs of Variables When One is Measured on an Ordinal and the Other on a Continuous Scale of Measurement

Author: Domenic V. Cicchetti, Nancy S. Lyons, Robert Heavens, Jr. and Ralph Horwitz

Source: *Educational and Psychological Measurement,* 1982, *42,* 209-213.

Description: To determine the correlation between a rank-ordered variable and one that is continuous, this program computes Jaspen's multiserial correlation coefficient for each comparison, proportion of cases at each rank, the *z*-score at each boundary between ranks, the mean *z* score for each rank, and summary statistics. The input consists of sample size, number of ranks for a specified comparison, maximum and minimum scores, and the ranked and continuous data. The article explains Jaspen's multiserial correlation coefficient in more detail and its benefits over the point-multiserial correlation coefficient.

Program Name: None Specified

Language: FORTRAN

Compatibility: IBM mainframes, IBM PC's and compatibles

Memory Requirements: None Specified

Cost of Program: No Charge

How to obtain a copy of the program:

Send a blank 3.5" diskette and a self-addressed, stamped mailer to:

Dr. Domenic V. Cicchetti
Senior Research Psychologist and Statistician
VA Medical Center and Yale University
950 Campbell Avenue
West Haven, CT 06516
e-mail: domenic.cicchetti@yale.edu

CORRELATION

Title: A Computer Program for Determining the Correlation Between Categorized Variables From a Bivariate Normal Distribution With a Given Correlation

Author: Robert M. O'Brien

Source: *Educational and Psychological Measurement,* 1984, *44,* 155-157.

Description: There are times when a researcher categorizes data that are ordinarily continuous. In order to determine the effects of this categorizing for two variables in terms of correlation, this program computes the Pearson product moment correlation and its square for equal distance scoring of the categories, normal scoring system, and the uniform or ridit scoring system (using the midpoint of the proportion of cases below the lower limit and upper limits of each category). The input consists of the number of categories for each variable and the cumulative proportion of cases falling below the upper extreme of each category.

Program Name: None Specified

Language: FORTRAN (uses IMSL subroutines)

Compatibility: DEC 1091

Memory Requirements: None Specified

Cost of Program: No Charge

How to obtain a copy of the program:

Send a blank 3.5" diskette and a
self-addressed, stamped mailer to:

Dr. Robert M. O'Brien
Department of Sociology
University of Oregon
Eugene, OR 97403
e-mail: bobrien@oregon.uoregon.edu

CORRELATION - AVERAGING

Title: A FORTRAN 77 Program for Averaging Correlation Coefficients

Author: N. Clayton Silver and Sarah C. Hollingsworth

Source: *Behavior Research Methods, Instruments, & Computers,* 1989, *21,* 647-650.

Description: This program computes the average correlation via the backtransformed average z procedure and its test of significance. This method could be used when one is attempting to obtain a stable estimate of the population correlation (or reliability) when small sample sizes and repeated testings are used.
A listing of the program is contained on pages 648-650.

Program Name: AVCOR

Language: FORTRAN

Compatibility: IBM PC's and compatibles

Memory Requirements: Less than 100K

Cost of Program: No Charge

How to obtain a copy of the program:

Send a formatted 3.5" diskette and
a self addressed, stamped mailer to:

Dr. N. Clayton Silver
Department of Psychology
University of Nevada, Las Vegas
Las Vegas, NV 89154-5030
e-mail: fdnsilvr@nevada.edu

CORRELATION - BOOTSTRAP

Title: MATRIXBOOT: A FORTRAN Program to Bootstrap Pearson Correlations Computed from Data Matrix Input

Author: Christy L. DeVader and Allan G. Bateson

Source: *Educational and Psychological Measurement*, 1991, *51*, 673-677.

Description: The bootstrap procedure is a nonparametric method of resampling a specific number of times (with replacement) from a set of observations and computing a certain statistic (e.g., correlation) with each iteration. The output of this interactive program consists of the number of bootstrap iterations, the mean, standard deviation, median, and 95% and 99% confidence intervals. The input is composed of any square matrix data set.

Program Name: MATRIXBOOT

Language: FORTRAN 77

Compatibility: VAX/VMS mainframes

Memory Requirements: None Specified

Cost of Program: No Charge

How to obtain a copy of the program:

Send a formatted 3.5" diskette and a self-addressed, stamped mailer to:

Dr. Allan G. Bateson
Department of Psychology
Towson State University
Towson, MD 21204
e-mail: e7p4bat@toe.towson.edu

CORRELATIONS - ILL-CONDITIONED

Title: Ill-Conditioned Correlation Analyzer

Author: William M. Holmes

Source: *Behavior Research Methods & Instrumentation,*
1982, *14*, 43.

Description: This program computes a number of statistics
designed to assess ill-conditioning in correlation matrices. Input
consists of a correlation matrix and the sample size upon which the
correlations are based. Output includes the determinant of the
matrix, the condition index, Haitovsky's test of multicollinearity,
and F tests of dependence and independence.

Program Name: ILK

Language: FORTRAN

Compatibility: Any computer having a FORTRAN
compiler. IBM, Apple, and mainframe
compatible

Memory Requirements: 28K

Cost of Program: No Charge

How to obtain a copy of the program:

Send a formatted 3.5" diskette and
a self-addressed, stamped mailer to:

Dr. William Holmes
Department of Criminal Justice
University of Massachusetts at Boston
100 Morrissey Blvd.
Boston, MA 02125
e-mail: holmes@umbsky.cc.ums.edu

CORRELATION - INDEPENDENT

Title: A FORTRAN 77 Program for Testing the Differences Among Independent Correlations

Author: N. Clayton Silver and Robert T. Burkey

Source: *Educational and Psychological Measurement*, 1991, *51*, 641-643.

Description: This program computes the Rao (1970) global test and the Levy (1976) subsequent multiple range procedure for testing the differences among independent correlations. The program is interactive and an output file is provided.

Program Name: INDEPCOR.FOR

Language: FORTRAN 77

Compatibility: VAX 8550, IBM PC's and compatibles (386 or greater) with math co-processor.

Memory Requirements: Less than 100K

Cost of Program: No Charge

How to obtain a copy of the program:

Send a formatted 3.5" diskette and
a self-addressed, stamped mailer to:

Dr. N. Clayton Silver
Department of Psychology
University of Nevada, Las Vegas
Las Vegas, NV 89154-5030
e-mail: fdnsilvr@nevada.edu

CORRELATION MATRICES

Title: CORRMTX: Generating Correlated Data Matrices

Author: T. Mark Beasley

Source: *Applied Psychological Measurement,* 1994,
18, 95.

Description: The program generates correlated data matrices for use in multivariate Monte Carlo simulations.

Program Name: CORRMTX

Language: SAS/IML

Compatibility: Any computer that implements SAS

Memory Requirements: None Specified

Cost of Program: No Charge

How to obtain a copy of the program:

Send a written request to:

Dr. T. Mark Beasley
DAIL School of Education
St. John's University
8000 Utopia Parkway
Jamaica, NY 11439
e-mail: beasleyt@sjuvm.stjohns.edu

CORRELATION MATRICES

Title: A FORTRAN 77 Program for Generating Sample
Correlation Matrices

Author: Gordon Rae

Source: *Educational and Psychological Measurement,* 1997,
57, 189-192.

Description: The program outputs sample correlation or
covariance matrices for use in Monte Carlo simulations (e.g.,
structural equation modeling, path analysis, factor analysis).

Program Name: None Specified

Language: FORTRAN 77

Compatibility: None Specified

Memory Requirements: None Specified

Cost of Program: No Charge

How to obtain a copy of the program:

Send a formatted 3.5"diskette and
a self-addressed, stamped mailer to:

Dr. Gordon Rae
School of Behavioral and Communication Sciences
University of Ulster
Coleraine
Northern Ireland
BT52 1SA

CORRELATION - MULTILEVEL DATA

Title: LEVEL: A FORTRAN IV Program for Correlational
Analysis of Group-Individual Data Structures

Author: David A. Kenny and James W. Stigler

Source: *Behavior Research Methods & Instrumentation*,
1983, *15*, 606.

Description: This program analyzes multilevel correlational data
that have been derived from hierarchically nested designs. In
particular, the program partitions variance into group and
individual effects and generates separate covariance and correlation
matrices for "persons within groups" and "groups controlling for
persons". The program can accommodate missing data and unequal
group sizes. Input includes the number of groups, the number of
persons per group, the number of variables, the number of
regression equations to be computed, and the specification of fixed
and random variables. For each level of analysis, the output
includes the covariance and correlation matrices, regression
coefficients (slope and beta) with corresponding t-tests, and the R^2
value.

Program Name: LEVEL

Language: Microsoft FORTRAN 5.0

Compatibility: IBM PC's and compatibles

Memory Requirements: 640K

Cost of Program: $150 (discounts are given to students)

How to obtain a copy of the program:

The program listing and a user's guide
may be obtained by contacting:

Dr. David A. Kenny
Department of Psychology
University of Connecticut
Storrs, CT 06269-1020
e-mail: kenny@uconnvm.uconn.edu

CORRELATION - ORDINAL

Title: Program CORFREE: A Program for Freeman's Family of Ordinal Correlation Coefficients

Author: Joseph L. Balloun and A. Ben Oumlil

Source: *Educational and Psychological Measurement*, 1990, *50*, 135-141.

Description: The program outputs three ordinal correlation coefficients (Kim's $d_{y.x}$, Wilson's e, and Goodman and Kruskal's gamma), a correction for the bias in gamma when the two variables are dichotomous, significance tests, estimates of the population correlation coefficients, robust/resistant estimates of the sampling variances of each coefficient, and the total number of observations for each correlation coefficient.

Program Name: CORFREE

Language: WATFOR 77

Compatibility: VAX/VMS mainframe, IBM PC's and compatibles

Memory Requirements: None Specified

Cost of Program: No Charge

How to obtain a copy of the program:

Send a formatted 3.5" diskette and a self-addressed, stamped mailer to:

Dr. Joseph L. Balloun
School of Business and Entrepreneurship
Nova Southeastern University
3100 SW 9th Avenue
Fort Lauderdale, FL 33315
e-mail: balloun@sbe.acast.nova.edu

CORRELATION - POLYCHORIC

Title: POLYCHR: A Computer Program to Calculate
Polychoric Correlation Coefficients from
Trichotomous Data

Author: C. David Vale

Source: *Applied Psychological Measurement*, 1980, *4*, 415.

Description: This program generates a matrix of polychoric
correlation coefficients from trichotomous data. The approach is
applicable whenever a bivariate normal relationship can be
assumed to underlie the trichotomized data. The program
calculates the determinant of the joint frequency matrix in order to
determine the sign of the obtained correlation. The primary output
consists of the lower diagonal correlation matrix.

Program Name: POLYCHR

Language: FORTRAN IV

Compatibility: IBM PC's and compatibles

Memory Requirements: At least 155K

Cost of Program: No Charge

How to obtain a copy of the program:

Send a formatted 3.5" diskette and
a self-addressed, stamped mailer to:

Dr. Malcolm Ree
AL/HRMA
7909 Lindbergh Drive
Brooks Air Force Base, TX 78235-5352
e-mail: ree@alhrm.brook.af.mil

CORRELATION - POOLING

Title: PIGCOR: A SAS Macro Program for Computing Pooled Intragroup Correlation Coefficients and Testing for Group Homogeneity

Author: Norman A. Constantine and Michael S. Shing

Source: *Applied Psychological Measurement,* 1988, *12,* 214.

Description: The program outputs a weighted and unweighted average of intragroup correlations, a significance test, and a test of homogeneity of the correlations across groups (Fisher, 1925). This program may have utility in meta-analytic procedures.

Program Name: PIGCOR

Language: SAS

Compatibility: Mainframe (should be adaptable for PC SAS)

Memory Requirements: None Specified

Cost of Program: No Charge

How to obtain a copy of the program:

Send a written request to:

Dr. Michael S. Shing
Advanced Strategies Group
Wells Fargo Nikko Investment Advising
45 Fremont St. #16F
San Francisco, CA 94105-2204

CORRELATION - TEACHING

Title: Understanding Correlations: Two Computer Exercises

Author: Miriam D. Goldstein and Michael J. Strube

Source: *Teaching of Psychology,* 1995, *22,* 205-206.

Description: The first program consists of students estimating the direction and magnitude of a correlation for nine successive scatterplots. The students receive an average absolute difference score between their estimates and the actual correlations presented. A second program allows students to produce scatterplots given a correlation of a specific direction and magnitude. These plots may be revised (either addition or deletion of points) so that the student can see how the magnitude of the correlation can change.

Program Name: None Specified

Language: QuickBASIC

Compatibility: IBM PC's and compatibles

Memory Requirements: 57K, 47K

Cost of Program: No Charge

How to obtain a copy of the program:

Send a formatted 3.5" diskette and
a self-addressed, stamped mailer to:

Dr. Miriam D. Goldstein
Department of Psychology
Washington University
St. Louis, MO 63130-4899
e-mail: miri@artsci.wustle.edu

CORRELATION - TRENDS

Title: A FORTRAN 77 Program for Testing Trends Among
Independent Correlations

Author: N. Clayton Silver, Michael S. Finger,
and Robert T. Burkey

Source: *Educational and Psychological Measurement*, 1992,
52, 109-111.

Description: This interactive program outputs the sum of squares
for each trend component and the probability that the particular
trend does not exist in the independent correlations. The input
consists of the independent correlations and sample sizes. The
program also computes trends for unequal sample sizes.

Program Name: TREND.FOR

Language: FORTRAN 77

Compatibility: IBM PC's and compatibles, IBM 4381
mainframe

Memory Requirements: Less than 100K

Cost of Program: No Charge

How to obtain a copy of the program:

Send a formatted 3.5" diskette and
a self-addressed, stamped mailer to:

Dr. N. Clayton Silver
Department of Psychology
University of Nevada, Las Vegas
4505 Maryland Pkwy
Las Vegas, NV 89154-5030
e-mail: fdnsilvr@nevada.edu

CORRESPONDENCE ANALYSIS

Title: CORV: A Microcomputer Program for Five Models of
Correspondence Analysis of Contingency Tables

Author: Bernard S. Gorman and Louis H. Primavera

Source: *Behavior Research Methods, Instruments, & Computers,*
1992, *24,* 580.

Description: Correspondence analysis is useful when the
researcher is interested in examining, for example, frequency
counts of various races across their different political party
affiliations (e.g., Democrat, Republican, Independent) in a
contingency table. In order to aid the researcher in interpretation,
the rows and columns of the contingency table are then depicted as
points in a graph using principal components analysis. This
program performs correspondence analysis using distance
normalization (Carroll et al, 1986), Greenacre's (1984)
normalization, "optimal" scaling (Nishisato, 1980), reciprocal
averaging normalization (Hill, 1971), and biplot normalization
(Gabriel, 1971; Maxwell, 1977). The output consists of the
eigenvalues, proportions of variance accounted for by each factor,
and approximate chi-square tests (for the entire contingency table
and for the individual factors). The input consists of either an
ASCII file or a contingency table entered via the keyboard.

Program Name: CORVD and CORVS

Language: QuickBASIC 4.5

Compatibility: IBM PC's and compatibles

Memory Requirements: 60K

Cost of Program: No Charge

How to obtain a copy of the program:

Send a formatted 3.5" diskette and
a self-addressed, stamped mailer to:

Dr. Bernard S. Gorman
Department of Psychology
1 Education Drive
Nassau Community College
Garden City, NY 11530
e-mail: bsgorman@pipeline.com

CORRESPONDENCE ANALYSIS

Title: MCA: A Simple Program for Multiple Correspondence
Analysis

Author: Bernard S. Gorman and Louis H. Primavera

Source: *Educational and Psychological Measurement,* 1993,
53, 685-687.

Description: This interactive program performs principal
components analysis on the cross-tabulation matrix of all
categories of all variables for examining patterns of association
among these categorical variables. This technique is also useful
subsequent to a log-linear analysis.   The input consists of the
sample size, number of categorical variables, the number of
categories for each variable, and either a subjects-by-variables
response matrix or a cross-tabulation matrix of all categories of all
variables. The program accommodates up to 70 categories (across
all variables).

Program Name: MCA

Language: QuickBASIC 4.5

Compatibility: IBM PC's and compatibles

Memory Requirements: 60K

Cost of Program: No Charge

How to obtain a copy of the program:

Send a formatted 3.5" diskette and
a self-addressed, stamped mailer to:

Dr. Bernard S. Gorman
Department of Psychology
1 Education Drive
Nassau Community College
Garden City, NY 11530
e-mail: bsgorman@pipeline.com

CORRESPONDENCE ANALYSIS

Title: COR.ANALYSIS: A P-STAT Macro for
Correspondence Analysis

Author: Wenzel Matiaske

Source: *Psychometrika,* 1991, *56,* 154.

Description: This program performs correspondence analysis of
contingency table data. The user input consists of the data matrix
and the number of dimensions to be analyzed. Output includes the
row and column profiles, inertias of the principal components and
associated chi-square statistic, the row and column contributions to
the overall model, and a factor map of the first and second
principal axes.

Program Name: COR.ANALYSIS

Language: Written for P-STAT (1988)

Compatibility: Any system that supports P-STAT

Memory Requirements: None Specified

Cost of Program: No Charge

How to obtain a copy of the program:

Send a formatted 3.5" diskette and
a self-addressed, stamped mailer to:

Dr. Wenzel Matiaske
Universitaet-Gesamthochschule Paderborn
Fachbereich 5
Warburger Straße 100
4790 Paderborn
West Germany
e-mail: ematil@pbhrzt.uucp

COVARIANCE STRUCTURAL MODELING

Title: Fuzzy Fit Index Tutoring System (FFITS): An
Intelligent System for Interpreting and Integrating
Covariance Structure Modeling Solutions

Author: J. Phillip Craiger and Michael D. Coovert

Source: *Applied Psychological Measurement,* 1991,
15, 292.

Description: The program provides help in evaluating the
goodness-of-fit, relative fit, and/or parsimony of the covariance
structure model. Furthermore, a tutorial is provided to aid users in
using the indices associated with evaluating covariance structure
models.

Program Name: FFITS-2

Language: C Language Integrated Production System

Compatibility: Any mainframe, IBM PC's and compatibles

Memory Requirements: 60K

Cost of Program: No Charge

How to obtain a copy of the program:

Send a formatted 3.5" diskette and
a self-addressed, stamped mailer to:

Dr. Michael D. Coovert
Department of Psychology
BEH 339
University of South Florida
Tampa, FL 33620-8200
e-mail: coovert@luna.cas.usf.edu

CRITERION-REFERENCED TESTS

Title: Determining the Lengths for Criterion-Referenced Tests

Author: Ronald K. Hambleton, Craig N. Mills, and Robert Simon

Source: *Journal of Educational Measurement,* 1983, *20,* 27-38.

Description: Discusses the use of the TESTLEN computer program (Mills & Simon, 1981) to generate a simulation program that examines the impact of test length on the decision consistency and accuracy of mastery vs. nonmastery decisions. The impact that other factors might have on the association between test length and the reliability and validity of criterion-referenced scores was also examined. Such factors included the method of item selection, the domain score distribution, and the statistical characteristics of the item pool (e.g., the item discrimination and difficulty parameters). Tables detailing the results of the simulation are presented in the article as are guidelines for tailoring one's use of the simulation program to meet particular user-defined specifications.

Program Name: TESTLEN was used to generate the computer simulation.

Language: None Specified

Compatibility: None Specified

Memory Requirements: None Specified

Cost of Program: A nominal fee (None Specified) is requested to cover the cost of handling and mailing.

How to obtain a copy of the program:

To obtain a copy of the computer simulation program, please send a written request to:

Ms. Bernadette McDonald
University of Massachusetts
Hills South, Room 152
Amherst, MA 01002
e-mail: rkh@educ.umass.edu

CRITICAL VALUES AND PROBABILITIES

Title: Probabilities and Critical Values for z, chi-square, r, t, and F

Author: Kevin E. O'Grady

Source: *Behavior Research Methods & Instrumentation,* 1981, *13,* 55-56.

Description: This program calculates probabilities and critical values for five commonly used statistics (z, chi square, r, t, and F). In order to estimate probability levels, the user inputs the probability distribution to be referenced, degrees of freedom, and the value of the test statistic. To obtain a critical value for a given probability level, the user indicates the relevant probability distribution, degrees of freedom, and the desired two-tailed significance level.

Program Name: None Specified

Language: FORTRAN IV

Compatibility: Runs on any system capable of supporting FORTRAN

Memory Requirements: None Specified

Cost of Program: No Charge

How to obtain a copy of the program:

A listing of the program can be obtained by contacting:

Dr. Kevin E. O'Grady
Department of Psychology
University of Maryland
College Park, MD 20742

CROSS-VALIDATION

Title: Computer Assisted Multicrossvalidation in Regression Analysis

Author: David J. Krus and Ellen A. Fuller

Source: *Educational and Psychological Measurement,* 1982, *42,* 187-193.

Description: This program computes a multicrossvalidation algorithm (i.e., repeatedly performing the standard crossvalidation technique to randomly selected subsamples of data). This approach compares favorably with the standard corrections for shrinkage.

Program Name: None Specified

Language: None Specified

Compatibility: None Specified

Memory Requirements: None Specified

Cost of Program: No Charge

How to obtain a copy of the program:

Send a formatted MS-DOS 5.25"diskette and a self-addressed, stamped mailer to:

Dr. David J. Krus
Educational Psychology Department
Arizona State University
Tempe, AZ 85287

CROSS-VALIDATION

Title: Cross-Validation with Gollob's Estimator: A
Computational Simplification

Author: John D. Morris

Source: *Educational and Psychological Measurement,* 1984,
44, 151-154.

Description: This program outputs Gollob's (1967) procedure for
estimating the population cross-validation coefficient of a sample
regression approach using the computational simplification
suggested by Allen (1971). The predicted score is also available.
Drehmer (1979) reported that Gollob's estimate was more efficient
than the Darlington (1968), Wherry (1931), and Olkin and Pratt
(1958) procedures and less biased than Darlington's (1968)
procedure with small samples (sample size of 20-60 and between
3-5 predictors).

Program Name: None Specified

Language: FORTRAN

Compatibility: None Specified

Memory Requirements: None Specified

Cost of Program: No Charge

How to obtain a copy of the program:

Send a formatted 3.5" diskette and
a self-addressed, stamped mailer to:

Dr. John D. Morris
Department of Education
Florida Atlantic University
Boca Raton, FL 33431

CUTTING SCORES

Title: UTIL: A BASIC Program for Determining Optimal
Cutting Scores Adjusted for Base Rates and
Classification Utility

Author: Dale E. Berger and Richard N. Tsujimoto

Source: *Educational and Psychological Measurement,* 1983,
43, 173-175.

Description: This menu-driven program is useful for determining
the optimal cutting score used to discriminate between two groups.
The input includes estimates of the population mean and variance
of each group, population base rates, and outcomes of the four
classification cells (true negative, false negative, true positive, and
false positive). The output consists of the expected proportion of
cases that will fall into each of the categories, will be misclassified
in each group, and will be misclassified overall. Moreover, the
optimal decision rule and a utility function for a specified set of
cutting scores are also given.

Program Name: UTIL

Language: BASIC

Compatibility: IBM PC's and compatibles and can be adapted for
mainframe use.

Memory Requirements: 4K

Cost of Program: $15

How to obtain a copy of the program:

Send a formatted 3.5" diskette, a self-addressed
stamped mailer, and payment to:

Dr. Dale Berger
Psychology Department
Claremont Graduate School
123 E. Eighth St.
Claremont, CA 91711
e-mail: bergerd@cgs.edu

DATA GENERATION AND ANALYSIS

Title: DATAGEN: A BASIC Program for Generating and
Analyzing Data for Use in Statistics Courses

Author: Leslie J. Cake and Roy C. Hostetter

Source: *Teaching of Psychology, 1986, 13,* 210-212.

Description: This program generates random samples of data in response to user-specified population parameters (means and standard deviations). In addition to population parameters, the user specifies the number of samples, the N for each sample, whether the samples are independent or dependent and, if the samples are dependent, the desired correlation between the two populations from which the samples are drawn. For each generated data set, a completely randomized one-way ANOVA can be performed. The ANOVA output and sample summary statistics can be printed separately (in somewhat different forms) for the instructor and the student.

Program Name: DATAGEN

Language: GWBASIC/BASICA/QuickBASIC

Compatibility: IBM PC's and compatibles

Memory Requirements: 640K

Cost of Program: No Charge

How to obtain a copy of the program:

Send a formatted 3.5" diskette and
a self-addressed, stamped mailer to:

Dr. Leslie Cake or Dr. Roy Hostetter
Department of Psychology
Sir Wilfred Grenfell College
University Drive
Corner Brook, Newfoundland
Canada, A2H 6P9
e-mail: lcake@beothuk.swgc.mun.ca
e-mail: rhostett@beothuk.swgc.mun.ca

DATA SORTING

Title: SELECT: A Pascal Program for Easy Data Manipulation

Author: Johannes Kingma and Johan Reuvekamp

Source: *Educational and Psychological Measurement,* 1987, *47,* 135-137.

Description: This program can rearrange the variable order in a data file. Moreover, this program allows for a selection of variables to be used from a big file in order for some microcomputers to handle data analysis. A separate output file is provided.

Program Name: SELECT

Language: Pascal

Compatibility: Apple II+

Memory Requirements: 18K

Cost of Program: None Specified

How to obtain a copy of the program:

Send a blank 3.5" diskette and a self-addressed, stamped mailer to:

Dr. Johannes Kingma
University Hospital at Groningen
Department of Traumatology
Groningen
Netherlands

DECISION THEORY - SOCIAL GROUPS

Title: SCHEME: An Interactive FORTRAN Program to Analyze and Simulate Group Decision Data

Author: Dennis H. Nagao and Verlin B. Hinsz

Source: *Behavior Research Methods & Instrumentation,* 1980, *12,* 484-486.

Description: This program evaluates the statistical adequacy (i.e., fit) of various models of group decision making by comparing different predicted group distributions of decisional preferences (differing on the basis of the social rule employed) against an observed group distribution. The program can also simulate the effects of group size, type of decision rule, and type of preference distribution on the distribution of group decisions. In executing simulations, the user may specify up to nine different distributions of individual preferences. The program is interactive and for each mode of analysis (model testing and simulation) the user is prompted for all relevant information.

Program Name: SCHEME

Language: CDC FORTRAN Extended Version 4

Compatibility: Initially designed to run in timesharing mode on a CDC 170 under the network operating system (NOS). The program can be modified to be compatible with other types of FORTRAN compilers.

Memory Requirements: None Specified

Cost of Program: No Charge

How to obtain a copy of the program:

The source code, a user's manual, and sample input and output may be obtained by contacting:

Dr. Dennis H. Nagao
Department of Management
Georgia Institute of Technology
225 North Avenue, NW
Atlanta, GA 30332-0001

DIAGNOSTIC EFFICIENCY STATISTICS

Title: Automated Calculation of Diagnostic Efficiency
Statistics

Author: Gary L. Canivez and Marley W. Watkins

Source: *Behavior Research Methods, Instruments, & Computers,*
1996, 28, 132-133.

Description: This program, written for Microsoft Excel,
computes sensitivity, positive and negative predictive power, false
positive rate, overall hit (correct classification) rate, kappa, the test
of significance, and its standard error.

Program Name: None Specified

Language: None Specified

Compatibility: Macintosh

Memory Requirements: None Specified

Cost of Program: $5; No charge if downloaded from America
OnLine BBS service

How to obtain a copy of the program:

Send a Macintosh formatted 3.5" diskette
and a self-addressed, stamped mailer to:

Dr. Gary L. Canivez
Department of Psychology
Eastern Illinois University
Charleston, IL 61920-3099
e-mail: cfglc@eiu.edu

DIAGNOSTIC EFFICIENCY STATISTICS

Title: A SAS Macro for Calculating Positive Predictive Values Across a Range of Base Rates

Author: Kevin P. Weinfurt

Source: *Applied Psychological Measurement,* 1996, *20,* 100.

Description: This macro program computes the positive predictive values (probability that a condition exists when it was predicted on the basis of the test result - such as would be found in the medical field). The input consists of the true and false positive rates and the output provides a plot of the positive predictive value as a function of the base rate.

Program Name: EFFIC.SAS

Language: SAS

Compatibility: Any system with SAS capabilities

Memory Requirements: None Specified

Cost of Program: No Charge

How to obtain a copy of the program:

Send a formatted 3.5" diskette and
a self-addressed, stamped mailer to:

Dr. Kevin P. Weinfurt
Department of Psychiatry
Georgetown University Medical Center
3750 Reservoir Road, NW
Washington, DC 20007
e-mail: kweinf01@gumedlib.dml.georgetown.edu

DIFFERENTIAL ITEM FUNCTIONING

Title: Lord_DIF: A Computer Program to Compute Lord's DIF Statistics

Author: Yuan Hwang Li

Source: *Applied Psychological Measurement,* 1995, *19,* 72.

Description: This interactive program computes the differential item functioning procedure (Lord, 1980) for detecting significant differences in item response functions among groups. That is, this program aids in examining differences across groups in determining the probability of obtaining a correct response for a given item. The input consists of the name of the input file (where the item statistics are stored for each group), transformation coefficients, and the name of the output file.

Program Name: LORD_DIF

Language: PASCAL

Compatibility: IBM PC's and compatibles

Memory Requirements: None Specified

Cost of Program: No Charge

How to obtain a copy of the program:

Send a formatted 3.5" diskette and
a self-addressed, stamped mailer to:

Dr. Yuan Hwang Li
Room 205
Test Development and Administration Office
Prince George's Public Schools
Upper Marlboro, MD 20772
e-mail: yuanhwan@wam.umd.edu

DIMENSIONALITY

Title: DIMTEST: A FORTRAN Program for Assessing Dimensionality of Binary Item Responses

Author: William Stout, Ratna Nandakumar, Brian Junker, Hua-Hua Chang, and Duane Steidinger

Source: *Applied Psychological Measurement,* 1992, *16,* 236.

Description: The program examines the hypothesis that the model associated with a matrix of dichotomous item responses (from a specified group of test takers) is unidimensional. The input includes test length and sample size. A partitioning of test items is available via IRTGO. The output consists of Stout's (1987) T statistic with the appropriate probability value, and the items that are included in the assessment and partitioning subtests.

Program Name: DIMTEST

Language: FORTRAN 77

Compatibility: UNIX mainframe systems, IBM PC's and compatibles

Memory Requirements: Need at least 640K memory and 10MB of hard drive

Cost of Program: $60 for students

How to obtain a copy of the program:

Send written request and payment to:

Dr. William Stout
Statistical Laboratory for Educational and Psychological Measurement
University of Illinois
101 Illini Hall
725 S. Wright Street
Champaign, IL 61820
e-mail: stoutdist@stat.uiuc.edu

DISCRIMINANT ANALYSIS

Title: Multiple Discriminant Analysis: A BASIC Program for Microcomputers

Author: Daniel Coulombe

Source: *Behavior Research Methods, Instruments, & Computers*, 1985, *17*, 135-136.

Description: Discriminant analysis allows for a linear combination of correlated variables to separate or classify groups of subjects. In performing multiple discriminant analysis, the output consists of the means and standard deviations for each group (and variables), the eigenvalues, discriminatory power index, Wilks' lambda, R^2, Bartlett's test of significance, discriminant functions (standardized and unstandardized) and the functions evaluated at group centroids, structural coefficients, discriminant scores for each individual, and the probability of each individual belonging to a particular group. The input consists of the number of variables, groups, and participants in each group. The raw data may be contained either in a file or manually entered. An example of the output is provided on pages 135-136.

Program Name: None Specified

Language: GW-BASIC

Compatibility: IBM PC's and compatibles, Tandy 2000

Memory Requirements: 7K

Cost of Program: $15

How to obtain a copy of the program:

Send a written request and payment to:

Dr. Daniel Coulombe
School of Psychology
University of Ottawa
275 Nicholas
Ottawa, Ontario
Canada
K1N 6N5

DISCRIMINANT ANALYSIS

Title: Implementation of Linear and Quadratic Discriminant
Analysis Incorporating Costs of Misclassification

Author: Ulrich Grouven, Felix Bergel, and Arthur Schultz

Source: *Computer Methods and Programs in Biomedicine*,
1996, *49*, 55-60.

Description: Performs both traditional linear discriminant
analysis (LDA) and quadratic discriminant analysis (QDA) as well
as variants of LDA and QDA that take into account
misclassification costs. The program is menu-driven and users can
specify, using mathematical expressions, the form of the cost
function desired (e.g., linear, quadratic, exponential). Output
includes the group-specific and pooled covariance matrices, the
estimated and true group membership, the classification table, and
the group-specific and overall resubstitution error rates.

Program Name: None Specified

Language: Borland PASCAL 7.0

Compatibility: IBM PC's and compatibles

Memory Requirements: At least 130 KB

Cost of Program: None Specified

How to obtain a copy of the program:

Send a formatted 3.5" diskette and
a self-addressed, stamped mailer to:

Dr. Ulrich Grouven
Hannover Medical School
Research Group Informatics and Biometry
Department Anaesthesia IV
Hospital Ostadt
Podbielskistraße 380
D-30659
Hannover, Germany

DISCRIMINANT ANALYSIS

Title: A Non-Parametric Variable Selection Algorithm for
Allocatory Linear Discriminant Analysis

Author: Samuel L. Seaman and Dean M. Young

Source: *Educational and Psychological Measurement*, 1990,
50, 837-841.

Description: The authors have developed an algorithm that selects
a subset of variables which minimizes the conditional probability
of misclassifications. This probability has been computed via the
leave-out method (Lachenbruch, 1967). The program output
consists of the conditional probabilities of misclassification for the
full set and subset of variables and a synopsis of the variables
retained by this non-parametric procedure. The input consists of
the sample size of each group, the number of variables, and the raw
data sorted by group membership.

Program Name: None Specified

Language: SAS (PROC MATRIX)

Compatibility: Any system using SAS. Initially tested on an
IBM 4361 machine

Memory Requirements: None Specified

Cost of Program: No Charge

How to obtain a copy of the program:

For the SAS listing, send a written request to:

Dr. Samuel L. Seaman
Information Sciences Department
Baylor University
500 Speight Avenue
Waco, TX 76798-0002

DISCRIMINANT ANALYSIS

Title: MAKE45: A User Interface for Multivariable Optimal
Discriminant Analysis Via SAS/OR

Author: Robert C. Soltysik and Paul R. Yarnold

Source: *Applied Psychological Measurement,* 1991,
15, 170.

Description: This interactive program writes the SAS/OR code to
perform two-category multivariable optimal discriminant analysis.
The input consists of a data file containing the binomial class
variable and the two continuous variables.

Program Name: MAKE45

Language: Turbo BASIC

Compatibility: VM/CMS mainframes and IBM PC's and
compatibles

Memory Requirements: 640K

Cost of Program: $25

How to obtain a copy of the program:

Send a formatted 3.5" diskette, a self-addressed
mailer, and payment to:

Dr. Paul R. Yarnold
Division of General Internal Medicine
Northwestern University Medical School
750 N. Lake Shore Drive
Room 626
Chicago, IL 60611
e-mail: paul.r.yarnold@uic.edu or laz@toad.net

DISCRIMINANT ANALYSIS - BOOTSTRAP

Title: A SAS Macro for Bootstrapping the Results of
Discriminant Analyses

Author: Lenard I. Dalgleish and David Chant

Source: *Educational and Psychological Measurement*, 1995,
55, 613-624.

Description: These macro programs perform the bootstrap
procedure for estimating standard errors and confidence intervals
on structure coefficients in discriminant function analysis. A
description of the bootstrap method is also provided.

Program Names: BSDA -   produces bootstrap values for
canonical correlations and
structure coefficients in a SAS
data set.

BSSTD -   provides bootstrap estimates of
standard error, zstatistics and
their probability values.

BCPCTL - gives the corrected bootstrap
confidence intervals for a
particular alpha.

Language: SAS

Compatibility: Any system that uses SAS

Memory Requirements: None Specified

Cost of Program: No Charge

How to obtain a copy of the program:

Send a formatted MS-DOS 3.5" diskette
and a self-addressed, stamped mailer to:

Dr. Lenard I. Dalgleish
Department of Psychology
University of Queensland
Brisbane, 4072
Queensland, Australia
e-mail: len@psych.psy.uq.oz.au

DISCRIMINANT ANALYSIS - BOOTSTRAP

Title: DISCSTRA: A Computer Program that Computes Bootstrap Resampling Estimates of Descriptive Discriminant Analysis Function and Structure Coefficients and Group Centroids

Author: Bruce Thompson

Source: *Educational and Psychological Measurement*, 1992, *52*, 905-911.

Description: This program provides bootstrap estimates of discriminant function and structure coefficients along with group centroids. The standard deviation and the coefficients of skewness and kurtosis are also provided for the function and structure coefficients.   An example and interpretation of the output is provided in the article.

Program Name: DISCSTRA

Language: FORTRAN 77

Compatibility: Mainframes that accommodate the IMSL package

Memory Requirements: None Specified

Cost of Program: No Charge

How to obtain a copy of the program:

Send an MS-DOS formatted 3.5" diskette and a self-addressed, stamped mailer to:

Dr. Bruce Thompson
Department of Educational Psychology
Texas A & M University
College Station, TX 77843-4225
e-mail: e100bt@tamvm1.tamu.edu

DISCRIMINANT ANALYSIS - JACKKNIFE

Title: A SAS Macro for Jackknifing the Results of Discriminant Analyses

Author: David Chant and Lenard I. Dalgleish

Source: *Multivariate Behavioral Research*, 1992, *27*, 323-333.

Description: This macro conducts jackknife analyses on the canonical correlations and structure coefficients from a discriminant analysis. The program utilizes the leave-one-out method (omitted subgroups are of size one) when selecting subsamples for jackknifing. The output consists of the jackknife estimates, the associated standard errors, and the *t*-values and p-values for each estimated canonical correlation and structure coefficient.

Program Name: JKCAND

Language: SAS

Compatibility: Any computer that supports SAS

Memory Requirements: None Specified

Cost of Program: No Charge

How to obtain a copy of the program:

Send a formatted 3.5" diskette and
a self-addressed, stamped mailer to:

Dr. Lenard I. Dalgleish
Department of Psychology
University of Queensland
Brisbane, 4072
Queensland, Australia
e-mail: len@psych.psy.uq.oz.au

DOMAIN SCORES

Title: LTDOMAIN: A Look-Up Table for the Corresponding Estimated One-Parameter Logistic Model Scale Score and the Unbiased Domain Score for Each Number-Correct Score

Author: Yuan Hwang Li

Source: *Applied Psychological Measurement,* 1995, *19,* 50.

Description: This interactive program generates a table for estimating a test taker's performance on a particular test without using their specific response pattern. This can be obtained by using theta (one-parameter logistic item response theory scale score -- usually the number-correct is a good estimate of this), the item difficulty, and proportion-correct score (unbiased estimated domain score). The input consists of the scaling factor and the names of the input and output files.

Program Name: LTDOMAIN

Language: PASCAL

Compatibility: IBM PC's and compatibles

Memory Requirements: None Specified

Cost of Program: No Charge

How to obtain a copy of the program:

Send a formatted 3.5" diskette and a self-addressed, stamped mailer to:

Dr. Yuan Hwang Li
Room 205
Test Development and Administration Office
Prince George's Public Schools
Upper Marlboro, MD 20772
e-mail: yuanhwan@wam.umd.edu

DRUG DOSE MONITORING

Title: MW/Pharm: An Integrated Software Package for
Drug Dosage Regimen Calculation and Therapeutic
Drug Monitoring

Author: Johannes H. Proost and Dirk K.F. Meijer

Source: *Computers in Biology and Medicine,* 1992, *22,*
155-163.

Description: After inputting a patient's personal information
(e.g., body weight, height, creatinine clearance) and medication
history, the program calculates several patient status variables (e.g.,
body surface area, lean body mass corrected for drug distribution
into fat tissue) as well as numerous pharmacokinetic parameters
(e.g., minimum and maximum effective concentrations, metabolic
and renal clearance rates, maximum elimination rate). Curve
fitting and/or Bayesian methods are then applied to these data in
order to calculate individualized pharmacokinetic parameters and a
theoretical dosing regimen for the patient.

Program Name: MW/Pharm (version 3.15). The program is
available in English, German, and Dutch
versions.

Language: None Specified

Compatibility: IBM PC's and compatibles

Memory Requirements: 600KB

Cost of Program: $1395

How to obtain a copy of the program:

For further information, contact:

Mediware B.V.
Industrieweg 11
8444 AS Heerenveen
The Netherlands
phone: (31) 51 3681789
fax: (31) 51 3681563

DRUG PHARMACOKINETICS

Title: Computation and Statistical Comparison of the Parameter Estimates of the Michaelis-Menten Model Using Nonlinear Optimization. ENZ 2.0, a User-Friendly Software Package

Author: Hedwig K. Stals and Peter E. Declercq

Source: *Computer Methods and Programs in Biomedicine, 1992, 37, 149-150.*

Description: Calculates the Michaelis-Menten constant K_m and the maximum elimination rate V_{max} for pharmacological/enzyme kinetic data using a nonlinear regression approach that incorporates the Davidson-Fletcher-Powell optimization method. A strength of the program is that it allows one to compare estimates of K_m and/or V_{max} across different data sets.

Program Name: ENZ 2.0

Language: Compiled BASIC

Compatibility: IBM PC's, PS2's, and compatibles

Memory Requirements: None Specified

Cost of Program: None Specified

How to obtain a copy of the program:

Send a written request to:

Dr. Peter E. Declercq
Katholieke Universiteit Leuven
Instituut voor Farmaceutische Wetenschappen
Laboratorium voor Klinische Chemie
E. Van Evenstraat 4, B-3000
Leuven, Belgium

DYADIC DATA

Title: Interpersonal Perception: A Social Relations Analysis

Author: David A. Kenny

Source: Book published by The Guilford Press in 1994.

Description: The book describes the analysis of interpersonal, dyadic data. The program SOREMO analyzes round-robin designs in which each individual communicates with or rates everyone in the group. The program BLOCKO analyzes block designs in which two subgroups of individuals are formed and each person rates everyone else in the other subgroup. Separate examples and the utility of each design are provided by the author.

Program Name: SOREMO and BLOCKO

Language: Microsoft FORTRAN 5.0

Compatibility: IBM PC's and compatibles

Memory Requirements: 640K

Cost of Program: $150 (discount for students)

How to obtain a copy of the program:

Send a written request to:

Dr. David A. Kenny
Department of Psychology
University of Connecticut
Storrs, CT 06269-1020
e-mail: kenny@uconnvm.uconn.edu

EFFECT SIZE

Title: A Computer Program to Calculate the Modified Glass Effect Size Estimator

Author: Stephen Powers

Source: *Educational and Psychological Measurement*, 1983, *43*, 843-844.

Description: This program computes a modification (Hedges, 1981) of Glass's estimate of effect size which is the sample mean difference divided by the standard deviation of the control group (Glass, 1976). The output includes the unbiased estimate of effect size, the weighted and unbiased estimator of the effect size across all experiments, the variance, and the 95% confidence interval. This program may be useful in meta-analysis work.

Program Name: None Specified

Language: BASIC

Compatibility: DECsystem-10 and compatibles

Memory Requirements: None Specified

Cost of Program: No Charge

How to obtain a copy of the program:

Send a blank 3.5" diskette and a
self-addressed, stamped mailer to:

Dr. Stephen Powers
Legal and Research Services
Tucson Unified School District
P.O. Box 40400
Tucson, AZ 85717

EFFECT SIZE

Title: A Program Which Computes a Multivariate Analog of Omega Squared

Author: Bruce Thompson

Source: *Educational and Psychological Measurement*, 1982, *42*, 201-204.

Description: This program computes the multivariate omega squared and a corrected multivariate omega squared (Tatsuoka, 1973) that eliminates the positive bias in multivariate omega squared. The output also includes estimates of variance accounted for and plots these values for aid in determining statistical significance. This application may be used in discriminant function analysis or multivariate analysis of variance.

Program Name: None Specified

Language: FORTRAN

Compatibility: None Specified

Memory Requirements: None Specified

Cost of Program: No Charge

How to obtain a copy of the program:

Send a blank 3.5" diskette and a
self-addressed, stamped mailer to:

Dr. Bruce Thompson
Department of Educational Psychology
Texas A & M University
College Station, TX 77843-4225
e-mail: e100bt@tamvm1.tamu.edu

EFFECT SIZE - META-ANALYSIS

Title: The Meta-Analysis Effect Size Calculator: A BASIC Program for Reconstructing Unbiased Effect Sizes

Author: William L. Curlette

Source: *Educational and Psychological Measurement*, 1987, *47*, 107-109.

Description: Computes the effect sizes for a meta-analysis in a number of ways depending upon the information provided in a research report. These procedures include Cohen's *d* (1977), and methodologies from Glass, McGaw, and Smith (1981) and Hedges (1981). An unbiased estimate of effect size is also output. Dr. Curlette has converted his uncompiled BASIC version to a compiled FORTRAN version.

Program Name: None Specified

Language: BASIC, FORTRAN

Compatibility: IBM PC's and compatibles

Memory Requirements: 13K memory (BASIC version)
30K memory (FORTRAN version)

Cost of Program: No charge for the paper copy of the BASIC version. $5 for the compiled FORTRAN version.

How to obtain a copy of the program:

Send a 3.5" diskette, payment (for FORTRAN version), and a self-addressed, stamped mailer to:

Dr. William L. Curlette
Department of Educational Policy Studies
Georgia State University
University Plaza
Atlanta, GA 30303
e-mail: wcurlette@gsu.edu

EFFECT SIZE, POWER, SAMPLE SIZE

Title: POWPAL: A Program for Estimating Effect Sizes, Statistical Power, and Sample Sizes

Author: Bernard S. Gorman, Louis H. Primavera, and David B. Allison

Source: *Educational and Psychological Measurement*, 1995, *55*, 773-776.

Description: Computes the effect sizes and power estimates of t, r, z, F, chi-square, or Cohen's (1988) d or f values using a modification of Darlington's (1990) formula. Effect sizes and power estimates are also provided for noncentrality parameters, sample sizes, or degrees of freedom from previous studies.

Program Name: POWPAL

Language: QuickBASIC 4.5

Compatibility: IBM PC's and compatibles

Memory Requirements: 60K disk space and less than 500K of RAM

Cost of Program: No Charge

How to obtain a copy of the program:

Send a blank 3.5" diskette and a self-addressed, stamped mailer to:

Dr. Bernard S. Gorman
Department of Psychology
1 Education Drive
Nassau Community College
Garden City, NY 11530
e-mail: bsgorman @pipeline.com

EFFECT SIZE, POWER, SAMPLE SIZE

Title: Power & Effect: A Statistical Utility for Macintosh and Windows Systems

Author: Glenn E. Meyer

Source: *Behavior Research Methods, Instruments, & Computers*, 1995, *27*, 134-138.

Description: This menu-driven interactive program computes the power, effect size, and sample size estimates of t, r, various ANOVA and ANCOVA designs, multiple regression, and chi-square. Moreover, tests of significance are available for r, testing r against a specified population correlation, one-, two-, and matched-sample t-tests, and slopes of regression lines (including testing the difference between two slopes). Additionally, opportunities are allowed to rectify incorrect entries and a help menu also is provided.

Program Name: POWER & EFFECT

Language: Hypercard 2.1 (for Macintosh); Windowcraft (for IBM PC Windows versions)

Compatibility: IBM PC's and compatibles (Windows 3.0 or 3.1) and Macintosh

Memory Requirements: None Specified

Cost of Program: $50 per copy. Site licenses are also available by contacting the author.

How to obtain a copy of the program:

Send a written request (specify either Macintosh or Windows versions) and payment to:

Dr. Glenn E. Meyer
Department of Psychology
Trinity University
715 Stadium Drive
San Antonio, TX 78212
e-mail: gmeyer@trinity.edu

EIGENVALUES

Title: EIGEN: A BASIC Program for Computing the Eigenvectors and Eigenvalues of a Real Symmetric Matrix

Author: Stephen Powers

Source: *Educational and Psychological Measurement,* 1987, *47,* 121-122.

Description: This program computes eigenvectors and eigenvalues of a real symmetric matrix using the JK method (Kaiser, 1972).

Program Name: EIGEN

Language: BASIC

Compatibility: TRS-80 Model 4 Microcomputer

Memory Requirements: 4.5K

Cost of Program: No Charge

How to obtain a copy of the program:

Send an MS-DOS formatted 3.5" diskette
and a self-addressed, stamped mailer to:

Dr. Stephen Powers
Legal and Research Services
Tucson Unified School District
P.O. Box 40400
Tucson, AZ 85717

EXPECTANCY TABLES

Title: A Theoretical Expectancy Table Calculator

Author: Brett Myors

Source: *Behavior Research Methods, Instruments, & Computers,*
1994, *26,* 467-469.

Description: This program provides simple, successive, and
cumulative expectancy tables . A successive expectancy table
provides the conditional probability of being in a particular column
given a particular row, whereas the cumulative probability is the
cumulative conditional probability of being in a particular column
given a particular row. These may be useful in selection validity.
The input consists of the correlation coefficient, number of rows
and columns in the table with the proportion in each row and
column. An example of the input and output is presented on page
468.

Program Name: EXPECT

Language: C (Compiled on Microsoft QuickC)

Compatibility: IBM PC's and compatibles

Memory Requirements: None Specified

Cost of Program: No Charge

How to obtain a copy of the program:

Send either a 3.5" or 5.25" diskette and
a self-addressed, stamped mailer to:

Dr. Brett Myors
School of Psychology
University of New South Wales
P.O. Box 1
Kensington NSW 2033
Australia
e-mail: b.hesketh@unsw.edu.au

EXPECTED NORMAL SCORES

Title: FORTRAN IV Functions to Compute Expected
Normal Scores

Author: William P. Dunlap and Susan G. Brown

Source: *Behavior Research Methods & Instrumentation,*
1983, *15,* 395-397.

Description: The two functions discussed in this article perform
types of normal scores tests which may be defined as
asymptotically efficient nonparametric alternatives to Student's *t*
test. The first function (SCR) calculates expected normal scores via
an approximate solution and the second function (SCOR) uses
numerical integration to obtain exact estimates of the expected
normal scores.

Program Name: SCR, SCOR

Language: FORTRAN IV

Compatibility: Designed for use on DEC-based systems. Can
be easily modified, however, to run on any
system with a FORTRAN compiler.

Memory Requirements: None Specified

Cost of Program: No Charge

How to obtain a copy of the program:

Send a formatted 3.5" diskette and
a self-addressed, stamped mailer to:

Dr. William P. Dunlap
Department of Psychology
Tulane University
New Orleans, LA 70118
e-mail: dunlap@mailhost.tcs.tulane.edu

FACTOR ANALYSIS

Title: INTERMAX: A Program for Orthogonal Analytical
Rotation by the Intermax Criterion

Author: Joseph L. Balloun and A. Ben Oumlil

Source: *Behavior Research Methods, Instruments, & Computers,*
1986, 18, 331-336.

Description: This program performs the intermax rotation
procedure, which maximizes the amount of squared factor loading
variation that is due to an interaction of variables and factors. The
output also includes the significance tests (e.g., tests for the
number of factors, significance of individual factor loadings) for
both parametric and jackknife solutions.

Program Name: INTERMAX

Language: WATFOR 77

Compatibility: IBM and VAX mainframes, IBM PC's and
compatibles

Memory Requirements: None Specified

Cost of Program: No Charge

How to obtain a copy of the program:

Send a formatted 3.5" diskette and
a self-addressed, stamped mailer to:

Dr. Joseph L. Balloun
School of Business and Entrepreneurship
Nova Southeastern University
3100 SW 9th Avenue
Fort Lauderdale, FL 33315
e-mail: balloun@sbe.acast.nova.edu

FACTOR ANALYSIS

Title: MBFACT: Multiple Battery Factor Analysis by
Maximum Likelihood

Author: Robert Cudeck

Source: *Applied Psychological Measurement,* 1980,
4, 417-418.

Description: This program factor analyzes two or more batteries
of variables that have been obtained on a single sample of subjects.
Results of the analysis allow for the stability of the obtained factors
to be evaluated. The primary input data consists of the covariance
matrix to be analyzed. Output includes the rotated factor pattern
matrix, the likelihood ratio test, Akaike's information criterion, and
the Tucker-Lewis (1973) reliability coefficient.

Program Name: MBFACT

Language: FORTRAN

Compatibility: IBM mainframe systems, IBM PC's and
compatibles (Windows or DOS).

Memory Requirements: None Specified

Cost of Program: No Charge

How to obtain a copy of the program:

Send a formatted 3.5" diskette and
a self-addressed, stamped mailer to:

Dr. Robert Cudeck
Department of Psychology
University of Minnesota
Minneapolis, MN 55455-0280
e-mail: racnlm@vx.cis.umn.edu

FACTOR ANALYSIS

Title: FACTREL: A General Program for Relating Factors Between Studies via the Kaiser-Hunka-Bianchini Method

Author: James S. Fleming

Source: *Educational and Psychological Measurement*, 1992, *52*, 113-115.

Description: This interactive program computes the Kaiser-Hunka-Bianchini (1971) method for comparing factors between studies which might have utility in meta-analytic studies when only factor loadings from previous studies are provided. The input file consists of orthogonal factor loadings or if oblique factors are compared, then the primary factor pattern or primary factor structure matrix and factor intercorrelations are entered. Moreover, the number of variables, number of factors in each study, and input file names are needed. The output consists of a between-studies factors cosine matrix, cosines between corresponding variables across studies with averages (median, mean, mean backtransformed r), and transformed loadings.

Program Name: FACTREL

Language: FORTRAN 77

Compatibility: UNIX, IBM PC's and compatibles

Memory Requirements: 640K

Cost of Program: No Charge

How to obtain a copy of the program:

Send a formatted 3.5" diskette and
a self-addressed, stamped mailer to:

Dr. James S. Fleming
Technology Center
California State University
Northridge, CA 91330-8280
e-mail: jfleming@csun.edu

FACTOR ANALYSIS

Title: DETFAC: A Program for Assessing Factor
Indeterminacy

Author: Sean M. Hammond

Source: *Behavior Research Methods, Instruments, & Computers,*
1987, *19,* 485-486.

Description: This program outputs the squared correlations
between the true and estimated factors and the Guttman (1955)
criterion for rotated factors in order to evaluate factor
indeterminacy. This situation results when there is more than one
set of adequate factor scores. The input consists of the k variable x
n factor matrix (unrotated) from a separate data file, the number of
variables, factors, and row format of the data matrix.

Program Name: DETFAC

Language: FORTRAN 77

Compatibility: IBM PC's and compatibles

Memory Requirements: None Specified

Cost of Program: No Charge

How to obtain a copy of the program:

Send a formatted 3.5" diskette and
a self-addressed, stamped mailer to:

Dr. Sean M. Hammond
Department of Psychology
University of Surrey
Guildford, England
GU2, 5XH
England

FACTOR ANALYSIS

Title: COMPCONG: Computation of Coefficient of
Congruence Between Two Solutions of Factor Analysis

Author: Soonmook Lee

Source: *Applied Psychological Measurement,* 1988,
12, 107.

Description: In order to compare the amount of agreement
between factors from two different studies, the program outputs a
matrix of congruency coefficients (amount of agreement) using the
equation found in Harman (1976) and a permuted and reflected
factor-loading matrix from the second study. The input consists of
the factor loading matrix from each of the two studies.

Program Name: COMPCONG

Language: FORTRAN 77

Compatibility: VAX/VMS, need IMSL (version 9.2 or higher)

Memory Requirements: None Specified

Cost of Program: No Charge

How to obtain a copy of the program:

Send a formatted 5.25" diskette and
a self-addressed, stamped mailer to:

Dr. Soonmook Lee
Department of Psychology
Fordham University
Fordham Road
Bronx, NY 10458

FACTOR ANALYSIS

Title: FACOM: A Library for Relating Solutions Obtained in Exploratory Factor Analysis

Author: Urbano Lorenzo and Pere J. Ferrando

Source: *Behavior Research Methods, Instruments, & Computers*, 1996, *28*, 627-630.

Description: A library of programs has been developed in order to compare factorial solutions when (a) two solutions are found with different methods using the same sample and variables; (b) two independent (or oblique) solutions are found using two different samples with the same variables. The input consists of storing the matrices (e.g., factor loading, factor weightings, transformation, and correlation) in separate ASCII files. Examples of output are shown on pages 629 and 630.

Program Name: FACOM

Language: SAS

Compatibility: IBM PC's and compatibles

Memory Requirements: 4 MB

Cost of Program: $8 (for diskette and manual to cover mailing costs)

How to obtain a copy of the program:

Send a written request and payment to:

Dr. Urbano Lorenzo
Departamento de Psicologia
Universitat Rovira I Virgilli
Ctra. de Valls s/n
43007 Tarragona
Spain
e-mail: uls@astor.urv.es

FACTOR ANALYSIS

Title: Matching Factor Structures Using Orthogonal Rotation to Congruence

Author: John R. Vokey

Source: *Behavior Research Methods, Instruments, & Computers,* 1989, *21,* 84-85.

Description: This program provides a procedure for orthogonally rotating principal components (Cliff, 1966) in order to best match a structure founded on theoretical expectation or it may be a replication of a previous factor solution. The output contains the original structure matrices (which may contain up to 20 variables), the orthogonal rotation of the matrix of component loadings which matches the target matrix, the rotations of both matrices for which the columns are as similar as possible, and the correlations between these columns.

Program Name: CLIFF

Language: ZBASIC

Compatibility: Macintosh, MS-DOS compatibles

Memory Requirements: None Specified

Cost of Program: No Charge

How to obtain a copy of the program:

Send a blank 3.5" diskette and a self-addressed, stamped mailer to:

Dr. John R. Vokey
Department of Psychology
University of Lethbridge
Lethbridge, Alberta
T1K, 3M4
Canada

FACTOR ANALYSIS

Title: COMPARE: A Program for Matching Factors Between Studies

Author: Niels G. Waller

Source: *Applied Psychological Measurement,* 1988, *12,* 210.

Description: In order to determine the amount of agreement between factors from two different studies, the program outputs correlation and congruence coefficients (Tucker, 1951) and the Kaiser, Hunka, and Bianchini (1971) measure of similarity. The input consists of separate data files of factor loading matrices for each study.

Program Name: COMPARE

Language: GAUSS

Compatibility: None Specified

Memory Requirements: None Specified

Cost of Program: No Charge

How to obtain a copy of the program:

Send either a formatted 3.5" or 5.25" diskette and a self-addressed, stamped mailer to:

Dr. Niels G. Waller
Department of Psychology
University of California
Davis, CA 95616
e-mail: ngwaller@ucdavis.edu

FACTOR ANALYSIS

Title: NOVAX 1.3: A PC-DOS Factor Analysis Program for
               Ordered Polytomous Data and Mainframe-Size Problems

Author: Niels G. Waller

Source: *Applied Psychological Measurement, 1994,*
             18, 195-196.

Description: The program computes iterated and noniterated
principal factors and principal components analyses on polychoric,
tetrachoric, or Pearson product-moment correlation matrices. The
output file includes the inputted correlation matrix, communalities,
ranked eigenvalues, scree plot, unrotated factor loadings, sorted
and unsorted varimax and promax rotated factor loadings.

Program Name: NOVAX

Language: FORTRAN 77

Compatibility: None Specified

Memory Requirements: None Specified

Cost of Program: $65

How to obtain a copy of the program:

Send a written request and payment to:

Dr. Niels G. Waller
Department of Psychology
University of California
Davis, CA 95616
e-mail: ngwaller@ucdavis.edu

FACTOR ANALYSIS

Title: Comparison of Correlations, Variances, Covariances, and Regression Weights With or Without Measurement Error

Author: C.E. Werts, D.A. Rock, R.L. Linn, and K.G. Jöreskog

Source: *Psychological Bulletin, 1976, 83,* 1007-1013.

Description: This program performs simultaneous maximum likelihood factor analysis across several groups or populations. By varying which parameters are constrained to be equal across groups, the program is capable of testing the equality of variance-covariance matrices, correlation matrices, and regression weights across populations. Regression weights can also be corrected for attenuation. Another program feature is that the ratio of one parameter to another within a given population can be examined for statistical significance (to evaluate, for example, whether the ratio of observed variances across parallel tests is as expected given the number of items and reliabilities of the two tests).

Program Name: SIFASP

Language: None Specified

Compatibility: None Specified

Memory Requirements: None Specified

Cost of Program: No Charge

How to obtain a copy of the program:

Send a blank formatted 3.5"diskette and a self-addressed, stamped mailer to:

Dr. K.G. Jöreskog
Department of Social Sciences
University of Uppsala
POB 256, 751 05
Uppsala, Sweden

FACTOR ANALYSIS - BOOTSTRAP

Title: Program FACSTRAP: A Program That Computes Bootstrap Estimates of Factor Structure

Author: Bruce Thompson

Source: *Educational and Psychological Measurement*, 1988, *48*, 681-685.

Description: This program provides bootstrap estimates of the principal components analysis of the correlation matrix, variance-covariance matrix, and/or the principal factors analysis of the correlation matrix. A varimax rotation is used. Three different analyses based on different sample sizes are provided. Moreover, the means and standard deviations of the first 15 eigenvalues and these changes (similar to the scree test for determining the number of factors) across the number of samples used are also output. Finally, the means and standard deviations for each of the structure matrix coefficients are also given. The input is a data file and the user needs to set the data format, the number of samples, and the types of analyses desired. This program has utility in determining the number of factors, estimating structure coefficients, and for examining the results across samples.

Program Name: FACSTRAP

Language: FORTRAN 77

Compatibility: Mainframes that accommodate the IMSL package

Memory Requirements: None Specified

Cost of Program: No Charge

How to obtain a copy of the program:

Send an MS-DOS formatted 3.5" diskette and a self-addressed, stamped mailer to:

Dr. Bruce Thompson
Department of Educational Psychology
Texas A & M University
College Station, TX 77843-4225
e-mail: e100bt@tamvm1.tamu.edu

FACTOR ANALYSIS - HIGHER ORDER

Title: Using SAS/PC for Higher Order Factoring

Author: William L. Johnson and Annabel M. Johnson

Source: *Educational and Psychological Measurement*, 1995,
              55, 429-434.

Description: The program, which orthogonally rotates the product matrix of the first and second order factors in computing the final solution for higher order factoring, is provided in the article. The output consists of the standard rotated factor pattern matrix. The article also provides an example and elaborates on the procedures used in higher order factoring.

Program Name: None Specified

Language: SAS for Windows

Compatibility: IBM mainframes, IBM PC's and
                    compatibles

Memory Requirements: 640K for 100 variables or less

Cost of Program: No Charge

How to obtain a copy of the program:

For additional information contact:

Dr. William L. Johnson
Ambassador University
P.O. Box 111
Big Sandy, TX 75755
e-mail: william_johnson@ambassador.edu

FACTOR ANALYSIS - LOADINGS

Title: FACLOD: A Program to Estimate the Statistical
Significance of Factor Loadings

Author: Randall M. Parker

Source: *Behavior Research Methods & Instrumentation,*
1978, 11, 393.

Description: This program utilizes a jackknife algorithm to
estimate the smallest statistically significant factor loading (at an
alpha level of .05) for an entire factor matrix. Input consists of a
factor-loading matrix with up to 100 variables and 50 factors.
Output consists of estimates for the smallest significant factor
loading as calculated via the following two methods: (1)
jackknifing the standard deviation of the loadings and (2)
jackknifing the logarithm of the standard deviation of the loadings.

Program Name: FACLOD

Language: CDC FORTRAN

Compatibility: Designed for use with MNF compilers but
with slight modifications should be adaptable
to other types of FORTRAN compilers.

Memory Requirements: None Specified

Cost of Program: No Charge

How to obtain a copy of the program:

The program listing can be obtained by contacting:

Dr. Randall M. Parker
Department of Special Education
EDB 306
University of Texas
Austin, TX 78712

FACTOR ANALYSIS - ROTATION

Title: Hyball: A Method for Subspace-Constrained Factor Rotation

Author: William W. Rozeboom

Source: *Multivariate Behavioral Research*, 1991, *26*, 163-177.

Description: This program allows the user to obliquely rotate one or more selected latent factors while simultaneously keeping other factor axes or subspaces invariant. This subspace-constrained factor rotation procedure is most useful in situations where the associations among variables (e.g., age, education, and intelligence) are thought to be mediated by one or more latent factors (e.g., maturation and training).

Program Name: HYBALL

Language: FORTRAN 77

Compatibility: IBM PC's and compatibles, UNIX source code is available

Memory Requirements: 512K

Cost of Program: $10

How to obtain a copy of the program:

Send a written request and payment to:

Dr. William W. Rozeboom
Department of Psychology
University of Alberta
Edmonton, Alberta T6G 2E9
Canada
e-mail: rozeboom@psych.ualberta.ca

FACTOR SCORES

Title: Estimation of Factor Scores Via FASCOR

Author: Craig A. Mason and Shihfen Tu

Source: *Educational and Psychological Measurement*, 1995, *55*, 791-794.

Description: Computes the factor scores from an ASCII file which contains a factor pattern matrix, a factor correlation matrix, and a correlation matrix among the variables. This program has utility for those interested in obtaining factor scores when performing confirmatory factor analysis. The user can input factor and variable names for additional clarification. Examples of the input and output are provided.

Program Name: FASCOR

Language: None Specified

Compatibility: IBM PC's and compatibles

Memory Requirements: None Specified

Cost of Program: No Charge

How to obtain a copy of the program:

Send a formatted 3.5" diskette and a
self-addressed, stamped mailer to:

Dr. Craig A. Mason
Department of Psychology
University of Miami
P.O. Box 248106
Coral Gables, FL 33124

FACTOR STRUCTURE COMPARISONS

Title: Sets of BASIC Programs for Factor Matrix
Comparisons: Ahmavaara Transformation, Congruence
Coefficient, Salient Variable Similarity Index

Author: Ralph Mason Dreger

Source: *Educational and Psychological Measurement,* 1985,
45, 167-171.

Description: These programs provide the Ahmavaara
transformation, the congruence coefficient, and Cattell's (1949)
Salient Similarity Index for determining if factor structures from
two distinct groups (or studies) are comparable. These programs
differ in whether the large or small matrices are stored and whether
the original (and/or intermediate) matrices should be printed or not.

Program Name: Eleven separate programs

Language: GWBASIC

Compatibility: IBM PC's and compatibles, Apple II

Memory Requirements: None Specified

Cost of Program: No Charge

How to obtain a copy of the program:

Send either a formatted 3.5" or 5.25" diskette
and a self-addressed, stamped mailer to:

Dr. Ralph Mason Dreger
Department of Psychology
Louisiana State University
Baton Rouge, LA 70803
e-mail: rdreger266@aol.com

FACTORIAL DESIGNS - CONFOUNDED

Title: A Computer Program for Confounded Factorial Designs

Author: Jamal Abedi

Source: *Behavior Research Methods & Instrumentation,* 1978, *11,* 600.

Description: This program is useful for the analysis of certain types of randomized block factorial and split-plot designs. In particular, this program analyzes confounded block factorial designs in which (a) the largest order interaction and the block factor are completely confounded, and (b) each factor has only two levels. The program can accommodate up to 10 factors and is capable of handling missing data. User output includes an ANOVA summary table, the means for blocks by replications, and the means and variances for all (main and interaction) effects.

Program Name: None Specified

Language: FORTRAN

Compatibility: Any computer capable of supporting FORTRAN. This includes Apple-based microcomputers (Apple IIe and up)

Memory Requirements: 1 MB

Cost of Program: $49

How to obtain a copy of the program:

Send a written request and payment to:

Dr. Jamal Abedi
1320 Moore Hall
UCLA
Graduate School of Education
Los Angeles, CA 90095-1522
jamal@cse.ucla.edu

FISHER'S EXACT TEST

Title: Exact Chi-Square and Fisher's Exact Probability Test for 3 by 2 Cross-Classification Tables

Author: Kenneth J. Berry and Paul W. Mielke, Jr.

Source: *Educational and Psychological Measurement*, 1987, *47*, 631-636.

Description: Using a recursive algorithm, subroutines are presented that compute exact chi-square and Fisher's exact tests for 3 x 2 contingency tables. These subroutines also provide probability values with large sample sizes.

Program Name: ECST, FEPT (subroutines)

Language: FORTRAN 77

Compatibility: IBM and UNIX mainframes, IBM PC's and compatibles

Memory Requirements: None Specified

Cost of Program: No Charge

How to obtain a copy of the program:

The authors prefer to e-mail the program, however, you may send a formatted 3.5" diskette and a self-addressed, stamped mailer to:

Dr. Kenneth J. Berry
Department of Sociology
Colorado State University
Fort Collins, CO 80523
e-mail: berry@lamar.colostate.edu

FISHER'S EXACT TEST

Title: Hypergeometric Tests for 2 x *k* Contingency Tables

Author: William P. Dunlap

Source: *Behavior Research Methods, Instruments, & Computers*, 1985, *17*, 432-434.

Description: This program, which is used for Case III data (both marginals are fixed), outputs an exact probability of an outcome that is as or more unlikely than the particular contingency table being evaluated. The input is the data from the two rows. For over 5000 tables that could be potentially generated, an approximation is provided. A listing of the program is contained on pages 433 and 434.

Program Name: HYPER

Language: FORTRAN IV

Compatibility: DEC-20, IBM PC's and compatibles

Memory Requirements: None Specified

Cost of Program: No Charge

How to obtain a copy of the program:

Send a formatted 3.5" diskette and
a self-addressed, stamped mailer to:

Dr. William P. Dunlap
Department of Psychology
Tulane University
New Orleans, LA 70118
e-mail: dunlap@mailhost.tcs.tulane.edu

FISHER'S EXACT TEST

Title: Fisher's Exact Probability Test for Cross-Classification Tables

Author: Paul W. Mielke, Jr. and Kenneth J. Berry

Source: *Educational and Psychological Measurement*, 1992, *52*, 97-101.

Description: Six subroutines are presented for computing Fisher's Exact Test for specific two-way contingency tables. The input is the observed cell frequency counts in the contingency table, whereas the output provided includes the exact probability value by cumulating probabilities of all tables that are as or more extreme than the observed table.

Program Name: ERWAY

Language: FORTRAN 77

Compatibility: IBM and UNIX mainframes, IBM PC's and compatibles

Memory Requirements: None Specified

Cost of Program: No Charge

How to obtain a copy of the program:

The authors prefer to e-mail the program, however, you may send a formatted 3.5" diskette and a self-addressed, stamped mailer to:

Dr. Kenneth J. Berry
Department of Sociology
Colorado State University
Fort Collins, CO 80523
e-mail: berry@lamar.colostate.edu

FISHER'S EXACT TEST

Title: Fisher's Exact Test of Mutual Independence for
2 x 2 x 2 Cross-Classification Tables

Author: Paul W. Mielke, Jr., Kenneth J. Berry, and
Daniel Zelterman

Source: *Educational and Psychological Measurement*, 1994,
54, 110-114.

Description: A subroutine (FEP222) computes Fisher's Exact
Test for 2 x 2 x 2 contingency tables. The input is the eight
observed cell frequency counts in the contingency table, whereas
the output provided includes the observed cell frequency counts,
the exact probability value of the table and exact significance level
by cumulating probabilities of all tables that are as or more
extreme than the observed table, and the number of possible tables
(with probabilities equal to or less than the observed table).

Program Name: FEP222 (subroutine)

Language: FORTRAN 77

Compatibility: IBM and UNIX mainframes, IBM PC's and
compatibles

Memory Requirements: None Specified

Cost of Program: No Charge

How to obtain a copy of the program:

The authors prefer to e-mail the program,
however, you may send a formatted 3.5"
diskette and a self-addressed, stamped mailer to:

Dr. Kenneth J. Berry
Department of Sociology
Colorado State University
Fort Collins, CO 80523
e-mail: berry@lamar.colostate.edu

FORECASTING

Title: Through a Glass, Clearly? A Computer Program for
Generalized Adaptive Filtering

Author: David J. Krus and Janet L. Jacobsen

Source: *Educational and Psychological Measurement,* 1983,
43, 837-841.

Description: This program performs generalized adaptive filtering
(Makridakis & Wheelwright, 1978), which is often used in
business forecasting where the purpose is to identify cyclical and
stochastic drifts. An application for the utility of this program is
provided in the article.

Program Name: None Specified

Language: FORTRAN

Compatibility: Terak 8510

Memory Requirements: None Specified

Cost of Program: No Charge

How to obtain a copy of the program:

Send a blank 3.5" diskette and a
self-addressed, stamped mailer to:

Dr. David J. Krus
Department of Educational Psychology
Arizona State University
Tempe, AZ 85287

G STATISTIC

Title: An Applesoft BASIC Program for the *G* Statistic: An Alternative to the Chi-Square Test

Author: Bernard C. Beins

Source: *Behavior Research Methods, Instruments, & Computers,* 1989, *21,* 627-629.

Description: This program computes the pooled, heterogeneity, and total *G* statistics. The *G* statistic tests for goodness-of-fit and examines the independence of frequencies for a p row x q column contingency table. The degrees of freedom and an adjusted *G* is also provided. According to the author, the major advantage of the *G* statistic is that it can address differences from theoretical expected frequencies for either subgroups of data or from the total data set. The input consists of entering the number of rows and columns followed by the data and expected frequencies if known. An example of the output is provided on page 628.

Program Name: None Specified

Language: BASIC

Compatibility: Apple II, Franklin 1200s, and Laser systems

Memory Requirements: None Specified

Cost of Program: No Charge

How to obtain a copy of the program:

Send a 5.25" diskette and a
self-addressed, stamped mailer to:

Dr. Bernard C. Beins
Psychology Department
Ithaca College
Ithaca, NY 14850

GENERALIZABILITY ANALYSIS

Title: GENOVA (A Program for Analysis of Variance and Generalizability Analyses)

Author: Joe E. Crick and Robert L. Brennan

Source: Elements of Generalizability Theory by R. L. Brennan (1992), Iowa City, IA: American College Testing.

Description: Performs generalizability analyses for univariate designs. The primary input consists of the data matrix to be analyzed. The output consists of information that is relevant for both G studies and D studies involving either norm-referenced or domain-referenced test score interpretations. The program can also use the results of a single G study to perform multiple D studies.

Program Name: GENOVA

Language: FORTRAN

Compatibility: Any mainframe, IBM PC's and compatibles, and any Apple-based system

Memory Requirements: 1 MB

Cost of Program: $35

How to obtain a copy of the program:

For the IBM PC version, send payment to:

Dr. Joe E. Crick
3750 Market St.
Philadelphia, PA 19014
e-mail: jcrick@mail.nbme.org

For the mainframe version, contact Dr. Brennan at (319) 335-5405.

For the Macintosh version, send payment, a formatted 3.5" diskette, and a self-addressed, stamped mailer to:

Dr. Robert L. Brennan
Director, Iowa Testing Programs
344A Lindquist Ctr. S.
University of Iowa
Iowa City, IA 52242
e-mail: robert-brennan@uiowa.edu

GOODMAN AND KRUSKAL'S GAMMA

Title: BASIC Programs for Computation of the Goodman-Kruskal Gamma Coefficient

Author: Thomas O. Nelson

Source: *Bulletin of the Psychonomic Society,* 1986, *24,* 281-283.

Description: Calculates Goodman and Kruskal's (1954) gamma coefficient (G) for three different types of data structure. In the first case, G can be calculated as a measure of association for any 2 x N data array in which two outcomes of interest are assessed for each individual. In the second case, G can be calculated as a measure of association for any ordered R x C cross-classification table. In the third case, G can be calculated as a measure of detection accuracy in any R x C matrix where the row variable indicates whether or not a trial contained a signal and the column variable indicates subjects responses to each trial ("yes" or "no"). The BASIC source code for all three applications is contained in the article.

Program Name: None Specified

Language: Applesoft BASIC. With only slight modifications to the code, other versions of BASIC may also be used.

Compatibility: Any computer supporting BASIC

Memory Requirements: None Specified

Cost of Program: No Charge

How to obtain a copy of the program:

For additional information, contact:

Dr. Thomas O. Nelson
Department of Psychology
University of Maryland
College Park, MD 20742-4411
e-mail: tnelson@glue.umd.edu

GOODMAN AND KRUSKAL'S TAU-B

Title: Goodman and Kruskal's Tau-B Statistic: A
FORTRAN-77 Subroutine

Author: Kenneth J. Berry and Paul W. Mielke, Jr.

Source: *Educational and Psychological Measurement*, 1986,
46, 645-649.

Description: This program computes Goodman and Kruskal's
tau-b statistic (which is used for bivariate cross-classifications of
categorical variables) and the nonasymptotic significance test. The
default for the rows and columns of the table is between 2 and 20,
however, it is modifiable.

Program Name: TAU (subroutine)

Language: FORTRAN 77

Compatibility: IBM and UNIX mainframes, IBM PC's and
compatibles

Memory Requirements: None Specified

Cost of Program: No Charge

How to obtain a copy of the program:

The authors prefer to e-mail the program,
however, you may send a formatted 3.5"
diskette and a self-addressed, stamped mailer to:

Dr. Kenneth J. Berry
Department of Sociology
Colorado State University
Fort Collins, CO 80523
e-mail: berry@lamar.colostate.edu

GOODNESS-OF-FIT - EXACT TEST

Title: Exact Goodness-of-Fit Probability Tests for Analyzing Categorical Data

Author: Paul W. Mielke, Jr. and Kenneth J. Berry

Source: *Educational and Psychological Measurement*, 1993, *53*, 707-710.

Description: Five subroutines are presented which compute an exact goodness-of-fit probability value for up to six unordered categories. That is, to determine the difference between the observed and expected frequencies. The input is composed of the number of categories, the observed cell frequencies, and expected cell proportions. An example as to when to use the program is provided in the article.

Program Name: EXGOF

Language: FORTRAN 77

Compatibility: IBM and UNIX mainframes, IBM PC's and compatibles

Memory Requirements: None Specified

Cost of Program: No Charge

How to obtain a copy of the program:

The authors prefer to e-mail the program, however, you may send a formatted 3.5" diskette and a self-addressed, stamped mailer to:

Dr. Kenneth J. Berry
Department of Sociology
Colorado State University
Fort Collins, CO 80523
e-mail: berry@lamar.colostate.edu

GRAPHICS

Title: SAS Macro Programs for Statistical Graphics

Author: Michael Friendly

Source: *Psychometrika*, 1992, *57*, 313-317.

Description: This collection of programs consists of 18 SAS macros for performing various types of graphical analyses and procedures. Most of the programs generate an output file containing the results. In addition to requiring the base SAS and SAS/GRAPH products, some of the macros also require SAS/STAT and/or SAS/IML

Program Name: GRAPHMAC (entire package). Each macro has its own name

Language: SAS

Compatibility: Any mainframe or PC with SAS capabilities

Memory Requirements: None Specified

Cost of Program: No Charge

How to obtain a copy of the program:

Access via e-mail using the UICSTAT archive (Bitnet: listserv@uicvm; Internet: listserv@uicvm.cc.uic.edu). To obtain the entire package, type the following command: GET GRAPHMAC PACKAGE.

For further information, contact:

Dr. Michael Friendly
Department of Psychology
York University
4700 Keele St.
N. York Ontario
Canada
M3J 1P3
e-mail: friendly@yorku.ca

GRECO-LATIN SQUARES

Title: Pairs of Latin Squares that Produce Digram-Balanced Greco-Latin Designs: A BASIC Program

Author: James R. Lewis

Source: *Behavior Research Methods, Instruments, & Computers,* 1993, *25,* 414-415.

Description: A digram-balanced Latin Square counterbalances immediate sequential effects (e.g., learning, fatigue). This program creates the pairs of squares (and stimuli) using an algorithm by Lewis (1989). The input consists of the number of conditions and an output file name. An example of the output is provided in the text.

Program Name: LATBUILD

Language: BASIC

Compatibility: IBM PC's and compatibles

Memory Requirements: 7K for the program

Cost of Program: No Charge

How to obtain a copy of the program:

Send a formatted 3.5" diskette and
a self-addressed, stamped mailer to:

Dr. James R. Lewis
1555 Palm Beach Lakes Blvd.
West Palm Beach, FL 33401
e-mail: jimlewis@vnet.ibm.com

GROWTH CURVE ANALYSIS

Title: Implementation of Hills' Growth Curve Analysis for Unequal-Time Intervals Using GAUSS

Author: Emet D. Schneiderman and Charles J. Kowalski

Source: *American Journal of Human Biology*, 1989, *1*, 31-42.

Description: Using Hills's (1968) method, this program estimates the population growth pattern from a single random sample of *N* individuals each of whom has been assessed over multiple time points. The program calculates velocity curves and acceleration curves for each individual as well as an averaged estimate across all individuals. Goodness of fit indices are also calculated for each polynomial order thereby allowing the user to select the lowest-order best fitting model. Hills's method differs from Rao's method in that Hills's procedure can accommodate time-dependent data that have been collected at either equally-spaced or unequally-spaced time intervals.

Program Name: HILLS.GCG

Language: GAUSS

Compatibility: IBM PC's and compatibles. Requires a math coprocessor from the 8087 family.

Memory Requirements: 4MB

Cost of Program: No Charge

How to obtain a copy of the program:

A listing of the GAUSS program is contained in the appendix of the source article. This program and other GAUSS programs are available for downloading on internet. For further information, contact:

Dr. Emet D. Schneiderman
Baylor College of Dentistry
Texas A&M University System
Dallas, TX 75266-0677
e-mail: emet@tambcd.edu

GROWTH CURVE ANALYSIS

Title: Rao's Polynomial Growth Curve Model for Unequal-
Time Intervals: A Menu-Driven GAUSS Program

Author: Emet D. Schneiderman, Stephen M. Willis,
Thomas R. Ten Have, and Charles J. Kowalski

Source: *International Journal of Biomedical Computing,* 1991*,
29*, 235-244.

Description: Using Rao's (1959) method, this program computes
the lowest order polynomial regression equation that adequately
fits a set of serial observations. The average fitted growth curve
and corresponding 95% confidence intervals are likewise
calculated. The data to be analyzed may be entered in either
ASCII or GAUSS format. Following data entry, the user specifies
the level of significance to be utilized and whether or not
observations were collected at equal time intervals. A unique
strength of the program is that it contains an automated error
checking routine that detects erroneous keyboard entries.

Program Name: RAO.GCG

Language: GAUSS

Compatibility: IBM PC's and compatibles A math coprocessor
is necessary.

Memory Requirements: 4 MB

Cost of Program: No Charge

How to obtain a copy of the program:

This program and other GAUSS programs are available
for downloading on internet. For further information, contact:

Dr. Emet D. Schneiderman
Baylor College of Dentistry
Texas A&M University System
Dallas, TX 75266-0677
e-mail:emet@tambcd.edu

GROWTH CURVE ANALYSIS

Title: PC Program for Analyzing One-Sample Longitudinal Data Sets Which Satisfy the Two-Stage Polynomial Growth Curve Model

Author: Thomas R. Ten Have, Charles J. Kowalski, and Emet D. Schneiderman

Source: *American Journal of Human Biology,* 1991, *3,* 269-279.

Description: This program conducts a two-stage polynomial growth curve analysis on a single sample of individuals in which the data have been collected longitudinally. The two-stage analysis proceeds by first calculating parameter estimates and confidence intervals for the individual growth curve models. The second step involves generating equations that express the relationship between the individual growth curves and the estimated population average growth curve (AGC). Goodness of fit indices allow the user to evaluate whether or not a two-stage model adequately fits the data or whether a one-stage model would be more appropriate. Prior to invoking the analysis, the user may select from among four different types of time design matrices. A sample run with output is contained in the appendix of the source article.

Program Name: 2STG.GCG

Language: GAUSS

Compatibility: IBM PC's and compatibles. Requires a math coprocessor from the 8087 family.

Memory Requirements: 4 MB

Cost of Program: No Charge

How to obtain a copy of the program:

This program and other GAUSS programs are available for downloading on internet. For further information, contact:

Dr. Emet D. Schneiderman
Baylor College of Dentistry
Texas A&M University System
Dallas, TX 75246
e-mail: emet@tambcd.edu

GUTTMAN'S LEAST SQUARE

Title: A BASIC Program to Compute Guttman's Least Square Weights for a Likert Scale

Author: Giovanni Battista Flebus

Source: *Educational and Psychological Measurement*, 1995, *55*, 442-444.

Description: Computes optimal weightings for questionnaire categories using Guttman's least squares method. The program also scores missing answers with optimal weight. The input consists of a file of raw data in fixed format, whereas the output provides the frequency and optimal weight for each category. This program is useful in detecting multifactorial items. A treatment of Guttman's least squares method is provided in the article.

Program Name: None Specified

Language: Macintosh TrueBasic

Compatibility: Macintosh (A Macintosh TrueBasic version is available that can be translated into a form of DOS BASIC)

Memory Requirements: Contingent on RAM availability. On a 4MB RAM Macintosh classic, more than 700 variables may be used (combination of number of items and alternatives, e.g., 70 10-point items).

Cost of Program: $10 for shipping.

How to obtain a copy of the program:

To receive a 3.5" disk with the program, send a written request and payment to:

Dr. Giovanni Battista Flebus
Istituto di Psicologia
Università di Urbino
Via Saffi 5
61029 Urbino (PS) Italy

HALF-NORMAL CRITICAL VALUES

Title: A FORTRAN IV Function for Computing Critical
Values of Ordered Half-Normal Scores

Author: William P. Dunlap and N. Clayton Silver

Source: *Behavior Research Methods, Instruments, & Computers,*
1989, *21,* 630-635.

Description: This program computes the critical values for
ordered half-normal scores. These critical values have utility for
testing individual correlations in a matrix via the rank adjusted
method (Stavig & Acock, 1978) or its modification (Silver, 1989),
which purportedly control the overall Type I error rate. Moreover,
these values can be used for evaluating ordered absolute values of
standardized linear contrasts in a 2^k design. A listing of the
program is contained on pages 634-635.

Program Name: CVHNS

Language: FORTRAN

Compatibility: IBM 3081 GX and IBM PC's and compatibles

Memory Requirements: None Specified

Cost of Program: No Charge

How to obtain a copy of the program:

Send a formatted 3.5" diskette and
a self addressed, stamped mailer to:

Dr. William P. Dunlap
Department of Psychology
Tulane University
New Orleans, LA 70118
e-mail: dunlap@mailhost.tcs.tulane.edu

HALF-NORMAL SCORES

Title: FORTRAN IV Functions for Computing Expected
Half-Normal Scores

Author: William P. Dunlap and Leann Myers

Source: *Behavior Research Methods, Instruments, &*
Computers, 1984, *16*, 401-404.

Description: This program calculates expected half-normal
scores or, more specifically, the expected value of the kth of N
ordered half-normal scores. Half-normal scores are derived from
the half-normal distribution which represents the distribution of the
absolute values of normally distributed data. The source code for
calculating expected half-normal scores is contained in the
appendix of the paper.

Program Name: HNS

Language: FORTRAN IV

Compatibility: Any system capable of supporting FORTRAN

Memory Requirements: None Specified

Cost of Program: No Charge

How to obtain a copy of the program:

Send a formatted 3.5" diskette and
a self-addressed, stamped mailer to:

Dr. William P. Dunlap
Department of Psychology
Tulane University
New Orleans, LA 70118
e-mail: dunlap@mailhost.tcs.tulane.edu

HIERARCHICAL LINEAR MODELING

Title: An Introduction to Hierarchical Linear Models

Author: Carolyn L. Arnold

Source: *Measurement and Evaluation in Counseling and Development*, 1992, *25*, 58-90.

Description: Along with other much more expensive commercial packages, this article discusses GENMOD (Mason, Anderson, & Hyat, 1988) which is a hierarchical linear modeling program that utilizes restricted maximum likelihood estimation and the EM algorithm. A particular strength of the program is that it allows for comparative analyses in situations where data at the within- and/or between-unit level consist of different variables in different formats (e.g., different categories of gender-race in different cities).

Program Name: GENMOD

Language: FORTRAN 77

Compatibility: Any computer supporting either MS-DOS or the MTS operating system.

Memory Requirements: At least 420K

Cost of Program: $50

How to obtain a copy of the program:

Send a written request and payment to:

Dr. William Mason
UCLA-Sociology
405 Hilgard Avenue
Los Angeles, CA 90024-1551

HIERARCHICAL LINEAR MODELING

Title: Application of Hierarchical Linear Models to
Assessing Change

Author: Anthony S. Bryk, Stephen W. Raudenbush, and
Richard T. Congdon (co-author of software)

Source: *Psychological Bulletin, 1987, 101,* 147-158.

Description: This program computes a number of indices that are
useful for assessing aspects of psychological change such as the
structure of an individual's mean growth trajectory, the degree of
individual variation around mean growth, the reliability of
measures for analyzing growth status and change, and the
correlation between initial status and rate of change. Variability in
growth trajectories as a function of demographics, individual
difference variables, and experimental treatments can also be
assessed.

Program Name: HLM version 4

Language: FORTRAN 77

Compatibility: UNIX mainframes, IBM PC's and compatibles

Memory Requirements: None Specified

Cost of Program: $400 for DOS extender
$430 for Windows 3.1+/95/NT versions

How to obtain a copy of the program:

For ordering information, contact:

Scientific Software International
1525 East 53rd Street
Suite 530
Chicago, IL 60615-4530
Phone: 1-800-247-6113   Fax: (312) 684-4979

For further information, contact:

Dr. Anthony S. Bryk
Department of Education
University of Chicago
5835 Kimbark Avenue
Chicago, IL 60637-1608

HOTELLING'S T^2

Title: An Approximate Hotelling's T^2 Test for Matched
Group Designs With SPSS

Author: William L. Deaton

Source: *Educational and Psychological Measurement*, 1982,
42, 219-221.

Description: This program outputs Hotelling's T^2 (for testing
whether two independent groups differ across two or more
dependent variables)for matched group designs using the
RELIABILITY routine of SPSS. The program is contained on
page 221.

Program Name: None Specified

Language: SPSS

Compatibility: Any machine with SPSS capability

Memory Requirements: None Specified

Cost of Program: No Charge

How to obtain a copy of the program:

Send a formatted 3.5" diskette and
a self-addressed, stamped mailer to:

Dr. William L. Deaton
Foundations of Education
Auburn University
Auburn, AL   36849

HOTELLING'S T^2

Title: A BASIC Program to Compute Hotelling's T^2 and Related Measures

Author: Andrew R. Gilpin

Source: *Behavior Research Methods, Instruments, & Computers,* 1985, *17,* 509.

Description: This program outputs Hotelling's T^2 (for testing whether two independent groups differ across two or more dependent variables), within-group (and combined group) covariance matrices and determinants, within-group (and combined group) means and standard deviations for each variable, Bartlett's chi-square test for equality of covariance matrices, its degrees of freedom and probability level, the squared multiple correlation, an F test, degrees of freedom and probability level for the multiple correlation and Hotelling's T^2, F-test for equality of profile variances, and separate t-tests for each dependent variable using a Bonferroni correction. The input consists of a data file or data input from the terminal.

Program Name: T-SQUARED

Language: Applesoft BASIC

Compatibility: Apple II+

Memory Requirements: None Specified

Cost of Program: $2 (payable to the University of Northern Iowa)

How to obtain a copy of the program:

Send a 3.5" diskette, a self-addressed stamped mailer, and payment to:

Dr. Andrew R. Gilpin
Department of Psychology
University of Northern Iowa
Cedar Falls, IA 50614
e-mail: gilpin@uni.edu

INFORMATION COMPLEXITY

Title: H-Comp: A Program to Calculate Information
Complexity

Author: Michael E. Nielsen

Source: *Behavior Research Methods, Instruments, & Computers,*
1996, *28,* 483-485.

Description: In order to examine the thought complexity of
ingroup or outgroup members or to examine self-complexity (e.g.,
describing oneself with a variety of adjectives), the statistic *H*
(Scott, 1969) is computed which measures the number of
independent dimensions gleaned from a set of dichotomous (0,1)
data. The input may be entered either from the keyboard or via an
ASCII file.

Program Name: H-COMP

Language: PowerBASIC

Compatibility: IBM PC's and compatibles

Memory Requirements: None Specified

Cost of Program: No Charge

How to obtain a copy of the program:

Send a formatted 3.5" diskette and
a self-addressed, stamped mailer to:

Dr. Michael E. Nielsen
Department of Psychology
Georgia Southern University
Statesboro, GA 30460-8041
e-mail: mnielsen@gasou.edu

It is also available from the COMPsych PC software library
(Hornby & Anderson, 1994) using an anonymous ftp
gluon.hawk.plattsburgh.edu. Path=pub/compsych/brmic

INTERNAL CONSISTENCY

Title: PRORATE: A BASIC Program for Calculating Minimum Test Length Given Internal Consistency Constraints

Author: Michael J. Strube

Source: *Behavior Research Methods, Instruments, & Computers,* 1985, *17,* 580.

Description: This program estimates the internal consistency for a test of *n* items or it provides a minimum test length needed in order to obtain a specific internal consistency. The input consists of the test length and the internal consistency of the test if one is interested in obtaining a minimum test length. This program can be used for estimating the internal consistency of a test when there are a number of missing responses. Hence, in order to enhance internal consistency, an average response could be used to obtain a full test total.

Program Name: PRORATE

Language: BASIC

Compatibility: IBM PC's and compatibles

Memory Requirements: None Specified

Cost of Program: No Charge

How to obtain a copy of the program:

Send a formatted 3.5" diskette and a self-addressed, stamped mailer to:

Dr. Michael J. Strube
Department of Psychology
Washington University
St. Louis, MO 63130
e-mail: mjstrube@artsci.wustl.edu

INTERRATER AGREEMENT

Title: A Computer Program to Determine Interobserver Reliability Statistics

Author: Edward Burns and Claire Cavallaro

Source: *Behavior Research Methods & Instrumentation,* 1982, *14*, 42.

Description: This program calculates several measures of interrater reliability for two observers when data are specified in a 2 by 2 format such that 0 indicates the nonoccurrence and 1 indicates the occurrence of a target behavior. The reliability statistics calculated are: 1) percent agreement, 2) effective percent agreement (occurrence), 3) effective percent agreement (nonoccurrence), 4) Cohen's kappa, and 5) the phi coefficient. Reliability can be calculated for each of a series of time periods as well as across all relevant time periods.

Program Name: None Specified

Language: BASIC

Compatibility: Designed for use on IBM systems

Memory Requirements: None Specified

Cost of Program: No Charge

How to obtain a copy of the program:

The program listing and sample input and output may be obtained by contacting:

Dr. Edward Burns
University of Washington
3900 7th Avenue, NE
Seattle, WA 98195

INTERRATER AGREEMENT

Title: Alternate Methods and Software for Calculating Interobserver Agreement for Continuous Observation Data

Author: William E. MacLean, Jon T. Tapp, and Willard L. Johnson

Source: *Journal of Psychopathology and Behavioral Assessment,* 1985, *7,* 65-73.

Description: Calculates interobserver agreement when the observations are based either upon discrete events or frequencies. The unique aspect of the program is that observations are logged in real time which allows the user to determine whether or not two observers recorded the same (or different) event within a particular time interval. The length of the time interval is specified by the user.

Program Name: None Specified

Language: BASIC

Compatibility: Any computer capable of supporting BASIC

Memory Requirements: None Specified

Cost of Program: No Charge

How to obtain a copy of the program:

Send a blank formatted 3.5"diskette and a self-addressed, stamped mailer to:

Dr. William E. MacLean, Jr.
Department of Psychology and Human Development
P.O. Box 158
Peabody College of Vanderbilt University
Nashville, TN 37203

INTERRATER AGREEMENT

Title: Interrater Agreement Statistics With the
Microcomputer

Author: Marley W. Watkins and Leon D. Larimer

Source: *Behavior Research Methods & Instrumentation,*
1980, *12,* 466.

Description: This program calculates Scott's (1955) pi and
Cohen's (1960) kappa coefficients which are chance-corrected
percentage of agreement measures. The two statistics differ only in
the way by which expected frequencies are calculated. Input
consists of the cross-tabulated matrix of ratings and output includes
pi and kappa, and the critical z values for both statistics.

Program Name: None Specified

Language: Applesoft BASIC

Compatibility: Apple IIe microcomputer

Memory Requirements: 48K

Cost of Program: No Charge

How to obtain a copy of the program:

Send a written request to:

Dr. Marley W. Watkins
Penn State University
227 Cedar Building
University Park, PA 16802
e-mail: mww10@psu.edu

INTERRATER AGREEMENT - CONJOINT

Title: A Computer Program for Assessing Conjoint
Interrater Agreement With a Correct Set of
Classifications

Author: Paul A. McDermott and Marley W. Watkins

Source: *Behavior Research Methods & Instrumentation,*
1978, 11, 607.

Description: This program calculates the level of interrater
agreement among a set of raters by comparing the raters responses
to a standard set of "correct" classifications. The degree of
correspondence between the two sets of ratings is assessed via
Light's (1971) G statistic. Input includes the number of cases,
number of categories, number of raters, the correct category choice
for each case, and the raters' category choices for each case. Output
includes the correct category choice for each case, the raters'
category choices for each case, and the G statistic and its
associated level of statistical significance. The program allows for
up to 160 cases assigned by 100 or fewer raters to a maximum of
10 categories.

Program Name: STANDARD

Language: FORTRAN IV (also in SAS version 6.11 and
lower)

Compatibility: IBM mainframes, IBM PC's and compatibles.

Memory Requirements: 1 MB

Cost of Program: No Charge

How to obtain a copy of the program:

The FORTRAN IV version is in paper copy only.

For the SAS version, send a formatted 3.5" diskette
and a self-addressed, stamped mailer to:

Dr. Paul A. McDermott
Graduate School of Education
University of Pennsylvania
3700 Walnut Street
Philadelphia, PA 19104-6216

INTERRATER RELIABILITY

Title: Interrater/Test Reliability System (ITRS)

Author: Jamal Abedi

Source: *Multivariate Behavioral Research,* 1996, *31,* 409-417.

Description: This program computes the interrater and test reliability for a group of n raters. Various descriptive statistics, Kendall's Tau, percent of agreement, Cronbach's alpha, Cohen's kappa, intraclass correlation, the generalizability coefficient (expanded over *p* tasks and *n* raters), and Williams' index of agreement compose the interrater reliability output. The test reliability output consists of frequencies for different item choices (and alerts the user to the disproportionality of certain choices), individual test scores (from the user key), means and standard deviations for the entire test and individual items, item-total and item-subset correlations, and alpha coefficients for the entire test and item subsets. The test reliability output is applicable to multiple-choice tests and those with a Likert-type format. The program also has options concerning missing data. Data can be input via an ASCII file, interactively, or an SPSS/SAS output file.

Program Name: None Specified

Language: None Specified

Compatibility: IBM PC's and compatibles and Macintosh computers

Memory Requirements: None Specified

Cost of Program: None Specified

How to obtain a copy of the program:

Send a blank 3.5" diskette and a self-addressed, stamped mailer to:

Dr. Jamal Abedi
1320 Moore Hall
UCLA
Graduate School of Education
Los Angeles, CA 90095-1522
e-mail: jamal@cse.ucla.edu

INTERRATER RELIABILITY

Title: Computing Interrater Reliability on the Apple Macintosh Computer

Author: John O. Brooks, III and Laura L. Brooks

Source: *Behavior Research Methods, Instruments, & Computers,* 1991, *23,* 82-84.

Description: This program computes the interrater reliability for *n* raters using the Spearman-Brown prophecy formula using the backtransformed average *z*. The input consists of a text or an ASCII data file. Furthermore, the number of raters, ratees, and items are supplied by the user. The program also provides options to compute reliabilities across ratees or items, with or without the backtransformed average *z*, and it saves the output as *r*s or *z*s. Examples of the Macintosh display and output are provided in the article.

Program Name: None Specified

Language: Microsoft QuickBASIC

Compatibility: Apple Macintosh

Memory Requirements: 1 MB RAM

Cost of Program: $6

How to obtain a copy of the program:

Send a written request and payment to:

Dr. John O. Brooks, III
Department of Psychiatry and Behavioral Sciences (C301)
Stanford University School of Medicine
Stanford, CA 94305-5717
e-mail: johnbrks@stanford.edu

INTERVAL SCALING

Title: THURSCAL: A Program for Interval Scaling Using Paired Comparisons or Paired Comparison Treatment of Complete Ranks Under Case III Assumptions

Author: John W. Bradford and Chester A. Schriesheim

Source: *Educational and Psychological Measurement*, 1990, *50*, 849-851.

Description: The program outputs matrices of input and ordered proportions, a matrix of ordered z-scores, the Case III scale values and standard deviations for each stimulus, and the Case III scale distances between stimuli. The input consists of complete unordered pairs, complete or incomplete preordered pairs, ordered pairs with Horst balanced values, or complete stimuli rankings. Either paired comparisons of stimuli or of complete ranks may be entered.

Program Name: THURSCAL

Language: Microsoft FORTRAN 4.0

Compatibility: IBM PC's and compatibles

Memory Requirements: 384K system memory

Cost of Program: No Charge

How to obtain a copy of the program:

Send a formatted 5.25"diskette and a self-addressed, stamped mailer to:

Dr. Chester A. Schriesheim
Department of Management
414 Jenkins
School of Business Administration
University of Miami
Coral Gables, FL 33124-9145

INTRACLASS CORRELATION

Title: A Note on the Unbiased Estimation of the Intraclass Correlation

Author: John R. Donoghue and Linda M. Collins

Source: *Psychometrika*, 1990, *55*, 159-164.

Description: Calculates Olkin and Pratt's (1958) unbiased estimator (h^*) of the intraclass correlation for any situation where the number of groups and the number of subjects per group are greater than or equal to 2. Because the program is written as a subroutine, it can be incorporated into other programs for different purposes, such as adjusting sequential observations for serial dependency. The listing of the program is available on pages 162-164.

Program Name: UNBIAS

Language: FORTRAN 77

Compatibility: IBM PC's and compatibles

Memory Requirements: None Specified

Cost of Program: No Charge

How to obtain a copy of the program:

The complete FORTRAN 77 source code is contained in the appendix of the original article. For further information contact:

Dr. John R. Donoghue
ENAR
ETS
Rosedale Road
Princeton, NJ 08541-0001

INTRACLASS CORRELATION

Title: Intraclass Correlations: There's More There Than Meets the Eye

Author: Mary Anne Lahey, Ronald G. Downey, and Frank E. Saal

Source: *Psychological Bulletin,* 1983, *93,* 586-595.

Description: The program discussed in this paper calculates the characteristic root test (Johnson & Graybill, 1972) to determine whether or not a rater by target interaction is present when calculating the intraclass correlation (ICC) among a set of raters. The test is most appropriate when (a) the interaction washes out the rater main effect thereby rendering the ICC nonsignificant, (b) the interaction is due to a single rater or ratee, or (c) the ratings were conducted in the absence of an experimental manipulation. A new version of the program found in the textbook <u>Analysis of Messy Data, Volume 2 - Nonreplicated Experiments</u> by Milliken and Johnson is offered.

Program Name: None Specified

Language: SAS (requires IML module to operate)

Compatibility: IBM PC's and compatibles

Memory Requirements: None Specified

Cost of Program: No Charge (however, a nominal fee is charged by SAS for Windows 95 version)

How to obtain a copy of the program:

Contact Dr. Johnson via e-mail:

Dr. Dallas Johnson
Department of Statistics
Kansas State University
Dickens Hall
Manhattan, KS 66506
e-mail: johnson@stat.ksu.edu

INTRACLASS CORRELATION

Title: INTRACLS: Application of the Intraclass Correlation to Computing Reliability

Author: F. Leon Paulson and Michael S. Trevisan

Source: *Applied Psychological Measurement,* 1990, *14,* 212.

Description: The program uses the intraclass correlation for computing an interrater reliability for more than two judges.

Program Name: INTRACLS

Language: C+

Compatibility: IBM PC's and compatibles

Memory Requirements: None Specified

Cost of Program: No Charge

How to obtain a copy of the program:

Send a formatted 3.5" diskette and a self-addressed, stamped mailer to:

Dr. Michael S. Trevisan
ELCP
P.O. Box 642136
Washington State University
Pullman. WA 99164-2136
e-mail: trevisan@mail.wsu.edu

INTRACLASS CORRELATION

Title: ICC: A BASIC Program for the Calculation of
Intraclass Correlations Based on Fixed Effects and
Random Effects Models

Author: Michael J. Strube

Source: *Behavior Research Methods, Instruments, & Computers,*
1985, 17, 578.

Description: The program computes the means and standard
deviations for all judges, an intercorrelation matrix (if more than
two judges), and an ANOVA summary table. The input consists of
a data file or the data can be manually entered into the program.

Program Name: ICC

Language: BASIC

Compatibility: IBM PC's and compatibles

Memory Requirements: None Specified

Cost of Program: No Charge

How to obtain a copy of the program:

Send a formatted 3.5" diskette and
a self-addressed, stamped mailer to:

Dr. Michael J. Strube
Department of Psychology
Washington University
St. Louis, MO 63130
e-mail: mjstrube@artsci.wustl.edu

INTRACLASS RELIABILITY

Title: RELCOEF: Testing the Equality of Intraclass Reliability Coefficients Obtained from Two Measurement Procedures

Author: Michael S. Trevisan and Glen Scymanski

Source: *Applied Psychological Measurement, 1993, 17, 72.*

Description: The program compares two independent intraclass reliability coefficients via the Alswalmeh and Feldt (1992) *F* test (converted to a *z*) and the associated probability value is given.

Program Name: RELCOEF

Language: Turbo Pascal

Compatibility: None Specified

Memory Requirements: None Specified

Cost of Program: No Charge

How to obtain a copy of the program:

Send a DOS formatted 3.5" diskette and a self-addressed, stamped mailer to:

Dr. Michael S. Trevisan
ELCP
P.O. Box 642136
Washington State University
Pullman, WA 99164-2136
e-mail: trevisan@mail.wsu.edu

ITEM ANALYSIS

Title: Some Simple Item Analysis Statistics
and Significance Tests

Author: Lewis R. Aiken

Source: *Journal of Research and Development in Education,*
1989, 22, 42-48.

Description: A set of three programs are discussed that calculate
a total of eight item analysis statistics that are most appropriate for
use with relatively small sample sizes ($n < 30$). Furthermore, these
programs are restricted to situations in which the items are
dichotomously scored using a (0,1) scoring format. Examples of
some of the indexes calculated include (1) item difficulty
estimates, (2) item discrimination indices, (3) the correspondence
between an examinee's response to an item and their responses to
other items, (4) the correspondence between an examinee's
response to an item and other examinees responses to the same
item, and (5) the uniformity of an examinee's responses to item
distractors. For each index, a test of significance and the
associated right-tail probability is provided.

Program Name: ITEMANAL

Language: BASIC and FORTRAN

Compatibility: IBM mainframes, IBM PC's and compatibles

Memory Requirements: None Specified

Cost of Program: No Charge

How to obtain a copy of the program:

Send a blank formatted 3.5" diskette and
a self-addressed, stamped mailer to:

Dr. Lewis R. Aiken
12449 Mountain Trail Court
Moorpark, CA 93021
Phone: (805) 523-8165

ITEM ANALYSIS

Title: Item Analysis with ITEMAN and RASCAL

Author: James P. Donnelly

Source: *Measurement and Evaluation in Counseling and Development*, 1994, *26*, 269-273.

Description: The program ITEMAN conducts both item and scale analyses on dichotomous data and on data collected using multipoint instruments with up to nine response options. The user inputs the number of items, the number of response alternatives, the codes for handling missing data, and the response key. The output includes the proportion of correct responses, the proportion endorsing each response option, the item to scale correlations, coefficient alphas, and over a dozen additional scale summary statistics. Written documentation is provided with the program.

Program Name: ITEMAN

Language: None Specified

Compatibility: IBM PC's and compatibles

Memory Requirements: At least 320K

Cost of Program: $99

How to obtain a copy of the program:

Send a written request and payment to:

Assessment Systems Corporation
2233 University Avenue
Suite 440
St. Paul, MN 55114

ITEM ANALYSIS

Title: INDEX: An Interactive Computer Program for Item Analysis of Objective Tests

Author: Harry A. King and Linvel E. Karres

Source: *Educational and Psychological Measurement,* 1981, *41,* 181-183.

Description: This program computes raw score means, the standard deviation, the Kuder-Richardson 20 reliability estimate, frequency of response to each choice, point-biserial correlation, Johnson-Findley index (based on the difference correct between the higher and lower scoring examinees), and defines the upper and lower 27%. The input consists of the number of examinees, the number of questions, and lists of the correct answers and answers by the examinees.

Program Name: INDEX

Language: DEC BASIC

Compatibility: IBM PC's and compatibles

Memory Requirements: 16K

Cost of Program: No Charge

How to obtain a copy of the program:

Send a blank 3.5" diskette and a self-addressed, stamped mailer to:

Dr. Harry A. King
Department of Physical Education
San Diego State University
San Diego, CA 92182

ITEM ANALYSIS

Title: TEST PAC: A Program for Comprehensive Item and Reliability Analysis

Author: Richard M. Luecht

Source: *Educational and Psychological Measurement,* 1987, *47,* 623-626.

Description: This menu-driven program provides descriptive statistics, item difficulties, discrimination indices, KR-20, Cronbach's alpha, Hoyt reliability, split-half reliability, and interitem phi coefficients. Moreover, a Rasch analysis (ability, item difficulty, and information parameter estimates) and generalizability analysis for fixed and random parameters under nested and crossed designs are also output. Finally, the program can aid in tracking student performance and assist in grading and test score reporting. The new version (ITEMSTAT) also performs item response theory calibrations.

Program Name: ITEMSTAT 1.2

Language: Compiled BASIC

Compatibility: IBM PC's and compatibles

Memory Requirements: 384K

Cost of Program: No Charge

How to obtain a copy of the program:

Send a formatted 3.5" diskette and
a self-addressed, stamped mailer to:

Dr. Richard M. Luecht
National Board of Medical Examiners
3750 Market St.
Philadelphia, PA 19104
e-mail: rluecht@mail.nbme.org

ITEM BIAS

Title: RUN: A Logistic-Based Interactive Program to Detect Patterns of Test Item Bias

Author: Michel G. Bougon and Robin I. Lissak

Source: *Behavior Research Methods & Instrumentation,* 1981, *13,* 755-756.

Description: This program assesses test item bias by estimating for each item an empirical characteristic curve (ECC) that is then evaluated against a corresponding ECC for a reference group of examinees. The B statistic (Bougon & Lissak, 1981) is the index used to compare each pair of ECC's. Input includes a list of the items to be examined for test bias, the number of data points in each ECC, and the two vectors of examinees' thetas (i.e., the ability parameters for the observed sample and the reference group). Output includes the B statistic for each item analyzed, a plot of each item's ECC, and (if desired) the vectors of thetas, differences, and t ratios of the ECC's.

Program Name: RUN

Language: APL

Compatibility: Any computer having APL in its system library

Memory Requirements: A minimum of 32K is recommended

Cost of Program: No Charge

How to obtain a copy of the program:

The program listing along with sample input and output can be obtained by contacting:

Dr. Michel Bougon
Management Department
Bryant College
1150 Douglas Pike
Smithfield, RI 02917
e-mail:mbougon@bryant.edu

ITEM RESPONSE THEORY

Title: Recognizing a Violation of the Assumption of Local Independence in the Analysis of Test Data

Author: David Andrich

Source: *Educational and Psychological Measurement,* 1983, *43,* 829-833.

Description: This program analyzes data according to a latent trait model. First, the program provides estimates of all parameters, two tests of fit for each subtest, and a test of fit for the response pattern for each individual. Moreover, a likelihood ratio test to determine whether all subtests have the same theta (cf. Rasch model) is also provided. Therefore, this program examines dependencies among responses.

Program Name: None Specified

Language: FORTRAN

Compatibility: None Specified

Memory Requirements: None Specified

Cost of Program: None Specified

How to obtain a copy of the program:

Send a written request to:

Dr. David Andrich
School of Education
Murdoch University
South Street
Murdoch
Western Australia 6150

ITEM RESPONSE THEORY

Title: Creating Item Characteristic Curves From LOGIST and BICAL Output

Author: Brooks Applegate and William G. LeBlanc

Source: *Educational and Psychological Measurement,* 1990, *50,* 581-584.

Description: The program augments the LOGIST and BICAL programs by outputting item and test characteristic curves, and item and test information functions for establishing ability estimates. The input is a raw data file which can be created by reentering the ability estimates from LOGIST or BICAL or by editing the output file created by these programs or by a procedure explained by LeBlanc (1989).

Program Name: None Specified

Language: SAS

Compatibility: IBM VM/CMS mainframe using SAS 5.18

Memory Requirements: None Specified

Cost of Program: No Charge

How to obtain a copy of the program:

Send either a formatted 3.5" or a 5.25" diskette and a self-addressed, stamped mailer to:

Dr. Brooks Applegate
University of Miami School of Medicine
1600 N.W. 10th Avenue
Division of Physical Therapy
Miami, FL 33136
e-mail: bapplega@umiamivm.1r.miami.edu

ITEM RESPONSE THEORY

Title: EQUATE 2.0: A Computer Program for the Characteristic Curve Method of IRT Equating

Author: Frank B. Baker

Source: *Applied Psychological Measurement,* 1993, *17*, 20.

Description: The program provides the test characteristic curve using graded (assigning item weights as either high to low or vice versa) , nominal (user pairs the anchor items), or dichotomous item scoring methods.

Program Name: EQUATE 2.1 (newest version)

Language: FORTRAN

Compatibility: IBM PC's and compatibles

Memory Requirements: 512K

Cost of Program: No Charge

How to obtain a copy of the program:

A program manual will also be included by sending a formatted 3.5" diskette and a self-addressed, stamped mailer to:

Dr. Frank B. Baker
Department of Educational Psychology
Educational Sciences Building
1025 W. Johnson Street
University of Wisconsin
Madison, WI 53706
e-mail: fbbaker@facstaff.wisc.edu

ITEM RESPONSE THEORY

Title: YeomanDG: A Data Generation Program (Version 1.0)

Author: Ralph De Ayala

Source: *Applied Psychological Measurement,* 1993,
17, 393.

Description: The program generates data for various item
response theory models (e.g., graded response, nominal response,
one-, two-, and three-parameter dichotomous models,
multidimensional models - up to four dimensions and five latent
classes). YeomanDG accommodates up to 32000 test takers and
150 (six-choice) items.

Program Name: YeomanDG (version 1.1)

Language: Pascal

Compatibility: Macintosh 68000 series

Memory Requirements: 2 MG of RAM, OS 6.0.2 (or higher),
68020 to 68040 CPU

Cost of Program: $10

How to obtain a copy of the program:

Send a written request and payment to:

Dr. Ralph De Ayala
Department of Measurement, Statistics, and Evaluation
Benjamin Building
University of Maryland
College Park, MD 20742
e-mail 400341@umdd

ITEM RESPONSE THEORY

Title: Item Parameter Estimation Via Marginal Maximum
Likelihood and an EM Algorithm: A Didactic

Author: Michael R. Harwell, Frank B. Baker,
and Michael Zwarts

Source: *Journal of Educational Statistics, 1988, 13, 243-271.*

Description: In the context of item response theory, this program
estimates item parameters using the marginal maximum likelihood
(MML) approach in conjunction with the expectancy maximization
(EM) algorithm. The MML/EM approach (Bock & Aitkin, 1981)
holds an advantage over the classic joint maximum likelihood
estimation (JMLE) procedure in that the MML/EM approach
integrates over the ability distribution and thus ensures consistent
item parameters across ability levels. Stated differently, the
MML/EM approach alleviates the Neyman-Scott problem.

Program Name: MML.EM

Language: BASIC

Compatibility: IBM PC's and compatibles

Memory Requirements: 512K

Cost of Program: No Charge

How to obtain a copy of the program:

A listing of the program is contained in the appendix of the source
article. Send a formatted 3.5" diskette and a self-addressed,
stamped mailer to:

Dr. Frank B. Baker
Department of Educational Psychology
Educational Sciences Building
1025 W. Johnson Street
University of Wisconsin
Madison, WI 53706
e-mail: fbbaker@facstaff.wisc.edu

ITEM RESPONSE THEORY

Title: DIMENSION: A Program to Generate Unidimensional
and Multidimensional Item Response Data

Author: John Hattie and Krzysztof Krakowski

Source: *Applied Psychological Measurement,* 1993,
17, 252.

Description: The program generates item response data for
compensatory and noncompensatory models. The input requires
the type of model, and the number of dimensions, items, and test
takers. The output consists of the correlation matrix among the
dimensions and the number correct.

Program Name: DIMENSION

Language: FORTRAN

Compatibility: IBM PC's and compatibles

Memory Requirements: 100K

Cost of Program: No Charge

How to obtain a copy of the program:

Send a formatted 3.5" diskette and
a self-addressed, stamped mailer to:

Dr. Krzysztof Krakowski
ECEL
University of Western Australia
Nedlands, WA 6907
Australia
e-mail: krzyszto@ecel.uwa.edu.au
        kkrakows@ecel.uwa.edu.oz

ITEM RESPONSE THEORY

Title: IRTDATA: An Interactive or Batch Pascal Program for
Generating Logistic Item Response Data

Author: George A. Johanson

Source: *Applied Psychological Measurement,* 1992,
16, 52.

Description: The program outputs a matrix of dichotomous
response vectors for up to 3000 simulated test takers responding to
a maximum of 200 items using the one-, two-, or three-parameter
logistic item response models. Output files for item and person
parameters are also provided. The user inputs the mean and
standard deviation of the item and person parameters. Moreover,
the distribution shape of the item parameter is also entered.

Program Name: IRTDATA

Language: Pascal

Compatibility: IBM PC's and compatibles

Memory Requirements: None Specified

Cost of Program: No Charge

How to obtain a copy of the program:

Send a formatted 3.5" diskette and
a self-addressed, stamped mailer to:

Dr. George A. Johanson
College of Education
201 McCracken Hall
Ohio University
Athens, OH 45701
e-mail: gjohanson1@ohiou.edu

ITEM RESPONSE THEORY

Title: IRTDIF: A Computer Program for IRT Differential Item Functioning Analysis

Author: Seock-Ho Kim and Allan S. Cohen

Source: *Applied Psychological Measurement,* 1992, *16,* 158.

Description: The program computes Lord's (1980) chi-square statistic with the appropriate probability value, and exact and closed-interval area measures for the one-, two-, and three-parameter item response theory models. The input consists of item parameter estimates and the variance-covariance matrix.

Program Name: IRTDIF

Language: FORTRAN

Compatibility: IBM PC's and compatibles (need math coprocessor)

Memory Requirements: None Specified

Cost of Program: No Charge

How to obtain a copy of the program:

Send a formatted 3.5" diskette and
a self-addressed, stamped mailer to:

Dr. Seock-Ho Kim or Dr. Allan S. Cohen
Testing and Evaluation
University of Wisconsin
1025 West Johnson Street
Madison, WI 53706
e-mail: shkim@tne.edsci.wisc.edu
cohen@tne.edsci.wisc.edu

ITEM RESPONSE THEORY

Title: MOKSCAL: A Program for a Nonparametric Item
Response Theory Model

Author: Johannes Kingma and Terry Taerum

Source: *Applied Psychological Measurement,* 1988,
12, 188, 200.

Description: This program uses a nonparametric item response
model (no assumptions about the functional form of the item trace
lines are made) for performing scale analysis (Mokken, 1971). The
output includes whether a specific set of items composes a
stochastic Mokken scale, three coefficients of scalability, four
different reliability coefficients, biserial and adjusted biserial
correlations and reliability for each item, tests for examining the
assumption of monotonicity in item difficulties among the scalable
items and that the item success probabilities and the latent trait also
have a monotonic function. An SPSS-X version is also available
(as indicated in *Educational and Psychological Measurement,*
1989, *49,* 101-136).

Program Name: MOKSCAL

Language: FORTRAN 77

Compatibility: IBM PC's and compatibles

Memory Requirements: 268K

Cost of Program: No Charge

How to obtain a copy of the program:

Two versions of the program are available: A separate program
compiled for a PC and another program to be used on SPSS-X

Send a formatted MS-DOS 5.25"diskette
and a self-addressed, stamped mailer to:

Dr. Johannes Kingma
University Hospital at Groningen
Department of Traumatology
Groningen
Netherlands

ITEM RESPONSE THEORY

Title: A FORTRAN Program for Assessing
Unidimensionality of Binary Data Using Holland and
Rosenbaum's Methodology

Author: Ratna Nandakumar

Source: *Multivariate Behavioral Research*, 1993, *28*, 63-66.

Description: In accord with Holland and Rosenbaum's (1986)
work indicating that item response data need to be characterized by
unidimensionality in order for items to be conditionally positively
associated, a program was developed to assess for
unidimensionality among binary item responses. The Mantel-
Haenszel (1959) statistic is computed for all item pairs thereby
allowing for all items to be evaluated simultaneously for the
presence of unidimensionality. The greater the proportion of
statistically nonsignificant Z-values, the greater the likelihood of
unidimensionality. In addition to the Mantel-Haenszel Z-values,
standard output also includes the corresponding Bonferroni-
corrected p-values for all item pairs.

Program Name: A test of unidimensionality using Holland
and Rosenbaum's procedure

Language: FORTRAN 77

Compatibility: IBM and UNIX mainframes, IBM PC's and
compatibles.

Memory Requirements: None Specified

Cost of Program: $5

How to obtain a copy of the program:

Send a written request and payment to:

Dr. Ratna Nandakumar
Department of Educational Studies
Willard Hall
University of Delaware
Newark, DE 19716
e-mail: nandakum@udel.edu

ITEM RESPONSE THEORY

Title: SIMUCAT: A Program to Simulate and Score Item Response Theory-Based Adaptive and Conventional Tests

Author: Walter P. Vispoel and Jon S. Twing

Source: *Applied Psychological Measurement*, 1990, *14*, 108.

Description: The program estimates the reliability and standard error of a theoretical adaptive or conventional test (up to 1700 test takers) for 17 theta levels (ranging from -3.2 to +3.2). The adaptive test is based on normal and rectangular theta distributions, whereas the conventional test focuses on a user selected set of items. A matrix of test item parameters (a,b,c values) comprises the input. This program aids test developers in discovering theta regions where the problems in reliability lie.

Program Name: SIMUCAT

Language: FORTRAN

Compatibility: IBM 4381 mainframe with MVS/OS

Memory Requirements: None Specified

Cost of Program: No Charge

How to obtain a copy of the program:

Send a formatted 3.5" diskette and a self-addressed, stamped mailer to:

Dr. Jon S. Twing
332 Lindquist Center
Iowa Testing Programs
University of Iowa
Iowa City, IA 52242

JACKKNIFE TECHNIQUE

Title: JACKKNIFE: A General-Purpose Package for Generating Multivariate Jackknife Analyses

Author: Joseph L. Balloun and A. Ben Oumlil

Source: *Behavior Research Methods, Instruments, & Computers,* 1986, *18,* 47-49.

Description: The jackknife technique is used to compute sample variance or confidence intervals and has particular utility when the assumptions are violated. This method reduces estimation bias and bias attributed to 1/N. The program computes the number of cases, mean, standard deviation (for each variable), the correlation matrix among all variables when one case at a time is dropped from the sample, jackknifed Fisher's zs, and jackknifed $\log_e$ 1 + standard deviations for each variable (for each individual). The JACKREG program provides jackknifed multiple regression analyses outputting unbiased estimates of slopes and multiple correlations, statistical significance tests when the usual assumptions are not met, parameter estimates and their correlations with each other, normality tests, and outlier detection. The input is a raw data file.

Program Name: JACKKNIFE, JACKREG

Language: WATFOR 77

Compatibility: IBM and VAX mainframes, IBM PC's and compatibles

Memory Requirements: None Specified

Cost of Program: No Charge

How to obtain a copy of the program:

Send a formatted 3.5" diskette and a self-addressed, stamped mailer to:

Dr. Joseph L. Balloun
School of Business and Entrepreneurship
Nova Southeastern University
3100 SW 9th Avenue
Fort Lauderdale, FL 33315
e-mail: balloun@sbe.acast.nova.edu

JAMES SECOND-ORDER TEST

Title: A SAS/IML Program for Applying the James Second-Order Test in Two-Factor Fixed Effect ANOVA Models

Author: Tung-Hsing Hsiung, Stephen Olejnik, and T. C. Oshima

Source: *Educational and Psychological Measurement*, 1994, *54*, 696-698.

Description: The program computes the James second-order test for examining main effects and interactions in two-between designs. The James second-order test is robust under heterogeneity of variance conditions for two-between designs (Hsiung & Olejnik, 1993). The first program analyzes raw data in an ASCII format, whereas the second program analyzes summary statistics also in ASCII. The output consists of the means and standard deviations, the James second-order test statistic, and the probability values.

Program Name: GOF (subroutine)

Language: SAS/IML

Compatibility: MVS/TSO, CMS, UNIX (using SAS 6.07 or later)

Memory Requirements: None Specified

Cost of Program: No Charge

How to obtain a copy of the program:

Send a formatted 3.5" diskette and a self-addressed, stamped mailer to:

Dr. Tung-Hsing Hsuing
325 Aderhold Hall
Department of Educational Psychology
University of Georgia
Athens, GA 30602
hsiung@moe.coe.uga.edu

JAMES SECOND-ORDER TEST

Title: A SAS Program for Testing the Hypothesis of the Equal Means Under Heteroscedasticity: James's Second-Order Test

Author: T. C. Oshima and James Algina

Source: *Educational and Psychological Measurement*, 1992, *52, 117-118.*

Description: The program computes the James second-order test for examining one-way designs which have violated the homogeneity of variance assumption. According to Wilcox (1988), under various conditions, this procedure controls Type I error better than other procedures. The input consists of a data file which includes sample sizes, means, and variances for up to 10 groups. The output consists of the data, the U statistic, and the critical values at various alpha levels.

Program Name: None Specified

Language: SAS/IML

Compatibility: IBM VM/CMS mainframe, IBM PC's and compatibles

Memory Requirements: None Specified

Cost of Program: No Charge

How to obtain a copy of the program:

Send a formatted 3.5" diskette and a self-addressed, stamped mailer to:

Dr. T. C. Oshima
Department of Educational Policy Studies
Georgia State University
University Plaza
Atlanta, GA 30303
e-mail: oshima@gsu.edu

JOHNSON-NEYMAN TECHNIQUE

Title: Comparing Two Non-Parallel Regression Lines With the Parametric Alternative to Analysis of Covariance Using SPSS-X or SAS -- The Johnson-Neyman Technique

Author: Mitchell B. Karpman

Source: *Educational and Psychological Measurement*, 1986, *46*, 639-644.

Description: This program computes the confidence interval for significant differences in prediction (Johnson-Neyman, 1936). The scores within the interval would indicate no significant differences on the independent variable when examining the separate regression lines of two groups. A listing of the program for SPSS-X and SAS is contained on pages 641 and 642. Programs for SPSS and BMDP are also available from the author. The listing for these programs is contained in *Educational and Psychological Measurement*, 1983, *43*, 141, 144-145.

Program Name: None Specified

Language: SPSS-X, SAS

Compatibility: Any system that uses SPSS-X or SAS

Memory Requirements: None Specified

Cost of Program: No Charge

How to obtain a copy of the program:

Send a written request to:

Dr. Mitchell B. Karpman
Sr. Operations Research Analyst
1808 Narrows Lane
Silver Spring, MD 20936-1137

JOHNSON-NEYMAN TECHNIQUE

Title: JOHN-NEY: An Interactive Program for Computing the Johnson-Neyman Confidence Region for Nonsignificant Prediction Differences

Author: Gary J. Lautenschlager

Source: *Applied Psychological Measurement,* 1987, *11,* 174,194.

Description: This program computes the confidence interval for significant differences in prediction (Johnson-Neyman, 1936). The scores within the interval would indicate no significant differences on the independent variable when examining the separate regression lines of two groups. The input consists of the sample sizes, means, between group and error sums of squares, regression coefficients, and slopes for the regression equation for each group.

Program Name: JOHN-NEY

Language: FORTRAN 77

Compatibility: Any mainframe or IBM PC and compatibles with a FORTRAN compiler

Memory Requirements: 640K

Cost of Program: No Charge

How to obtain a copy of the program:

Send a formatted 3.5" diskette and
a self-addressed, stamped mailer to:

Dr. Gary J. Lautenschlager
Department of Psychology
University of Georgia
Athens, GA 30602-3013
e-mail: garylaut@uga.cc.uga.edu

JOHNSON-NEYMAN TECHNIQUE

Title: A BASIC Program to Determine Regions of
Significance Using the Johnson-Neyman Technique

Author: Charles T. Scialfa

Source: *Behavior Research Methods, Instruments, & Computers,*
1987, 11, 349-352.

Description: This program computes the confidence interval for
significant differences in prediction (Johnson-Neyman, 1936).
That is, it examines the homogeneity of regression. This procedure
is similar to a test of simple effects in an interaction. The output is
composed of the point of intersection (equivalent performance for
the two groups) and the regions of significance in which there are
significant group differences for a particular covariate value. For
each group, the input consists of the sample sizes, predictor means,
standard deviations, error sums of squares, slope, and Y-intercept
estimates. A listing of the program can be found on pages 350-
352.

Program Name: None Specified

Language: BASIC

Compatibility: None Specified

Memory Requirements: None Specified

Cost of Program: No Charge

How to obtain a copy of the program:

Send a written request to:

Dr. Charles T. Scialfa
Department of Psychology
University of Calgary
2500 University Drive
Calgary, Alberta
TZN 1N4
Canada

KAPPA - GENERALIZED

Title: An Easy to Use BASIC Program for Agreement Amongst Many Raters

Author: Paul R. Jackson

Source: *British Journal of Clinical Psychology,* 1983, *22,* 145-146.

Description: Using Fleiss's (1971) formulae, this program calculates the generalized kappa coefficient and its asymptotic standard error estimate. Conceptually, the generalized kappa coefficient is equivalent to calculating the average value of Cohen's kappa across all pairs of raters. The program has an internal error check procedure that is applied to inputted data and the user has the option of entering data via several short-hand procedures.

Program Name: HANDY KAPPA

Language: Microsoft BASIC

Compatibility: Runs on APPLE, PET, and Z80-based machines

Memory Requirements: None Specified

Cost of Program: No Charge

How to obtain a copy of the program:

A listing of the program, instructions, and a worked example may be obtained by contacting:

Dr. Paul R. Jackson
University of Sheffield
Institute of Work Psychology
Sheffield S10 2TN
England

KAPPA - SIGNIFICANCE

Title: A DBASE III Program That Performs Significance
Testing for the Kappa Coefficient

Author: Tim S. C. Chan

Source: *Behavior Research Methods, Instruments, & Computers,*
1987, *19,* 53-54.

Description: This program outputs the observed frequency matrix, kappa, weighted kappa, and a percentage of agreement. Furthermore, the output also includes testing the computed kappa value against zero (or some other value) and its probability value. The standard errors of kappa and weighted kappa are also provided. The input consists of creating a data file, inputting frequencies in the form of a matrix, or reading from a DBASE III file. The program accommodates up to eight raters and rating points.

Program Name: None Specified

Language: DBASE III

Compatibility: None Specified

Memory Requirements: 6K

Cost of Program: No Charge

How to obtain a copy of the program:

Send a 5.25" diskette and a
self-addressed, stamped mailer to:

Dr. Tim S. C. Chan
Dental Data Processing Unit
Faculty of Dentistry
University of Hong Kong
34 Hospital Rd.
Hong Kong

KAPPA - SIGNIFICANCE

Title: A Computer Program for Determining the Significance of the Difference Between Pairs of Independently Derived Values of Kappa or Weighted Kappa

Author: Domenic V. Cicchetti and Robert Heavens, Jr.

Source: *Educational and Psychological Measurement*, 1990, *41*, 189-193.

Description: This program would be useful, for example, when one would compare the kappas between experienced and inexperienced judges. The output consists of observed and chance agreements, kappa (or weighted kappa, which would be used when partial rater agreement is possible), standard errors, and variance. Moreover, the z statistic and its probability level for determining if the two kappas are different are given. The input consists of the sample size, rating scale, type of rating scale, number of categories of classification, the format, and the data.

Program Name: None Specified

Language: FORTRAN 77

Compatibility: IBM mainframes, IBM PC's and compatibles

Memory Requirements: None Specified

Cost of Program: No Charge

How to obtain a copy of the program:

Send a formatted 3.5" double-density diskette and a self-addressed, stamped mailer to:

Dr. Domenic V. Cicchetti
Senior Research Psychologist and Biostatistician
VA Medical Center and Yale University
950 Campbell Avenue
West Haven, CT 06516
e-mail: domenic.cicchetti@yale.edu

KAPPA - WEIGHTED KAPPA

Title: KAPPO: A Program for Assessing the Reliability of Criterion-Referenced Tests

Author: Lewis R. Aiken

Source: *Applied Psychological Measurement,* 1988, *12,* 104.

Description: The program outputs the statistical significance of weighted or unweighted kappa and the coefficient of agreement (proportion of scores falling above or below a specified level on both tests) for up to 5 x 5 matrices. The number of rows and columns in the frequency table, each cell frequency, a choice of weighted or unweighted kappa, and the disagreement weight (for weighted kappa only) are inputted.

Program Name: KAPPO

Language: BASIC, PASCAL

Compatibility: IBM PC's and compatibles

Memory Requirements: None Specified

Cost of Program: No Charge

How to obtain a copy of the program:

Mention whether you want either the BASIC or PASCAL versions

Send a formatted 3.5" diskette and
a self-addressed, stamped mailer to:

Dr. Lewis R. Aiken
12449 Mountain Trail Court
Moorpark, CA 930 21
Phone (805) 523-8165

KAPPA - WEIGHTED KAPPA

Title: A Computer Program for Calculating Subject-by-Subject Kappa or Weighted Kappa Coefficients

Author: Domenic V. Cicchetti, Donald Showalter, and Paul McCarthy

Source: *Educational and Psychological Measurement*, 1990, *50*, 153-158.

Description: This program outputs each variable name and a rater x rater contingency table that includes the observed and expected number of cases, the agreement weight, the magnitude of kappa (or weighted kappa) for each cell, proportion of observed and expected agreement, kappa, the standard error of kappa, the probability value, and tests indicating whether one rater is biased when compared to another. This program handles up to 21 raters and 1820 objects per variable for up to 16 response categories. The input consists of various parameter lines followed by the data.

Program Name: None Specified

Language: FORTRAN 77

Compatibility: IBM PC's and compatibles

Memory Requirements: 223K of RAM

Cost of Program: No Charge

How to obtain a copy of the program:

Send a formatted 3.5" double-density diskette and a self-addressed, stamped mailer to:

Dr. Domenic V. Cicchetti
Senior Research Psychologist and Biostatistician
VA Medical Center and Yale University
950 Campbell Avenue
West Haven, CT 06516
e-mail: domenic.cicchetti@yale.edu

KAPPA - WEIGHTED KAPPA

Title: A Computer Program for Calculating Rater
Agreement and Bias Statistics Using Contingency
Table Input

Author: Robert Heavens and Domenic V. Cicchetti

Source: *Proceedings of the American Statistical Association,*
1978, *Statistical Computing Section,* 366-370.

Description: Calculates kappa and weighted kappa coefficients
from contingency table data as measures of overall (chance-
corrected) reliability and reliability for individual categories. The
user has the option of examining the effects that combining and/or
deleting categories has upon levels of chance-corrected agreement
and interrater bias.

Program Name: RATCAT

Language: FORTRAN

Compatibility: Mainframes and IBM PC's and compatibles

Memory Requirements: None Specified

Cost of Program: No Charge

How to obtain a copy of the program:

Send a formatted 3.5" diskette and
a self-addressed, stamped mailer to:

Dr. Domenic V. Cicchetti
Senior Research Psychologist and Biostatistician
VA Medical Center and Yale University
950 Campbell Avenue
West Haven, CT 06516
e-mail: domenic.cicchetti@yale.edu

KAPPA - WEIGHTED KAPPA

Title: Computing Cohen's Kappa Coefficients Using SPSS
MATRIX

Author: Claude A. M. Valiquette, Alain D. Lesage, Mirelle Cyr,
and Jean Toupin

Source: *Behavior Research Methods, Instruments, & Computers,*
1994, *26,* 60-61.

Description: The SPSS MATRIX program outputs the raw and
weighted kappa for symmetric or asymmetric disagreement
weights. Matrices for the contingency table and the disagreement
weights are used in this process. The program listings for raw and
weighted kappas are provided in the article.

Program Name: None Specified

Language: SPSS (MATRIX routine)

Compatibility: Any computer with SPSS capabilities

Memory Requirements: None Specified

Cost of Program: No Charge

How to obtain a copy of the program:

For further information contact:

Dr. Mirelle Cyr
Department of Psychology
Universite de Montreal
C.P. 6128
Succ. A.
Montreal, Quebec
Canada H3C 3J7

KENDALL'S TAU

Title: Kendall's Tau and Kendall's Partial Correlation: Two BASIC Programs for Microcomputers

Author: John P. Galla

Source: *Behavior Research Methods, Instruments, & Computers,* 1987, *19,* 55-56.

Description: This program computes Kendall's tau, S (the numerator of the tau statistic, which is a measure of lack of agreement in the rankings), the *z* test, and the appropriate probability and Kendall's partial correlation. No significance test is provided for Kendall's partial correlation. The input consists of reading data from data statements.

Program Name: None Specified

Language: BASIC

Compatibility: IBM PC's and compatibles

Memory Requirements: None Specified

Cost of Program: No Charge

How to obtain a copy of the program:

Send a formatted 3.5" diskette and
a self-addressed, stamped mailer to:

Dr. John P. Galla
Social Science Division
Widener University
Chester, PA 19013
e-mail: galla@pop1.science.widener.edu

LAG SEQUENTIAL ANALYSIS

Title: Computing Lag Sequential Statistics on Dyadic Time Interval Data: The TLAG Program

Author: Douglas K. Symons, Richard D. Wright, and Greg Moran

Source: *Behavior Research Methods, Instruments, & Computers,* 1988, *20,* 343-346.

Description: This program computes normal curve statistics for each subject-dyad as the square root of the chi-square statistic for the 2 x 2 contingency table of the change or no change in behavior of the two variables. The output includes measures of autocorrelation, measures of sequential dependency for x lags, and *z* scores adjusted and unadjusted for autocorrelation. The input consists of the data specified as a number of coded behaviors x number of time blocks array. A listing of the program is contained on pages 344-345.

Program Name: TLAG

Language: BASIC

Compatibility: IBM PC's and compatibles

Memory Requirements: 256K

Cost of Program: $5

How to obtain a copy of the program:

Send either a 3.5"or 5.25" diskette, a self-addressed stamped mailer, and payment to:

Dr. Douglas K. Symons
Department of Psychology
Acadia University
Wolfville, NS
Canada
BOP 1XO
e-mail: dsymons@ace.acadiau.ca

LATENT TRAIT MODELS

Title: MAXLOG: A Computer Program for the Estimation of the Parameters of a Multidimensional Logistic Model

Author: Robert L. McKinley and Mark D. Reckase

Source: *Behavior Research Methods & Instrumentation,* 1983, *15,* 389-390.

Description: This program utilizes an algorithm developed by Reckase and McKinley that extends the two-parameter logistic (2PL) latent trait model for use with dichotomously scored multidimensional tests. Using maximum likelihood estimation, the program first estimates the ability parameters and then calculates the item parameters. Input includes the number of examinees and the number of items. Output includes the item and person parameters, the estimated standard errors for each parameter estimate, and an analysis of the residuals.

Program Name: MAXLOG

Language: FORTRAN IV

Compatibility: IBM PC's and compatibles

Memory Requirements: None Specified

Cost of Program: No Charge

How to obtain a copy of the program:

Send a blank formatted 3.5" diskette and a self-addressed, stamped mailer to:

Dr. Robert L. McKinley
Director of Research
Test Development and Research
Law School Admission Services
P.O. Box 40
Newtown, PA 18940-0040

LINEAR REGRESSION - BOOTSTRAP

Title: BOOTSREG: An SAS Matrix Language Program for
Bootstrapping Linear Regression Models

Author: Xitao Fan and William G. Jacoby

Source: *Educational and Psychological Measurement*, 1995,
55, 764-768.

Description: Computes the regression statistics and bootstrap
distributions for R^2, adjusted R^2, regression coefficients and beta
weights. Each bootstrap distribution includes summary statistics
(e.g., mean, median, mode, skewness, kurtosis, standard deviation,
variance, maximum and minimum values, first and third quartiles,
interquartile range, and confidence intervals).   In this program, the
user provides the name of the raw data file, the number of
independent variables used in the regression model, the number of
bootstrap samples to be drawn, and the size of each sample.

Program Name: BOOTSREG

Language: SAS

Compatibility: Any system that uses SAS

Memory Requirements: None Specified

Cost of Program: No Charge

How to obtain a copy of the program:

Send a formatted 3.5" diskette and
a self-addressed, stamped mailer to:

Dr. Xitao Fan
Department of Psychology
Utah State University
Logan, UT 84322-2810
e-mail fafan@cc.usu.edu

LOG-LINEAR MODELS

Title: GENLOG II: A General Log-Linear Model Program for the Personal Computer

Author: Douglas G. Bonett, M. L. Brecht, and J. Arthur Woodward

Source: *Educational and Psychological Measurement,* 1985, *45,* 617-621.

Description: This interactive program can be used when examining a q x k design in which there are ordered categories. The input consists of entering the number of variables and the number of levels of each variable. Moreover, testing main effects or contrasts for planned comparisons are also possible. The output consists of the Wald test and probability values for main effects and planned comparisons. Either weighted least squares or maximum likelihood estimation can be employed. The program also provides the observed and predicted cell frequencies, standardized residual frequencies, and the Pearson and likelihood ratio statistics.

Program Name: GENLOG II

Language: BASIC

Compatibility: IBM PC's and compatibles or Apple Microcomputers

Memory Requirements: 64K

Cost of Program: None Specified

How to obtain a copy of the program:

Send a written request to:

Dr. Mary Lynn Brecht
University of California
School of Nursing
10833 Le Conte Ave
Los Angeles, CA 90024-1300
e-mail: lbrecht@sonnet.ucla.edu

LOG-LINEAR MODELS

Title: CONSCAL: Program for Testing Structural
              Hypotheses

Author: Mark L. Davison and Stephen J. Thoma

Source: *Applied Psychological Measurement*, 1980, *4*, 8.

Description: Uses an iterative proportional fitting algorithm to fit
the following four models to contingency table data: (1) learning
hierarchies in dichotomous test data, (2) patterns in rank order
preference data, (3) patterns in score profiles, and (4) cluster
structures in confusion data. Input includes the contingency table
cell frequencies and a list of the cells associated with each
parameter of the loglinear model. Output includes the expected cell
frequencies, the chi-square and likelihood ratio fit statistics, and
the model parameter estimates.

Program Name: CONSCAL

Language: FORTRAN

Compatibility: Initially designed for the CDC Cyber 74
                     machine. Will run with slight modifications on
                     most systems.

Memory Requirements: None Specified

Cost of Program: $5

How to obtain a copy of the program:

The program listing and user's manual can be obtained by sending
a written request and a check (made payable to the University of
Minnesota) to:

Dr. Mark L. Davison
Department of Social, Psychological, and Philosophical
Foundations of Education
178 Pillsbury Drive S.E.
Minneapolis, MN 55455
e-mail: mld@vx.cis.umn.edu

LOG-NORMAL DISTRIBUTION

Title: BES: An Algorithm for Estimation in Log-Normal
Distributions

Author: Cees H. Elzinga

Source: *Behavior Research Methods, Instruments, & Computers,*
1985, *17,* 505-507.

Description: This program uses the Bessel function for obtaining
uniform minimum-variance unbiased estimates for log-normal
distributions. An application of this program may be used for
magnitude-estimation experiments (e.g., making several judgments
of different stimulus intensities). A listing of the subroutine is
contained on page 507.

Program Name: BES

Language: FORTRAN

Compatibility: None Specified

Memory Requirements: None Specified

Cost of Program: No Charge

How to obtain a copy of the program:

Send a written request to:

Dr. Cees H. Elzinga
Department of Psychology
Catholic University of Nijmegen
Comeniuslaan 4
P.O. Box 9102
6500 HC Nijmegen
The Netherlands

LONGITUDINAL CHANGE

Title: The Trilinear Program: A Program to Analyze
Longitudinal Change on the Macintosh

Author: John O. Brooks, III

Source: *Behavior Research Methods, Instruments, & Computers,*
1993, *25,* 485-486.

Description: In a trilinear model, measurements follow a stability-
change-stability sequence. According to the author, the trilinear
model is more general and provides estimates of more parameters
than the linear model.   Hence, this program provides estimates of
stability, when the change starts and finishes, and the average rate
of change.

Program Name: None Specified

Language: None Specified

Compatibility: Macintosh

Memory Requirements: 4 MB RAM

Cost of Program: No Charge

How to obtain a copy of the program:

Send a written request to:

Dr. John O. Brooks, III
Department of Psychiatry and Behavioral Sciences (C301)
Stanford University School of Medicine
Stanford, CA 94305-5717
e-mail: johnbrks@stanford.edu

MAIN EFFECTS AND INTERACTIONS

Title: Topics in Research Methods: Main Effects and Interactions

Author: Brian S. Rushton

Source: *Science Software Quarterly,* 1984, *Fall,* 42-44.

Description: This interactive menu-driven program was designed as an instructional tool for teaching about factorial experiments and the analysis of main effects and interactions for two- and three-factor experimental designs. Sample factorial designs are contained within the program and the user may examine the data either numerically or graphically. The program includes written documentation.

Program Name: None Specified

Language: None Specified

Compatibility: Apple II+ and IIe machines

Memory Requirements: None Specified

Cost of Program: $50

How to obtain a copy of the program:

Send a written request and payment to:

Marcey Levine
Marketing Department
Oxford University Press
198 Madison Avenue
New York, NY 10016

MANN-WHITNEY U-TEST

Title: Action Research, the Mann-Whitney *U*, and Thou

Author: Joseph C. Ciechalski

Source: *Elementary School Guidance & Counseling,* 1990, *25,* 54-63.

Description: Given ranked data, this program calculates the lower value of the Mann-Whitney *U*-Test which can then be evaluated for statistical significance by comparing the obtained value against a table of critical values for the Mann-Whitney *U*. The user is prompted to enter the appropriate ranks for the experimental and control groups. The number of ranks contained within each group may be equal or unequal.

Program Name: MWU

Language: BASIC

Compatibility: Any computer with a BASIC interpreter or compiler

Memory Requirements: None Specified

Cost of Program: No Charge

How to obtain a copy of the program:

A listing of the program is contained in the appendix of the source article or send a self-addressed, stamped envelope to:

Dr. Joseph C. Ciechalski
Department of Counselor and Adult Education
Steight 142
School of Education
East Carolina University
Greenville, NC 27858-4353
e-mail: 74130.3426@compuserve.com

MANOVA

Title: Two-Way Multivariate Analysis of Variance: A BASIC Program for Microcomputers

Author: Daniel Coulombe

Source: *Behavior Research Methods, Instruments, & Computers*, 1985, *17*, 137-138.

Description: This program performs a two-way MANOVA in which the output consists of the means and standard deviations and the sums of squares and cross products matrices for the row, column, interaction, and error terms. Furthermore, the determinant values are provided for each cell. Moreover, the program outputs a MANOVA summary table consisting of Wilks' lambda, Bartlett's and Rao's statistical significance tests along with the discriminant function analysis containing the eigenvalues, discriminatory power index, Wilks' lambda, R^2, Bartlett's test of significance, standardized discriminant functions and group centroids. The input consists of the number of rows, columns, variables, groups, and participants in each group. The raw data may be contained either in a file or manually entered. An example of the output is provided on pages 137-138.

Program Name: None Specified

Language: GW-BASIC

Compatibility: IBM PC's and compatibles, Tandy 2000

Memory Requirements: 9K memory

Cost of Program: $15

How to obtain a copy of the program:

Send a written request and payment to:

Dr. Daniel Coulombe
School of Psychology
University of Ottawa
275 Nicholas
Ottawa, Ontario
Canada
K1N 6N5

MANOVA - NONPARAMETRIC

Title: NMANOVA: Nonparametric Multivariate One-Way Analysis of Variance

Author: Vincent J. Samar and Carol Hoppe

Source: *Applied Psychological Measurement*, 1981, *5*, 516.

Description: This program performs a nonparametric multivariate extension of the Kruskal-Wallis test with the only assumption being that the multivariate cumulative distribution functions are continuous. After testing whether the mean population ranks of the c groups on the p variables are equal, users may perform any number of univariate and multivariate post-hoc contrasts. Input consists of a subject by variable raw data matrix that includes a grouping variable specifying group membership. Output includes the chi-square statistic, univariate confidence intervals, and multivariate simultaneous confidence intervals.

Program Name: NMANOVA

Language: FORTRAN 77

Compatibility: Any computer capable of supporting FORTRAN

Memory Requirements: None Specified

Cost of Program: No Charge

How to obtain a copy of the program:

The program listing with documentation and sample data and output may be obtained by contacting:

Dr. Vincent J. Samar
Rochester Institute of Technology
National Technical Institute for the Deaf
Communication Research Department
Rochester, NY 14623
e-mail: vjsncr@rit.edu

MANTEL-HAENSZEL STATISTIC

Title: DIF: A Computer Program for the Analysis of Differential Item Performance

Author: Eckhard Klieme and Heinrich Stumpf

Source: *Educational and Psychological Measurement*, 1991, *51*, 669-671.

Description: To determine whether a focal group of test takers responds differently to a specific item than the reference group, the program outputs the Mantel-Haenszel Statistic for detecting differential item functioning, difficulty (p-value) and discrimination (point-biserial correlation) values for each group, effect size values for the differences between these groups, and z-tests for determining item difficulty and discrimination, and a plot of the classical difficulty index for each score with the respective score for the reference and focal groups is also provided. The input is found in a parameter file and a data file.

Program Name: DIF

Language: FORTRAN 77

Compatibility: IBM PC's and compatibles

Memory Requirements: None Specified

Cost of Program: No Charge

How to obtain a copy of the program:

Send a formatted 3.5" diskette and
a self-addressed, stamped mailer to:

Dr. Eckhard Klieme
Institute for Educational Research
Kobelenzer Strasse 77
D-53777
Bonn
Germany
e-mail: team@ibf.bn.evnet.de

MANTEL-HAENSZEL STATISTIC

Title: A FORTRAN 77 Program for Detecting Differential Item Functioning Through the Mantel-Haenszel Statistic

Author: Ratna Nandakumar

Source: *Educational and Psychological Measurement*, 1993, *53*, 679-684.

Description: This program outputs the Mantel-Haenszel Statistic for detecting differential item functioning, the common odds ratio, delta, and the proportion of items over the total number of items that are significant (e.g., whether the item favors a specific group). The input file consists of the names and codes for the reference and focal groups, number of items, test takers, data format, and lower and upper criteria for determining the groups. The program accommodates up to 60 items and 5000 test takers. An example of the input is provided in the text.

Program Name: DIFMH

Language: FORTRAN

Compatibility: All mainframes and IBM PC's and compatibles

Memory Requirements: None Specified

Cost of Program: $5

How to obtain a copy of the program:

Send a formatted 3.5"diskette, a self-addressed stamped mailer, and payment to:

Dr. Ratna Nandakumar
Department of Educational Studies
University of Delaware
Willard Hall
Newark, DE 19716
e-mail: nandakum@udel.edu

MANTEL-HAENSZEL STATISTIC

Title: MH: A FORTRAN 77 Program to Compute the Mantel-Haenszel Statistic for Detecting Differential Item Functioning

Author: H. Jane Rogers and Ronald K. Hambleton

Source: *Educational and Psychological Measurement*, 1994, *54*, 101-104.

Description: This program computes the Mantel-Haenszel statistic for detecting differential item functioning. It uses a total test score or a "purified" test score as the internal criterion or allows for an external criterion for matching examinees. Descriptive statistics, classical item difficulty statistics, delta-diff values, MH chi-square values, and weighted *p*-diff squared values are provided. Two input files are needed to run the MH program: one for the specifications file (provided) and the other for the data. MH handles up to 100 items.

Program Name: MH

Language: None Specified

Compatibility: Mainframe or PC. PC version includes the Dorans and Kulick (1986) standardization indices.

Memory Requirements: None Specified

Cost of Program: $75

How to obtain a copy of the program:

Send a written request and payment to:

Dr. Ronald K. Hambleton
Laboratory of Psychometric and Evaluative Research
Hills South
Room 152
University of Massachusetts
Amherst, MA 01003
e-mail: rkh@educ.umass.edu

MARGINAL HOMOGENEITY

Title: A MINITAB Macro for Testing Marginal Homogeneity
in Contingency Tables

Author: Glyn M. Collis

Source: *Behavior Research Methods, Instruments, & Computers,*
1986, *18,* 66-67.

Description: This program outputs Stuart's Q, Bhapkar's Q (for
larger contingency tables), and McNemar's chi-square (for the 2 x
2 case) when testing whether the row totals are about the same as
the column totals in a contingency table (marginal homogeneity).
The user assigns values to the number of categories, the first of p
columns of the contingency table, and the first of p columns of
workspace. A listing of the program is contained on page 67.

Program Name: MARGHOMO.MTB

Language: MINITAB

Compatibility: MINITAB release 82.1 or later

Memory Requirements: None Specified

Cost of Program: No Charge

How to obtain a copy of the program:

Send a written request to:

Dr. Glyn M. Collis
Department of Psychology
University of Warwick
Coventry CV4 7AL
England

MARKOV CHAIN ANALYSIS

Title: A Statistical Analysis System (SAS) Computer Program for Markov Chain Analysis

Author: Stephen V. Faraone

Source: *Journal of Psychopathology and Behavioral Assessment*, 1986, *8*, 367-379.

Description: Conducts a Markov chain analysis on a sequence of user-specified behavior codes. The program tests a series of hypotheses regarding first-order and second-order transition frequencies and transition probabilities. Pearson and likelihood-ratio chi-square statistics are used to evaluate competing models of serial dependency (i.e., random sequence vs. first-order Markov chain vs. second-order Markov chain).

Program Name: None Specified

Language: SAS

Compatibility: Any computer which uses SAS

Memory Requirements: None Specified

Cost of Program: No Charge

How to obtain a copy of the program:

The complete SAS code is contained in the appendix of the article.

For further information contact:

Dr. Stephen V. Faraone
385 Old Trail Rd.
Sanibel, FL 33957-6408
e-mail: 74020.1725@compuserve.com

MARKOV MODEL

Title: Markov Count: A Program for Computing the Learning
Statistics of Two-Stage Markov Learning Experiments

Author: Johannes Kingma and Johan Reuvekamp

Source: *Educational and Psychological Measurement,* 1987,
47, 89-97.

Description: A two-stage Markov model consists of an unlearned
state (all errors), a combination of successes and errors, and a
learned state in which there are only successes. This program
outputs transition counts, total counts for the second and
subsequent trials, and learning statistics. This output is provided
for each category. A data input file is required.

Program Name: None Specified

Language: Pascal

Compatibility: Apple II+

Memory Requirements: 34K

Cost of Program: None Specified

How to obtain a copy of the program:

Send a formatted 5.25" diskette and
a self-addressed, stamped mailer to:

Dr. Johannes Kingma
University Hospital at Groningen
Department of Traumatology
Groningen
Netherlands

MARKOV MODEL

Title: Markov Model: A Package for Computing the Parameters of One-Stage and Two-Stage Learning Models and Hypothesis Testing

Author: Johannes Kingma and Johan Reuvekamp

Source: *Educational and Psychological Measurement,* 1987, *47,* 99-105.

Description: This program is concerned with determining if a specific type of model (e.g., one-stage) consisting of an initial unlearned state (errors and successes occur) followed by a terminal state in which only successes occur, accounts for fitting the data. A necessity test is provided which examines whether a larger stage model would be more appropriate. Finally, hypothesis tests for experimentwise, conditionwise, and parameterwise issues are performed for between and within conditions. The input consists of a starting parameter (e.g., .50), maximum number of iterations, and stepsize for convergence of the minimization procedure.

Program Name: ONESTAGE, TWOSTAGE (estimates parameters for and likelihood for one- and two-stage learning models, respectively)

BETWEEN, WITHIN (provides hypothesis tests between and within conditions, respectively)

Language: FORTRAN 77

Compatibility: Cyber, DEC, VAX, Ahmdahl mainframes

Memory Requirements: None Specified

Cost of Program: None Specified

How to obtain a copy of the program:

Send a formatted MS-DOS 5.25" diskette and a self-addressed, stamped mailer to:

Dr. Johannes Kingma
University Hospital at Groningen
Department of Traumatology
Groningen
Netherlands

MARKOV MODEL

Title: Fix-Count: A Program for Computing the Error-Success Transitions in Fixed-Trial Two-Stage Markov Learning Experiments

Author: Johannes Kingma and Kees P. Van den Bos

Source: *Educational and Psychological Measurement*, 1987, *47*, 649-653.

Description: This program outputs the total number of counts and summary statistics for each response pattern of two-stage learning models with fixed trials. One may be able to use this program to examine the success-error patterns of the first k trials across different populations which cannot meet strict learning criteria. The default is a maximum of five fixed trials and six categories.

Program Name: FIX.COUNT

Language: FORTRAN 77

Compatibility: Apple II+, IBM PC's and compatibles

Memory Requirements: 28K

Cost of Program: No Charge

How to obtain a copy of the program:

Send a formatted MS-DOS 5.25" diskette and a self-addressed, stamped mailer to:

Dr. Johannes Kingma
University Hospital at Groningen
Department of Traumatology
Groningen
Netherlands

MARKOV MODEL

Title: Markov-Fixed: Four Programs for Computing the Parameters of One-Stage and Two-Stage Learning Models and Hypothesis Testing in Fixed-Trial Experiments

Author: Johannes Kingma and Kees P. Van den Bos

Source: *Educational and Psychological Measurement,* 1987, *47,* 655-671.

Description: Four separate programs are provided for computing the parameters for one- and two-stage Markov models, and for testing hypotheses concerning parameter differences between and within experimental conditions for fixed-trial experiments. Goodness-of-fit, necessity, and sufficiency tests are provided. The input consists of two files: The first file consists of the frequencies of error-success patterns and the second file contains the theoretical parameter, maximum number of iterations, and a stepsize for convergence for minimization.

Program Name: FIXONE, FIXTWO (estimates parameters for and likelihood for one- and two-stage learning models, respectively)

BETWEEN, WITHIN (provides hypothesis tests between and within conditions, respectively)

Language: FORTRAN 77

Compatibility: Amdahl, Cyber, and VAX mainframes

Memory Requirements: 51K for each program

Cost of Program: None Specified

How to obtain a copy of the program:

Send a formatted MS-DOS 5.25" diskette and a self-addressed, stamped mailer to:

Dr. Johannes Kingma
University Hospital at Groningen
Department of Traumatology
Groningen
Netherlands

MARKOV MODEL

Title: Markov-Forget: A Package for Parameter Estimation and Hypothesis Testing of 5,7,8,9,and 10-Parameter Two-Stage Forgetting Models

Author: Johannes Kingma and Kees P. Van den Bos

Source: *Educational and Psychological Measurement,* 1987, *47,* 673-687.

Description: Programs for computing the parameters of a particular model, and testing hypotheses about parameter differences between and within conditions are provided for each of five models. The output includes the chi-square statistic, probabilities of occurrence of error-success response patterns in a certain condition, and the estimated frequencies of these patterns. The input consists of two files: the first file includes the frequency counts of error-success patterns for each experimental condition and the other file consists of parameters for determining the optimal model (e.g., maximum number of iterations, stepsize for convergence of the minimization).

Program Name: 15 separate programs (e.g., Forget9.within)

Language: FORTRAN 77

Compatibility: Amdahl, Cyber, and VAX mainframes

Memory Requirements: 55K for each program

Cost of Program: None Specified

How to obtain a copy of the program:

Send a formatted MS-DOS 5.25" diskette and a self-addressed, stamped mailer to:

Dr. Johannes Kingma
University Hospital at Groningen
Department of Traumatology
Groningen
Netherlands

MATRIX ALGEBRA

Title: MATRICKS: Matrix Algebra for Applesoft BASIC

Author: John R. Vokey

Source: *Behavior Research Methods, Instruments, & Computers,* 1986, *18,* 409-411.

Description: This program allows for numerous matrix algebra techniques to be used for demonstrating multiple regression, canonical correlation, multiple discriminant function analysis, and MANOVA, for example. Moreover, it aids in simplifying rotations and scaling of two- and three-dimensional graphics.

Program Name: MATRICKS

Language: 6502 assembler language; Applesoft BASIC

Compatibility: Apple II

Memory Requirements: None Specified

Cost of Program: No Charge

How to obtain a copy of the program:

Send a 3.5" Apple-compatible floppy diskette and a self-addressed, stamped mailer to:

Dr. John R. Vokey
Department of Psychology
University of Lethbridge
Lethbridge, Alberta
Canada
T1K 3M4

MATRIX COMPARISONS

Title: MATFIT: A FORTRAN Subroutine for Comparing
Two Matrices in a Subspace

Author: J. O . Ramsay

Source: *Psychometrika,* 1990, *55,* 551-553.

Description: This program optimizes the correlation between two
matrices in a subspace by either maximizing the squared
correlation, or minimizing the squared distance, between the
relevant transformation matrices. The program is perhaps most
useful for comparing matrices of similarity judgments or
preference ratings. The matrices generated by the program
can also be evaluated via simulation in order to examine the
sampling properties of the two fitting criteria (i.e., correlational
and distance approaches).

Program Name: MATFIT

Language: FORTRAN 77

Compatibility: IBM PC's and compatibles

Memory Requirements: None Specified

Cost of Program: No Charge

How to obtain a copy of the program:

Send a formatted 3.5" diskette and
a self-addressed, stamped mailer to:

Dr. J. O. Ramsay
Department of Psychology
McGill University
1205 Dr. Penfield Avenue
Montreal, Quebec
Canada
H3A 1B1
e-mail: ramsay@psych.mcgill.ca

MATRIX MANIPULATIONS

Title: The Use of Matrix Manipulation Programs in
Teaching Statistical Methods

Author: N. John Castellan

Source: *Behavior Research Methods & Instrumentation,*
1980, *12,* 172-177.

Description: This computer package manipulates and analyzes
matrices and arrays of real or randomly-generated data. The
program can perform 48 different matrix manipulation operations
(e.g., duplicate matrix, transpose matrix, remove matrix diagonal
and store as a vector, calculate eigenvectors and eigenvalues) and
23 statistical operations (e.g., descriptives, regression, chi-square,
rank correlations, time series analysis). The program can
accommodate user-written FORTRAN subroutines.

Program Name: Symbolic Matrix Interpretive System and
Statistical Interpretive System (SMIS/SIS).

Language: None Specified

Compatibility: None Specified

Memory Requirements: None Specified

Cost of Program: None Specified

How to obtain a copy of the program:

For ordering and cost information, contact:

Dr. Don Robinson
Department of Psychology
Indiana University
Bloomington, IN 47405

MEANS AND VARIANCES

Title: A BASIC Program for Generating Integer
Means and Variances

Author: Bernard C. Beins

Source: *Teaching of Psychology,* 1989, *16,* 230-231.

Description: This program creates datasets with integer means
and variances. The user may specify the sample size, the range of
scores, and whether the variance is calculated using N or N-1 in the
denominator. Standard output includes the raw data, means,
variances, and standard deviations using both N and N-1.

Program Name: None Specified

Language: Applesoft BASIC

Compatibility: Any computer within the Apple II family

Memory Requirements: None Specified

Cost of Program: No Charge

How to obtain a copy of the program:

A listing of the program may be obtained by contacting:

Dr. Bernard C. Beins
Department of Psychology
Ithaca College
Ithaca, NY 14850

MEDIATING VARIABLES

Title: A SAS Program for Testing the Statistical Significance
of a Mediating Variable

Author: Ting Hsiang Lin

Source: *Educational and Psychological Measurement*, 1997, *57*,
186-188.

Description: This interactive program computes a significance
test for a mediating variable by examining the equality of two
regression coefficients. A mediator variable is one which is
significantly related to both the predictor and the criterion
variables. When it is controlled for, however, the relationship
between the predictor and the criterion is significantly reduced.
The user specifies the independent, dependent, and mediator
variable. This input consists of either a SAS data file or summary
statistics. The output consists of the *t* value, its significance level,
and the effect size for the mediator variable.

Program Name: None Specified

Language: SAS

Compatibility: Any computer that supports SAS

Memory Requirements: None Specified

Cost of Program: No Charge

How to obtain a copy of the program:

A listing of the program may be obtained by writing:

Dr. Ting Hsiang Lin
New England Research Institutes
9 Galen Street
Watertown, MA 02172

MEDIANS - SKEWED DISTRIBUTIONS

Title: Sorting Data Sets and Computing Medians for Skewed Distributions

Author: Ralph Mason Dreger

Source: *Educational and Psychological Measurement*, 1995, *55*, 785-790.

Description: Computes the medians of clustered or unclustered data using the Shell-Metzner sort algorithm (Dreger, 1989). The user inputs the name of the cluster, the number of rows and columns, the name of the file, and whether or not an ID number is present. The output includes the cluster name, a listing of the original and reordered data matrices, and a list of medians.

Program Name: SHELMEDS.BAS

Language: GWBASIC

Compatibility: IBM PC's and compatibles

Memory Requirements: 1K

Cost of Program: No Charge

How to obtain a copy of the program:

Send either a formatted 3.5" or 5.25" diskette and a self-addressed, stamped mailer to:

Dr. Ralph Mason Dreger
Department of Psychology
Louisiana State University
Baton Rouge, LA 70803
e-mail: rdreger266@aol.com

META-ANALYSIS

Title: A Computer Program for Performing Meta-Analyses When the Outcome Variable is Dichotomous: Relevance to Neuropsychology and Biomedical Research

Author: Domenic V. Cicchetti, Donald Showalter, and Bruce E. Wexler

Source: *The Clinical Neuropsychologist*, 1993, 7, 454-459.

Description: This program calculates measures of association and performs meta-analyses on data with dichotomous outcomes that can be presented in the form of 2 x 2 contingency tables. Input consists of the number of study groups and the cell counts for each fourfold table. Output includes for each fourfold table (i.e., each separate study) the chi-square statistic, the odds ratio, the Phi coefficient, and the Phi/Phi max coefficient which adjusts for the "usual" case. Three different (meta-) analyses of the combined tables are conducted using the Log Odds ratio, Cornfield/Gart, and Mantel-Haenszel methods. For each meta-analysis, the chi-square tests of homogeneity and association are performed and the probabilities pertaining to each test are computed.

Program Name: None Specified

Language: C

Compatibility: Any computer capable of supporting C

Memory Requirements: None Specified

Cost of Program: No Charge

How to obtain a copy of the program:

A listing of the C source code with documentation, and sample applications, can be obtained by contacting:

Dr. Domenic V. Cicchetti
Senior Research Psychologist and Biostatistician
West Haven VA Medical Center & Yale University
950 Campbell Avenue
West Haven, CT 06516
e-mail: domenic.cicchetti@yale.edu

META-ANALYSIS

Title: A Microcomputer Program Package for Meta-Analysis

Author: Bernard S. Gorman and Louis H. Primavera

Source: *Behavior Research Methods & Instrumentation,*
               1983, *15,* 617.

Description: This package contains four separate computer programs. Effect Size calculates Friedman's (1982) magnitude-of-effect index (r_m). Rosenthal computes average effect sizes from various effect-magnitude indexes and is capable of performing chi-square tests for both diffuse differences and focused contrasts. Cumulative Analysis calculates from a series of effect sizes and sample sizes a weighted average effect size and an analysis of the variability among studies. Regression Synthesis allows for the analysis of linear regression models in which effect sizes serve as dependent variables and the independent variables consist of the design characteristics from the individual studies. All four programs are menu driven and completely interactive.

Program Name: EFFECT SIZE, ROSENTHAL,
                    CUMULATIVE ANALYSIS, REGRESSION
                    SYNTHESIS

Language: QuickBASIC 4.5

Compatibility: Designed for use with Apple II+ systems and
                    IBM PC's and compatibles

Memory Requirements: A minimum of 60K

Cost of Program: No Charge

How to obtain a copy of the program:

Send a blank 3.5" diskette and a
self-addressed, stamped mailer to:

Dr. Bernard S. Gorman
Department of Psychology
1 Education Drive
Nassau Community College
Garden City, NY 11530
e-mail: bsgorman@pipeline.com

META-ANALYSIS

Title: Conducting Meta-Analysis Using the PROC MEANS
Procedure in SAS

Author: Allen I. Huffcutt, Winfred Arthur, Jr.,
and Winston Bennett

Source: *Educational and Psychological Measurement,* 1993,
53, 119-131.

Description: SAS listings are provided using the PROC MEANS
procedure for performing a meta-analysis (e.g., Hunter & Schmidt,
1990). These listings also correct for sampling error, provide
artifact distributions with compound attenuation and compound
variance computations, the appropriate summary statistics (e.g.,
population correlation, variance of the corrected population
correlation), and allow for an examination of moderator variables.

Program Name: None Specified

Language: SAS

Compatibility: Any mainframe computer that implements SAS,
and IBM PC's and compatibles that have the PC
version of SAS

Memory Requirements: None Specified

Cost of Program: No Charge

How to obtain a copy of the program:

Listings of the various SAS procedures are provided
in the text. For further information, send a written request to:

Dr. Allen I. Huffcutt
Department of Psychology
Bradley University
Peoria, IL 61625
e-mail: huffcutt@bumail.bradley.edu

META-ANALYSIS

Title: META-RAND: A SAS Macro Program for Randomly Generated Meta-Analysis

Author: Meni Koslowsky and Abraham Sagie

Source: *Educational and Psychological Measurement,* 1992, *52,* 915-917.

Description: This program generates random correlations for a simulation study in which various assumptions can be tested in a meta-analysis. The input consists of the subpopulation means, population reliabilities of the predictor and criterion, sample size, number of correlations, number of meta-analyses, and the ratio of the sample to population standard deviation. The output consists of a summary of the input, various uncorrected and corrected statistics, namely average correlation, variance, error, and true components. Moreover, tests of homogeneity or heterogeneity of the observed correlations such as Hunter and Schmidt's (1990) 75% rule, bounds for credibility intervals, and the *U*-test and *Q*-test, and indicators of adequacy for each test are also outputted.

Program Name: META-RAND

Language: SAS

Compatibility: IBM-MVS, VM, and UNIX mainframes

Memory Requirements: Between 500K and 5000K

Cost of Program: No Charge

How to obtain a copy of the program:

Send a formatted 3.5" diskette and
a self-addressed, stamped mailer to:

Dr. Abraham Sagie
School of Business Administration
Bar-Han University
Ramat-Gan 52900
Israel
e-mail: sagiea@ashur.cc.biu.ac.il

META-ANALYSIS

Title: A BASIC Program for Meta-Analysis Using Stouffer's
Formula

Author: Brian Mullen

Source: *Behavior Research Methods & Instrumentation,*
1982, 14, 551.

Description: This program uses Stouffer's (1949) method to
perform meta-analyses of independent studies. Input consists of a
one-tailed p value and a weight for each study. After transforming
probability levels into weighted *z* scores (standard normal
deviates), the program outputs the standard normal deviate for
meta-analysis (Z_{ma}), its associated p value, and the fail-safe number
for the .05 level of significance.

Program Name: None Specified

Language: Level II BASIC

Compatibility: Can be modified to be compatible with most
versions of BASIC

Memory Requirements: A minimum of 1.4K

Cost of Program: No Charge

How to obtain a copy of the program:

A listing of the program may be obtained by contacting:

Dr. Brian Mullen
Department of Psychology
Syracuse University
Syracuse, NY 13244
e-mail: bmullen@syr.edu

META-ANALYSIS

Title: META_SAS: A Method for Detecting Moderators After a Meta-Analysis

Author: Abraham Sagie and Meni Koslowsky

Source: *Psychometrika,* 1992, *57,* 316.

Description: This program tests for the existence of moderators in a meta-analysis using the Schmidt and Hunter 75% rule for corrected and uncorrected rs, the Q (Hunter & Schmidt, 1990) and U statistics (Spector & Levine, 1987) and credibility intervals around the corrected r (Whitener, 1990). The program also corrects for sampling error, range restriction, and predictor and criterion reliabilities. The input file consists of a correlation matrix.

Program Name: META_SAS

Language: SAS

Compatibility: Any system that uses SAS

Memory Requirements: None Specified

Cost of Program: $50

How to obtain a copy of the program:

Send a formatted 3.5" diskette, a self-addressed stamped mailer, and payment to:

Dr. Abraham Sagie
School of Business Administration
Bar-Han University
Ramat-Gan 52900
Israel
e-mail: sagiea@ashur.cc.biu.ac.il

META-ANALYSIS

Title: Meta-Analysis Programs

Author: Ralf Schwarzer

Source: *Behavior Research Methods, Instruments, & Computers,*
1988, *20,* 338.

Description: This program allows for data file management,
combination of effect sizes for means and correlations, cluster
analysis of means and correlations, weighted means, a
transformation of statistics into effect sizes, combining
probabilities (when effect sizes are not available), significance tests
for correlations, and stem-and-leaf displays for correlations.

Program Name: META 5.3

Language: Pascal

Compatibility: IBM PC's and compatibles

Memory Requirements: 300K RAM and 212K storage space

Cost of Program: $10 for overseas postage and handling

How to obtain a copy of the program:

Send a formatted 3.5"diskette, a self-addressed
stamped mailer, and payment to:

Dr. Ralf Schwarzer
Freie Universitat Berlin
Fachbereich Erziehungswissenschaft
Psychologie und Sportwissenschaft
Institut für Arbeits-, Organizations - u
Gesundheitspsychologie (WE 10)
Habelschwerdter Allee 45
14195 Berlin
West Germany
e-mail: health@zedat.fu-berlin.de

META-ANALYSIS

Title: A Graphical User Interface Psychometric Meta-Analysis
Program for DOS

Author: Joseph M. Stauffer

Source: *Educational and Psychological Measurement,* 1996, *56,*
675-676.

Description: This interactive program using a Windows-type
interface, performs meta-analysis using the Hunter and Schmidt
(1990) algorithms. The features include a full-screen editor in
which one can copy, cut, and paste, etc. in a fashion similar to
Windows.

Program Name: METAQUIK 16 v.1.1

Language: Object Pascal (Delphi)

Compatibility: IBM PC's and compatibles (for Windows)

Memory Requirements: 4 MB

Cost of Program: No Charge

How to obtain a copy of the program:

Send a formatted 3.5" diskette and
a self-addressed, stamped mailer to:

Dr. Joseph Stauffer
Department of Management and Finance
Indiana State University
Terre Haute, IN 47809-5402
e-mail: mfstauf@befac.indstate.edu

May download mq16zip.exe at:
ftp://mama.indstate.edu/users/stauffer/

META-ANALYSIS

Title: Correlational Meta-Analysis Using Minitab

Author: Hoben Thomas

Source: *Applied Psychological Measurement,* 1990,
14, 82.

Description: These Minitab exec files use mixture model
procedures (Thomas, 1989) for estimating:
  1. the posterior probability of *r* coming from component j,
  2. the posterior mean for each sample *r* via Bayesian methods,
  3. the mean and variance of the population correlation.
The input consists of independent pairs of correlations with their
corresponding sample sizes.

Program Name: None Specified

Language: Minitab

Compatibility: All computers using any version of Minitab

Memory Requirements: None Specified

Cost of Program: No Charge

How to obtain a copy of the program:

Send a formatted 3.5" diskette and
a self-addressed, stamped mailer to:

Dr. Hoben Thomas
Department of Psychology
513 Bruce V. Moore Building
The Pennsylvania State University
University Park, PA 16802
e-mail: hxt@psu.edu

META-ANALYSIS - VOTE-COUNTING

Title: A Procedure for Combining Sample Correlation Coefficients and Vote Counts to Obtain an Estimate and a Confidence Interval for the Population Correlation Coefficient

Author: Brad J. Bushman and Morgan C. Wang

Source: *Psychological Bulletin*, 1995, *117*, 530-546.

Description: In response to the problem of missing correlational effect size estimates in meta-analysis and the need for an appropriate solution, this program conducts vote-counting procedures (Bushman, 1994) on those samples (i.e., studies) for which either the direction of an effect is presented (e.g., a positive or negative correlation) or the statistical significance of the results is noted. The program can be used to meta-analyze studies that have either equal or unequal sample sizes. The vote-count results can be used to supplement the calculated effect sizes in order to estimate with as little bias as possible, and provide a narrow confidence interval for the population correlation coefficient.

Program Name: COMBINE.SAS

Language: SAS

Compatibility: IBM PC's and compatibles, VMS/VAX, IBM, and UNIX mainframes

Memory Requirements: None Specified

Cost of Program: $10 (shipping and handling)

How to obtain a copy of the program:

Send a formatted 3.5" diskette, a self-addressed stamped mailer, and payment to:

Dr. Chung-Ching Morgan Wang
Department of Statistics
University of Central Florida
Orlando, FL 32816-2370
e-mail: cwang@pegasus.cc.ucf.edu

META-ANALYSIS VOTE-COUNTING

Title: A Microsoft FORTRAN 77 Program for Determining the Confidence Interval Around the Estimate of the Population Correlation Coefficient for the Vote-Counting Method

Author: Morgan C. Wang and N. Clayton Silver

Source: *Educational and Psychological Measurement*, 1994, *54*, 105-109.

Description: Used in the vote-counting method of meta-analysis, this program computes the confidence interval around the estimate of the population correlation coefficient using the normal (Sachs, 1982) and chi-square approximations (Hedges & Olkin, 1985) for large sample sizes and an exact method (binomial distribution) for small sample sizes. The user inputs the number of studies examined, the significance level (one or two-tailed), the number of studies that provide positive (or negative) results, the sample size for each study, and the technique used for averaging sample sizes. The output consists of the number of studies, number of positive significant studies, the average sample size, and the 90%, 95%, and 99% confidence intervals for all three methods.

Program Name: METAVOTE.SAS

Language: SAS

Compatibility: IBM PC's and compatibles, IBM, UNIX, and VAX/VMS mainframes

Memory Requirements: None Specified

Cost of Program: $10 (shipping and handling)

How to obtain a copy of the program:

Send a formatted 3.5" diskette, a self-addressed stamped mailer, and payment to:

Dr. Chung-Ching Morgan Wang
Department of Statistics
University of Central Florida
Orlando, FL 32816-2370
e-mail: cwang@pegasus.cc.ucf.edu

MINIMUM MULTIVARIATE FUNCTION

Title: PRAXIS: Brent's Algorithm for Function Minimization

Author: Karl R. Gegenfurtner

Source: *Behavior Research Methods, Instruments, & Computers,*
1992, 24, 560-564.

Description: This program minimizes a multivariate function,
through a modification of the direction-set method (Powell, 1964),
which can be used, for example, to fit a psychometric function
through a set of data points. A similar program, LOCALMIN,
minimizes a univariate function. For example, this program aids in
determining a maximum-likelihood estimate of a statistic.

Program Name: PRAXIS (multivariate), LOCALMIN
   (univariate). These are subroutines.

Language: C, Turbo-Pascal

Compatibility: UNIX mainframe, IBM PC's and compatibles,
   Apple-based systems

Memory Requirements: None Specified

Cost of Program: No Charge

How to obtain a copy of the program:

Send a formatted 3.5" diskette and
a self-addressed, stamped mailer to:

Dr. Karl Gegenfurtner
MPI for Biological Cybernetics
Spemannstraße 38
D-72076 Tubingen
Germany
e-mail: karl@mpik-tueb.mpg.de

MISSING DATA ESTIMATION

Title: A FORTRAN IV Program for the Estimation of
Missing Data

Author: Martijn P.F. Berger

Source: *Behavior Research Methods & Instrumentation,*
1978, 11, 395-396.

Description: This program estimates missing data by first
partitioning a correlation matrix into two submatrices (X_1, which
consists of missing data and X_2, which contains all available data)
and then by regressing X_1 on X_2. The initial correlation matrix can
be estimated via either Wilks' (1932) method or Glasser's (1964)
method. A program assumption is that the data are missing at
random. Furthermore, the regression-based estimates may be
inaccurate when the proportion of missing data is large (i.e., >.20).
Input includes the raw data matrix, the choice of method for
computing the correlation matrix, the number of iterations, and the
code for missing entries. Output includes, for each iteration, the
correlation matrix, the data matrix with estimates for missing
values, and the means and standard deviations for each variable.

Program Name: There are several named subroutines

Language: FORTRAN IV

Compatibility: Any system that supports FORTRAN

Memory Requirements: At least 67K

Cost of Program: No Charge

How to obtain a copy of the program:

The program listings may be obtained by contacting:

Dr. Martijn P.F. Berger
University of Twente
Department of Education
P.O. Box 217
7500 AE Enschede
Netherlands

MIXTURE MODELS

Title: Analyses of Multinomial Mixture Distributions: New Tests for Stochastic Models of Cognition and Action

Author: Steven Yantis, David E. Meyer, and J.E. Keith Smith

Source: *Psychological Bulletin*, 1991, *110*, 350-374.

Description: Given separate samples of observations drawn from two or more basis distributions and from the postulated mixture distributions, this program calculates the probability-density functions and summary statistics for each distribution using an approach known as multinomial maximum likelihood mixture (MMLM) analysis. Standard output includes estimates of the mixing probabilities and a goodness-of-fit statistic that indicates how well the hypothesized mixture accounts for the obtained data.

Program Name: MLEMIX

Language: Turbo Pascal

Compatibility: IBM PC's and compatibles

Memory Requirements: 640K

Cost of Program: No Charge

How to obtain a copy of the program:

Send a formatted 3.5" diskette and a self-addressed, stamped mailer to:

Dr. Steven Yantis
Department of Psychology
Johns Hopkins University
3400 N. Charles St.
Baltimore, MD 21218-2608
e-mail: yantis@jhu.edu

MODERATOR EFFECTS

Title: Improving the Estimation of Moderating Effects by Using Computer-Administered Questionnaires

Author: Herman Aguinis, William H. Bommer, and Charles A. Pierce

Source: *Educational and Psychological Measurement,* 1996, *56,* 1045-1049.

Description: This program improves the accuracy in estimating moderating effects of questionnaire responses by avoiding transcriptional errors and scale coarseness. Hence, this program allows the user to administer questionnaires via computer rather than paper-and-pencil means. The input consists of an ASCII file which includes instructions, questions, and debriefing information. Moreover, anchors such as agree-disagree or satisfied-dissatisfied are given. The output consists of numerical responses using six digits.

Program Name: CAQ

Language: Turbo C

Compatibility: IBM PC's and compatibles

Memory Requirements: None Specified

Cost of Program: No Charge

How to obtain a copy of the program:

Send either a formatted 3.5" or 5.25"diskette and a self-addressed, stamped mailer to:

Dr. Herman Aguinis
Department of Psychology
University of Colorado at Denver
P.O. Box 173364
Denver, CO 80217-3364
e-mail: haguinis@castle.cudenver.edu

MOKKEN TEST

Title: Mokken Test for the Robustness of Nonparametric Stochastic Mokken Scales

Author: Johannes Kingma and Johan Reuvekamp

Source: *Educational and Psychological Measurement,* 1986, *46,* 679-685.

Description: This program is useful for scaling political knowledge, social attitudes, developmental concepts, and problem solving tasks, for example. The output consists of response patterns, the number of identical response patterns and the percentage of the total number of observed response patterns, the expected and observed probabilities, coefficient of scalability, and statistic of robustness. Two input files are needed: the first consists of the actual data file (e.g., dichotomous items) followed by the variables; the second file consists of the number of variables, the positive alternative, the variables used in the analysis, number of groups, and the group variable.

Program Name: None Specified

Language: Pascal

Compatibility: Apple II+

Memory Requirements: 64K

Cost of Program: None Specified

How to obtain a copy of the program:

Send a formatted 5.25" diskette and a self-addressed, stamped mailer to:

Dr. Johannes Kingma
University Hospital at Groningen
Department of Traumatology
Groningen
Netherlands

MONOTONICITY

Title: Mononeonic Hypotheses in Multiple Group Designs:
A Monte Carlo Study

Author: Sanford L. Braver and Virgil L. Sheets

Source: *Psychological Bulletin, 1993, 113, 379-395.*

Description: This program calculates tests of monotonicity on
actual sample data (or simulated data) drawn from a variety of
different population conditions. When evaluating monotonically
increasing data, the program can detect a variety of different shapes
including linear, approximately linear, concave, and ogive patterns.
The following types of test statistics, along with their respective
significance values, can be calculated: omnibus tests only, multiple
significance tests with uncorrected alphas, multiple significance
tests with corrected alphas, and trend tests.

Program Name: None Specified

Language: SAS

Compatibility: Any system that supports the SAS language

Memory Requirements: None Specified

Cost of Program: No Charge

How to obtain a copy of the program:

Send a blank formatted 3.5"diskette and
a self-addressed, stamped mailer to:

Dr. Sanford L. Braver
Department of Psychology
Arizona State University
Tempe, AZ 85287-1104

MULTICOLLINEARITY

Title: MULTCO: Computation of the Degree of
Multicollinearity

Author: Soonmook Lee and Scott Hershberger

Source: *Applied Psychological Measurement,* 1988,
12, 324.

Description: The program outputs the multiple correlation and the squared multiple correlation of one variable with all other variables in order to examine the degree of multicollinearity in a data set.

Program Name: MULTCO

Language: FORTRAN 77

Compatibility: VAX/VMS (IMSL - version 9.2 or higher)

Memory Requirements: None Specified

Cost of Program: No Charge

How to obtain a copy of the program:

Send a written request to:

Dr. Soonmook Lee
Department of Psychology
Fordham University
Fordham Road
Bronx, NY 10458

MULTIDIMENSIONAL SCALING

Title: The Determination of the Underlying Dimensionality
of an Empirically Obtained Matrix of Proximities

Author: Ian Spence and Jed Graef

Source: *Multivariate Behavioral Research*, 1974, *9*,
331-341.

Description: In relation to Monte Carlo derived stress values, the
program evaluates the goodness of fit of up to five user-inputted
empirically obtained stress values. By comparing the obtained
values against the predicted (Monte Carlo) values and examining
the residual error, the program determines whether the empirically
derived proximities matrix is best accounted for by a one-, two-,
three-, or four-dimensional solution.

Program Name: M-SPACE

Language: FORTRAN IV

Compatibility: All computers that support FORTRAN

Memory Requirements: None Specified

Cost of Program: No Charge

How to obtain a copy of the program:

All inquiries regarding M-SPACE should be addressed to:

Dr. Ian Spence
Department of Psychology
University of Toronto
Toronto, Ontario
M5S 1A1
Canada
e-mail: spence@psych.utoronto.ca

MULTIDIMENSIONAL SCALING

Title: IDSORT: An Individual Differences Multidimensional Scaling Program for Sorting Data

Author: Yoshio Takane

Source: *Behavior Research Methods & Instrumentation,* 1982, *14,* 546.

Description: This program fits the INDSCAL (Carroll & Chang, 1970) weighted euclidean distance model to sorting data. The program simultaneously derives a similarity measure from the sorting data and searches for a stimulus representation from the derived similarity measure. Input includes the number of stimuli, subjects and dimensions, and the original sorting data for each subject. Output includes the stimulus coordinates and individual differences weights for each specified dimensionality.

Program Name: IDSORT

Language: FORTRAN IV

Compatibility: IBM mainframes

Memory Requirements: None Specified

Cost of Program: No Charge

How to obtain a copy of the program:

Available through e-mail only. For further information contact:

Dr. Yoshio Takane
Department of Psychology
McGill University
1205 Avenue Docteur Penfield
Montreal, Quebec H3A 1B1
Canada
e-mail: takane@takane2.psych.mcgill.ca

MULTIDIMENSIONAL SCALING

Title: MDSORT: A Special-Purpose Multidimensional Scaling Program for Sorting Data

Author: Yoshio Takane

Source: *Behavior Research Methods & Instrumentation*, 1981, *13*, 698.

Description: This program performs nonmetric multidimensional scaling (MDS) on raw sorted data by following a two-step process. The sorted values are first converted to similarity data (i.e., euclidean distances) and then represented in multidimensional space using a common clustering criterion. Input includes the number of stimuli, subjects and dimensions, and the sorted data for all subjects. Output includes the chi-square statistic for each dimensionality, the stimulus coordinates, and the cluster centroids. The program can accommodate missing data.

Program Name: MDSORT

Language: FORTRAN IV

Compatibility: IBM mainframes

Memory Requirements: None Specified

Cost of Program: No Charge

How to obtain a copy of the program:

Available through e-mail only. For further information contact:

Dr. Yoshio Takane
Department of Psychology
McGill University
1205 Avenue Docteur Penfield
Montreal, Quebec H3A 1B1
Canada
e-mail: takane@takane2.psych.mcgill.ca

MULTIDIMENSIONAL SCALING

Title: Multidimensional Successive Categories Scaling: A Maximum Likelihood Method

Author: Yoshio Takane

Source: *Psychometrika*, 1981, *46*, 9-28.

Description: This program utilizes a maximum likelihood estimation procedure to perform two different types of multidimensional scaling (metric and nonmetric) under two different error distributional assumptions (additive and multiplicative). In addition to calculating the asymptotic chi-square and log likelihood ratio statistics as goodness-of-fit indices, the program also computes Akaike's (1973) information criterion (AIC) statistic. The AIC statistic is useful for determining which of the two error models provides a better fit to the data.

Program Name: MAXSCAL-2.1

Language: FORTRAN

Compatibility: Any computer that supports FORTRAN

Memory Requirements: None Specified

Cost of Program: No Charge

How to obtain a copy of the program:

Available through e-mail only. For further information contact:

Dr. Yoshio Takane
Department of Psychology
McGill University
1205 Avenue Docteur Penfield
Montreal, Quebec H3A 1B1
Canada
e-mail: takane@takane2.psych.mcgill.ca

MULTINOMIAL DISTRIBUTION

Title: Exact Cumulative Probabilities for the Multinomial Distribution

Author: Kenneth J. Berry and Paul W. Mielke, Jr.

Source: *Educational and Psychological Measurement*, 1995, *55*, 769-772.

Description: Computes the exact point and cumulative probabilities for the multinomial distribution. The input includes the number of categories, observed frequencies for each category, and the probabilities for each category.

Program Name: MULT

Language: FORTRAN 77

Compatibility: IBM and UNIX mainframes, IBM PC's and compatibles

Memory Requirements: None Specified

Cost of Program: No Charge

How to obtain a copy of the program:

The authors prefer to e-mail the program, however, you may send a formatted 3.5" diskette and a self-addressed, stamped mailer to:

Dr. Kenneth J. Berry
Department of Sociology
Colorado State University
Fort Collins, CO 80523
e-mail: berry@lamar.colostate.edu

MULTINOMIAL PROBABILITIES

Title: Exact Multinomial Probabilities for One-Way
Contingency Tables

Author: William P. Dunlap, Leann Myers,
and N. Clayton Silver

Source: *Behavior Research Methods, Instruments, & Computers,*
1984, *16,* 54-56.

Description: This program computes the exact multinomial probabilities for one-way contingency tables. For example, if a researcher wanted to test a pre-experimental bias for rats to prefer one arm of a radial maze or if a horse racing aficionado would be interested in determining if there is an equal opportunity to win a race regardless of post position, then this program would be applicable. A listing of this program is contained on pages 55-56.

Program Name: MP

Language: FORTRAN

Compatibility: DEC-2060 and IBM PC's and compatibles

Memory Requirements: None Specified

Cost of Program: No Charge

How to obtain a copy of the program:

Send a formatted 3.5" diskette and
a self-addressed, stamped mailer to:

Dr. William P. Dunlap
Department of Psychology
Tulane University
New Orleans, LA 70118
e-mail: dunlap@mailhost.tcs.tulane.edu

MULTIPLE COMPARISONS

Title: A Computer Program for the Games-Howell Multiple Comparison Procedure

Author: Stephen Powers and Richard L. Lopez, Jr.

Source: *Educational and Psychological Measurement*, 1986, *46*, 163-165.

Description: This program computes the Games-Howell procedure (recommended by Jaccard, Becker, & Wood, 1984) for making multiple comparisons among group means with unequal variances and sample sizes. The output consists of the means, variances, standard errors, sample sizes, degrees of freedom, the q statistic, and its statistical significance indicated by an asterisk. The input is composed of the number of groups and alpha level. A file containing the means, variances, and sample sizes of each group is also needed.

Program Name: None Specified

Language: Pascal

Compatibility: TRS-80 Model IV microcomputer

Memory Requirements: 2.5 KB

Cost of Program: No Charge

How to obtain a copy of the program:

Send a written request to:

Dr. Stephen Powers
Legal and Research Services
Tucson Unified School District
P.O. Box 40400
Tucson, AZ 85717

MULTIPLE COMPARISONS - PERITZ

Title: PERITZ: A FORTRAN Program for Performing Multiple Comparisons of Means Using the Peritz Q Method

Author: Samuel A. Martin and Larry E. Toothaker

Source: *Behavior Research Methods, Instruments, & Computers,* 1989, *21*, 465-472.

Description: This program computes the Peritz Q which is a multiple comparison stepdown procedure, similar to the Student Newman-Keuls approach. However, it purports to control Type I errors better than the Student Newman-Keuls method. The user is queried for the number of groups, the mean square error, the degrees of freedom error, the alpha rate, and names of each group. The output is composed of a summary of the input, the mean difference, the Q value, and whether it is significant at the particular alpha rate. The program is provided in Appendix A on pages 466-472.

Program Name: PERITZ

Language: FORTRAN

Compatibility: VAX 8600 VAX/VMS operating system

Memory Requirements: None Specified

Cost of Program: No Charge

How to obtain a copy of the program:

Send a written request to:

Dr. Larry E. Toothaker
Department of Psychology
University of Oklahoma
900 Asp Avenue
Norman, OK 73069
e-mail: ltoothaker@ou.edu

MULTIPLE CORRELATION

Title: A FORTRAN 77 Program for Determining the Minimum Significant Increase of the Multiple Correlation Coefficient

Author: N. Clayton Silver and Michael S. Finger

Source: *Educational and Psychological Measurement,* 1993, *53, 703-706.*

Description: This interactive program computes the minimum multiple correlation coefficient needed for significance when an extra predictor is added to the regression equation (Dutoit & Penfield, 1979) coupled with the Wherry (1940) and Olkin and Pratt (1958) corrections for shrinkage. The input consists of the multiple correlation, sample size, number of predictors in the study, and significance level.

Program Name: MINCOR.FOR

Language: FORTRAN 77

Compatibility: IBM PC's and compatibles

Memory Requirements: Less than 100K

Cost of Program: No Charge

How to obtain a copy of the program:

Send a formatted 3.5" diskette and a self-addressed, stamped mailer to:

Dr. N. Clayton Silver
Department of Psychology
University of Nevada, Las Vegas
4505 Maryland Pkwy
Las Vegas, NV 89154-5030
e-mail: fdnsilvr@nevada.edu

MULTIPLE-CUE LEARNING

Title: MCPL: A Program for Describing Performance in Multiple-Cue Probability Learning

Author: Terry L. Dickinson and Ray W. Cooksey

Source: *Behavior Research Methods & Instrumentation,* 1981, *13*, 60.

Description: This program describes an individual's performance on multiple-cue probability learning (MCPL) tasks. MCPL tasks require individuals to utilize information provided by multiple cues in order to make inferences about the values of some learning criterion. Over the course of several trials, the program's algorithm estimates the degree of linear predictability of the criterion based on the multiple cues. Input includes the multiple-cue and criterion values and subjects' inferences. Output includes the correlations for each subject broken down by trial block as well as across trials, and the Fisher z transforms of the correlation coefficients.

Program Name: MCPL

Language: FORTRAN IV

Compatibility: Any computer that supports FORTRAN

Memory Requirements: A minimum of 54K

Cost of Program: No Charge

How to obtain a copy of the program:

The program listing and sample input and output may be obtained by contacting:

Dr. Terry L. Dickinson
Department of Psychology
Old Dominion University
Norfolk, VA 23529-1000
e-mail: tld200f@oduvm.cc.odu.edu

MULTIPLE REGRESSION

Title: BASIC BACKSTEP: A Simple Backward-Selection Multiple-Regression Program for Minicomputers and Microcomputers

Author: Bernard S. Gorman and Louis H. Primavera

Source: *Behavior Research Methods & Instrumentation,* 1981, *13,* 703.

Description: This program performs backward-selection multiple regression analysis. After the data have been entered, variables may be deleted either by (a) employing Darlington's (1968) usefulness criterion, or (b) specifying the order of variable deletion (forced deletion). Standard output includes means and standard deviations, the correlation matrix, its inverse and its determinant, F-tests for each model step, beta weights, partial correlations, and squared semipartial correlations.

Program Name: BACKSTEP

Language: QuickBASIC 4.5

Compatibility: Designed for Apple II machines. The program can be modified to run on IBM PC's and compatibles.

Memory Requirements: At least 60K

Cost of Program: No Charge

How to obtain a copy of the program:

Send a blank 3.5" diskette and a self-addressed, stamped mailer to:

Dr. Bernard S. Gorman
Department of Psychology
1 Education Drive
Nassau Community College
Garden City, NY 11530
e-mail: bsgorman@pipeline.com

MULTIPLE REGRESSION - BEST SUBSET

Title: A Program for Approximating R^2 Probability Values in Best Subset Multiple Regression

Author: Jeffrey Lee Rasmussen

Source: *Behavior Research Methods, Instruments, &, Computers,* 1984, *16*, 61-62.

Description: This program calculates exact probability values for given values of R^2 that are derived via best subset multiple regression. Given that best subset regression often yields positively biased estimates by capitalizing on chance covariation between the predictors and criterion, and given that such biased regression estimates typically "shrink" upon cross-validation, exact probability values that correct or adjust for positive bias are necessary. In calculating probability values, the present program utilizes a modified version of an algorithm developed by Diehr and Hoflin (1974).

Program Name: None Specified

Language: FORTRAN IV

Compatibility: Can be modified to run on any system capable of supporting the FORTRAN language

Memory Requirements: None Specified

Cost of Program: No Charge

How to obtain a copy of the program:

The program listing may be obtained by contacting:

Dr. Jeffrey Lee Rasmussen
Department of Psychology
Purdue School of Science at Indianapolis
402 North Blackford Street
Indianapolis, IN 46202-3275
e-mail: irhfl00@indyvax.iupui.edu

MULTIPLE REGRESSION - TEACHING

Title: Unique Multiple Linear Regression Problems for Each Student

Author: George E. Counts

Source: *Journal of Experimental Education*, 1976, *44*, 24-27.

Description: This program generates random samples from a simulated dataset with a known multiple correlation coefficient (MCC). The user determines the MCC by specifying the intercorrelations among the variables of interest. The purpose of the program is to allow the user to examine the variability in regression-based results that occur when different variable intercorrelations and hence different MCC's are specified. The program output includes the MCC, the variable intercorrelations, the sample means, and the sample standard deviations.

Program Name: None Specified

Language: None Specified

Compatibility: IBM mainframes, IBM PC's and compatibles

Memory Requirements: None Specified

Cost of Program: No Charge

How to obtain a copy of the program:

The program listing may be obtained by contacting:

Dr. George E. Counts
Department of Educational Administration and Counseling
Southeast Missouri State University
1 University Plaza
Cape Girardeau, Missouri 63701-4710

MULTISTAGE BONFERRONI

Title: A PASCAL Program to Perform the Bonferroni
Multistage Multiple-Correlation Procedure

Author: John Crosbie

Source: *Behavior Research Methods, Instruments, & Computers,*
1986, *18,* 327-329.

Description: This program computes the multistage Bonferroni
procedure for controlling the Type I error rate when examining a
set of correlations in a matrix. The output consists of the
correlations, the correlations that are found to be significant, the
sample sizes, alpha rate, z and t values, and the critical value of r.

Program Name: BONFER

Language: Turbo Pascal

Compatibility: IBM PC's and compatibles

Memory Requirements: 640K

Cost of Program: No Charge

How to obtain a copy of the program:

Send a formatted 3.5" diskette and
a self-addressed, stamped mailer to:

Dr. John Crosbie
Department of Psychology
West Virginia University
Morgantown, WV 26506-6040

The author prefers to e-mail requests at:
e-mail: jcrosbie@wvu.edu

MULTITRAIT-MULTIMETHOD MATRIX

Title: MTMM.EXE: A Program for Analyzing Multitrait-Multimethod Matrices

Author: Ron D. Hays and Toshi Hayashi

Source: *Applied Psychological Measurement,* 1986, *10,* 104.

Description: This program outputs the average convergent validity correlation and separate *t*-tests for examining discriminant validity. The input file consists of the title, number of traits, methods, observations, and the correlation matrix.

Program Name: MTMM.EXE

Language: FORTRAN

Compatibility: IBM PC's and compatibles

Memory Requirements: 120K

Cost of Program: No Charge

How to obtain a copy of the program:

Send a 3.5" formatted diskette and a self-addressed, stamped mailer to:

Dr. Ron D. Hays
The RAND Corporation
1700 Main Street
P.O. Box 2138
Santa Monica, CA 90407-2138
Internet: Ronald_Hays@rand.org

MULTIVARIATE ANALYSES

Title: The Use of a Simulated Statistics Laboratory in the Teaching of Multivariate Statistics

Author: Steve M. Bajgier and MaryAnne Atkinson

Source: *Collegiate Microcomputer*, 1989, 7, 240-250.

Description: This program provides a simulated learning environment (SLE) that allows students to conduct random experiments using various bivariate probability models. The program is interactive and users begin by (a) selecting random samples of specified size and (b) selecting the parameters of one or more bivariate distributions. Parameters to be specified include the number of bivariate populations or groups, the centroid of each group, standard deviations and confidence intervals for each group, and the x,y correlation for each group. The group data are presented visually and students can perform several types of analyses including the construction of 90%, 95% or 99% confidence ellipses, the construction of a separating hyperplane (for a two group case), and the calculation of Fisher discriminant and quadratic discriminant analyses. Either type of discriminant analysis may also be performed on a holdout sample.

Program Name: MVWORLD

Language: Pascal

Compatibility: Designed for use on the Apple Macintosh system

Memory Requirements: 500K

Cost of Program: $49.95

How to obtain a copy of the program:

Send a written request and payment to:

Dr. Steve M. Bajgier
Quantitative Methods Department
College of Business and Administration
Drexel University
Chestnut St.
Philadelphia, PA 19104-2816
e-mail:bajgiesm@duvm.ocs.drexel.edu

MULTIVARIATE DYADIC DATA

Title: MDyad: Multivariate Analysis of Dyadic Behavior

Author: Jorge L. Mendoza

Source: *Applied Psychological Measurement,* 1990,
             14, 107.

Description: The program computes the Mendoza and Graziano (1982) method for analyzing multivariate dyadic data. In outputting the results, users may assume homogeneity or heterogeneity of the dispersion matrices.

Program Name: MDyad

Language: SAS Proc Matrix ; SAS Proc IML

Compatibility: IBM PC's and compatibles, IBM mainframes

Memory Requirements: None Specified

Cost of Program: No Charge

How to obtain a copy of the program:

Send a formatted 3.5" diskette and
a self-addressed, stamped mailer to:

Dr. Jorge L. Mendoza
Department of Psychology
University of Oklahoma
900 Asp Avenue
Norman, OK 73069
e-mail: jmendoza@ou.edu

MULTIVARIATE LINEAR MODELING

Title: MGLM: A PASCAL Program for Multivariate Linear Modeling

Author: J. Gary Lutz and Leigh A. Cundari

Source: *Educational and Psychological Measurement,* 1993, *53,* 699-701.

Description: This interactive program computes:

1. discriminant analyses
2. goodness-of-fit tests for the beginning model
3. interval and least squares estimates of the model parameters
4. tests of specific hypotheses (repeated measures and other parametric functions)
5. most significant parametric function

The user inputs the observation and full rank, fixed design matrices. The program works for up to nine parameter models and nine dependent variables and can be used as a tool for teaching multivariate modeling.

Program Name: MGLM

Language: Turbo Pascal 5.0

Compatibility: IBM PC's and compatibles

Memory Requirements: 4 MB

Cost of Program: $10 (check or money order to Lehigh University)

How to obtain a copy of the program:

Send either a 3.5" or 5.25" diskette, a self-addressed stamped mailer, and payment to:

Dr. J. Gary Lutz
Lehigh University
Iacocca Hall
Bethlehem, PA 18015
e-mail: jgl3@lehigh.edu

MULTIVARIATE NORMAL

Title: A SAS Program for Assessing Multivariate Normality

Author: Xitao Fan

Source: *Educational and Psychological Measurement*, 1996,
56, 668-674.

Description: In order to check for multivariate normality, which is
assumed in multivariate statistical significance tests, this program
outputs the proportion of Mahalanobis D^2 values beyond the 50th
percentile of the chi-square distribution, a normalized estimate of
multivariate kurtosis, and a graphic plot. Moreover, instructions
concerning the interpretation of output are also provided. The
input consists of the data filename and number of variables.

Program Name: None Specified

Language: SAS (need IML module)

Compatibility: PC, mainframe, or Windows

Memory Requirements: None Specified

Cost of Program: No Charge

How to obtain a copy of the program:

Send a formatted 3.5" diskette and
a self-addressed, stamped mailer to:

Dr. Xitao Fan
Department of Psychology
Utah State University
Logan, UT 84322-2810
e-mail: fafan@cc.usu.edu

MULTIVARIATE NORMAL

Title: NORMUL: A FORTRAN Program for Testing Multivariate Normality

Author: Ronald R. Holden and Michael Parent

Source: *Behavior Research Methods, Instruments, & Computers,* 1995, *27*, 400-403.

Description: This program provides a summary of the input data (e.g., number of variables and sample size), Mahalanobis D^2 values with the ordered chi-square percentiles, correlations between the ordered chi-square percentiles and the Mahalanobis D^2, and their probabilities. Moreover, the mean, standard deviation, standard error of the mean, and ordered random multivariate normal correlations are provided. An example of the output is given in the article.

Program Name: NORMUL

Language: VS FORTRAN (and IMSL)

Compatibility: VMS mainframes that have FORTRAN compilers and IMSL capabilities

Memory Requirements: None Specified

Cost of Program: No Charge

How to obtain a copy of the program:

Send a formatted 3.5" diskette and a self-addressed, stamped mailer to:

Dr. Ronald R. Holden
Department of Psychology
Queen's University
Kingston, Ontario
K7L 3N6
Canada
e-mail: holdenr@pavlov.psych.queensu.ca

MULTIVARIATE NORMAL

Title: MULTINOR: A FORTRAN Program That Assists in
Evaluating Multivariate Normality

Author: Bruce Thompson

Source: *Educational and Psychological Measurement*, 1990,
50, 845-848.

Description: In order to use various structural equation model
testing procedures (e.g., LISREL), an assumption is that data
should be multivariate normal. The program outputs the
variance/covariance matrix, an inverted variance/covariance
matrix, sorted and unsorted Mahalanobis D^2 values with the chi-
square values and percentiles, and a scatterplot of the Mahalanobis
D^2 and chi-square values. Summary information including the
variable means, job parameters, and input data are also provided.
The default version of the program accommodates 20 variables and
1000 subjects.

Program Name: MULTINOR

Language: FORTRAN

Compatibility: None Specified

Memory Requirements: None Specified

Cost of Program: No Charge

How to obtain a copy of the program:

Send a formatted 3.5" diskette and
a self-addressed, stamped mailer to:

Dr. Bruce Thompson
Department of Educational Psychology
Texas A& M University
College Station, TX 77843
e-mail: e100bt@tamvm1.tamu.edu

MULTIVARIATE NORMAL SCORES

Title: A QuickBASIC Program for Generating Correlated
Multivariate Random Normal Scores

Author: Herman Aguinis

Source: *Educational and Psychological Measurement*, 1994,
54, 687-689.

Description: The program generates multivariate random normal
scores with a specified intercorrelation. The utility of this program
is found in Monte Carlo simulations. The input consists of sample
size, the correlations above the diagonal in a specified matrix, and
the number of samples for each variable. The first output file
consists of the multivariate random normal scores, whereas the
second output file consists of the means, standard deviations, and
intercorrelations for each vector.

Program Name: MULTIVAR.BAS

Language: QuickBASIC

Compatibility: IBM PC's and compatibles

Memory Requirements: None Specified

Cost of Program: No Charge

How to obtain a copy of the program:

Send either a 3.5" or 5.25" formatted diskette
and a self-addressed, stamped mailer to:

Dr. Herman Aguinis
Department of Psychology
University of Colorado at Denver
Campus Box 173
P.O. Box 173364
Denver, CO 80217-3364
e-mail: haguinis@castle.cudenver.edu

NONPARAMETRIC ANCOVA

Title: Quade's Nonparametric Analysis of Covariance by
Matching

Author: Gordon Rae

Source: *Behavior Research Methods, Instruments, & Computers,*
1985, *17,* 421-422.

Description: This program outputs Quade's (1982) rank analysis
of covariance by matching which includes the sums of squares,
degrees of freedom, F ratios, matched differences in group means
and probability along with the standard errors and critical ratios.
Means for adjusted scores are also provided. In order to apply this
technique, one need not bother with the traditional analysis of
covariance assumptions (e.g., the conditional distribution of the
dependent variable is normal with regard to the covariate), but only
to provide a rule for determining whether two individuals are
comparable when matching. The input consists of the number of
covariates, number of treatments, sample sizes, the maximum
amount by which two individuals may differ on the covariate, but
still be considered matched, and values of the covariates and
dependent variable. A listing of the output is contained on page
422.

Program Name: None Specified

Language: FORTRAN 77

Compatibility: VAX-11

Memory Requirements: None Specified

Cost of Program: No Charge

How to obtain a copy of the program:

Send a blank 3.5" diskette and a
self-addressed, stamped mailer to:

Dr. Gordon Rae
School of Behavioral and Communication Sciences
University of Ulster
Coleraine
Northern Ireland
BT52 1SA

NONPARAMETRIC ANOVA

Title: Analysis of Variance Procedures Based on a
Proximity Measure Between Subjects

Author: L.J. Hubert, R.G. Golledge, and C.M. Costanzo

Source: *Psychological Bulletin*, 1982, *91*, 424-430.

Description: Performs a nonparametric version of analysis of
variance (ANOVA) for a dataset comprised of k-dependent
samples where the observations are of a type that is not appropriate
for parametric ANOVA (e.g., paired comparisons, rankings, sorted
objects). Given as input a proximity matrix (e.g., Pearson rs or
Euclidean distances) that represents the degree of correspondence
among all pairs of subjects, the program computes the standard F
ratio for examining between-condition differences but assumes a
random allocation of observations model when calculating the
level of statistical significance. In particular, the program conducts
a randomization-type test by repeatedly permutating the
observations (i.e., blocks of data points) and then calculating the
significance level after each permutation. The end result is that an
approximate permutation distribution is created and used to
evaluate the statistical significance of the F ratio.

Program Name: None Specified

Language: None Specified

Compatibility: IBM PC's and compatibles

Memory Requirements: None Specified

Cost of Program: No Charge

How to obtain a copy of the program:

Send a blank formatted 3.5"diskette and
a self-addressed, stamped mailer to:

Dr. Lawrence J. Hubert
Department of Psychology
University of Illinois
603 E. Daniel St.
Champaign, IL 61820

NONPARAMETRIC - PAGE TEST

Title: Program Page: Using SPSS-X to Generate the L
Statistic for the Page Test of Ordered Alternatives

Author: Pietro J. Pascale

Source: *Educational and Psychological Measurement,* 1993,
53, 95-97.

Description: The program provides the Page test (Page, 1963),
which is a nonparametric technique for ranked or ordinal data
testing the ordered hypotheses for three or more groups, and its
probability value. This technique is similar to examining the linear
component in trend analysis from a parametric standpoint. The
output also includes the initial (number of observations x number
of groups) matrix and the ranks matrix.

Program Name: None Specified

Language: SPSS-X

Compatibility: Any computer that uses SPSS-X (can be used on
SPSS-PC)

Memory Requirements: None Specified

Cost of Program: No Charge

How to obtain a copy of the program:

Send a formatted MS-DOS 3.5" diskette
and a self-addressed, stamped mailer to:

Dr. Pietro J. Pascale
Department of Education
Youngstown State University
410 Wick Avenue
Youngstown, OH 44555-0001
e-mail: fr161002@ysub.edu

NONPARAMETRIC - PAGE TEST

Title: PAGE: A PASCAL Program for the Nonparametric Test for Ordered Alternatives

Author: Pietro J. Pascale

Source: *Educational and Psychological Measurement,* 1993, *53,* 99-101.

Description: The program provides the Page test (Page, 1963), which is a nonparametric technique for ranked or ordinal data testing the ordered hypotheses for three or more groups, and its probability value. This technique is similar to examining the linear component in trend analysis from a parametric standpoint. The output also includes the initial (number of observations x number of groups) matrix and the ranks matrix. The input consists of the number of conditions, sample size, and the raw data matrix. The program accommodates from 3 to 12 groups and a sample size from 2 to 12.

Program Name: PAGE

Language: PASCAL

Compatibility: IBM or compatible mainframes. Small adjustments in the program are needed for IBM PC's and compatibles

Memory Requirements: None Specified

Cost of Program: No Charge

How to obtain a copy of the program:

Send a formatted MS-DOS 3.5" diskette and a self-addressed, stamped mailer to:

Dr. Pietro J. Pascale
Department of Education
Youngstown State University
Youngstown, OH 44555-0001
e-mail: fr161002@ysub.edu

NONPARAMETRIC STATISTICS

Title: CBASIC Programs for Nonparametric Statistical Analysis

Author: Thomas E. Hannan

Source: *Behavior Research Methods, Instruments, & Computers,* 1986, *18,* 403-404.

Description: The program computes the sign test, Wilcoxon matched-pairs signed-ranks test, one- and two- and k-sample multinomial tests, Mann-Whitney U test, Friedman two-way ANOVA, Kruskal-Wallis one-way ANOVA, and Kendall's tau. The input consists of entering the filename, the number of independent samples, the number of subjects in each sample, and the title for each sample. An example of the input and output are shown on page 404.

Program Name: None Specified

Language: CBASIC

Compatibility: IBM PC's and compatibles

Memory Requirements: 128K, 16-bit machine

Cost of Program: No Charge

How to obtain a copy of the program:

Send a formatted 3.5" diskette and a self-addressed, stamped mailer to:

Dr. Thomas E. Hannan
Department of Psychology: Experimental
Duke University
Durham, NC 27706-8001
e-mail: thannan@acpub.duke.edu

NONPARAMETRIC STATISTICS

Title: Implementation of Nonparametric Multivariate Statistics with S

Author: Ching-Fan Sheu and Suzanne Curry

Source: *Behavior Research Methods, Instruments, & Computers,* 1996, *28,* 315-318.

Description: The programs listed in the article compute multivariate analogs of the sign test, one-sample signed-rank test, and two-sample rank-sum test. Examples in the use of these techniques are also provided.

Program Name: Nonparametric Multivariate Statistics with S

Language: S-Plus 3.2

Compatibility: UNIX mainframes, IBM PC's and compatibles. Need to have access to S.

Memory Requirements: None Specified

Cost of Program: No Charge

How to obtain a copy of the program:

Send a written request to:

Dr. Ching-Fan Sheu
Department of Psychology
DePaul University
2219 N. Kenmore Ave.
Chicago, IL 60614-3504
e-mail: csheu@condor.depaul.edu

NORMAL CURVE

Title: The Last Normal Curve Programs

Author: D. Louis Wood

Source: *Behavior Research Methods, Instruments, & Computers,* 1987, *19,* 338-344.

Description: This program computes the normal curve area with higher degrees of accuracy. The program provides options for performing a two-tailed z test plus the population mean to the z area, an area over a particular range (e.g., between z = -.5 and .3), a percentile rank, and the z test for determining whether the population correlation equals zero. A listing of the programs are available on pages 342-344. The author is willing to furnish a copy of GWBASICA upon request.

Program Name: NORMLCV.BAS

Language: GWBASICA

Compatibility: IBM PC's and compatibles

Memory Requirements: Less than 1 MB

Cost of Program: No Charge

How to obtain a copy of the program:

Send either a 3.5" or 5.25" formatted diskette and a self-addressed, stamped mailer to:

Dr. D. Louis Wood
University of Arkansas at Little Rock
2801 South University
Little Rock, AK 72204

ORDER ANALYSIS

Title: ORDER2: A Program to Perform Ordering-Theoretic
               Data Analysis

Author: Richard F. Antonak, William M. Bart,
               and Kaustubh Lele

Source: *Behavior Research Methods & Instrumentation,*
               1978, *11,* 457-458.

Description: This program uses ordering-theoretic data analysis
as a means of identifying the best-fitting linear or nonlinear
hierarchical network from among a set of items or task responses.
The program relies upon a type of scalogram analysis in which
response patterns are identified and then arranged hierarchically.
The user may specify a tolerance level for random error
occurrences in the item response patterns. Input includes the
number of subjects, the number of items, and the item scoring keys
(e.g., 1=success, 0=failure). Output includes descriptive scale and
item statistics, the matrices of item response patterns, reliability
indices, tables of percentages of confirmatory responses for various
types of item-to-item relations (e.g., P implies Q), and a summary
of the response pattern hierarchies.

Program Name: ORDER2

Language: FORTRAN 10

Compatibility: Any system that can run FORTRAN 10

Memory Requirements: None Specified

Cost of Program: No Charge

How to obtain a copy of the program:

Send a formatted 3.5" diskette and
a self-addressed, stamped mailer to:

Dr. Richard F. Antonak, Associate Dean
Department of Education
University of North Carolina at Charlotte
9201 University City
Charlotte, NC 28223-0001
e-mail:rantonak@email.uncc.edu

ORTHOGONAL COMPARISONS

Title: Orthogonal Comparisons

Author: Allen H. Wolach and Maureen A. McHale

Source: *Behavior Research Methods, Instruments, & Computers,* 1988, *20*, 337.

Description: This program outputs sets of orthogonal coefficients (or comparisons), all possible comparisons, or it determines if the comparisons inputted by the user are orthogonal (and all possible sets of orthogonal comparisons using the comparisons supplied by the user), and a tutorial on orthogonal comparisons. This program could be used when performing subsequent tests for ANOVA when three or more groups are used.

Program Name: ORTHOGON

Language: BASIC

Compatibility: IBM PC's and compatibles

Memory Requirements: 128K memory

Cost of Program: No Charge

How to obtain a copy of the program:

Send either a 3.5" or 5.25" formatted diskette and a self-addressed, stamped mailer to:

Dr. Allen H. Wolach
Department of Psychology
Illinois Institute of Technology
3300 S. Federal St.
Chicago, IL 60616

ORTHOGONAL POLYNOMIALS

Title: Orthogonal Polynomial Coefficients and Trend Analysis for Unequal Intervals and Unequal *N*s: A Microcomputer Application

Author: Daniel Coulombe

Source: *Behavior Research Methods, Instruments, & Computers,* 1985, *17*, 441-442.

Description: This program performs trend analysis by generating orthogonal polynomials. The output consists of summary statistics (mean of each group, treatment and error sums of squares), orthogonal polynomials, the trend analysis summary table, and the goodness-of-fit tests for each trend. The input consists of the number of treatment levels (or groups), the sample size for each group, group mean, group name, and treatment and error sums of squares. A listing of the program is available on page 441 and sample output is provided on page 442.

Program Name: TRENDAN.BAS

Language: Microsoft GW-BASIC

Compatibility: Any microcomputer with BASIC capability

Memory Requirements: 8K RAM

Cost of Program: No Charge

How to obtain a copy of the program:

Send a blank 3.5" diskette and a self-addressed, stamped mailer to:

Dr. Daniel Coulombe
School of Psychology
University of Ottawa
275 Nicholas
Ottawa, Ontario,
Canada
K1N 6N5

PARALLEL ANALYSIS

Title: Determining the Number of Common Factors in Factor
Analysis: A Review and Program

Author: Michael D. Coovert and Kathleen McNelis

Source: *Educational and Psychological Measurement,* 1988,
48, 687-692.

Description: The program determines the number of components
to keep in a principal components analysis by using a combination
of parallel analysis and discriminability analysis. The input
consists of the sample size, number of variables, and eigenvalues.
The output for the parallel analysis includes the observed and
random eigenvalue coupled with the suggested number of
components to retain. The output for the discriminability analysis
includes slope analysis of each eigenvalue pair. The article also
includes a review of other approaches for determining the number
of factors to retain.

Program Name: NFACTOR

Language: BASIC

Compatibility: Any mainframe (via uploading), IBM PC's and
compatibles, Apple-based system (if the code is
retyped)

Memory Requirements: 4K

Cost of Program: No Charge

How to obtain a copy of the program:

Send a formatted 3.5"diskette and
a self-addressed, stamped mailer to:

Dr. Michael D. Coovert
Department of Psychology
BEH 339
University of South Florida
Tampa, FL 33620-8200
e-mail: coovert@luna.cas.usf.edu

PARALLEL ANALYSIS

Title: PAR: Parallel Analysis Routine for Random Data Eigenvalue Estimation

Author: Ronald R. Holden, R. Stewart Longman, Albert A. Cota, and G. Cynthia Fekken

Source: *Applied Psychological Measurement,* 1989, *13,* 192.

Description: The program determines the number of components to keep in a principal components analysis by using parallel analysis of random data matrices. The program uses techniques by Allen and Hubbard (1986) and Longman, Cota, Holden, and Fekken (1989) for estimating mean eigenvalues. The output consists of mean eigenvalue estimates for both techniques and the 95% confidence interval for the Longman et al. estimate. The program is compatible for 5 to 50 variables and for 50 to 1000 test takers.

Program Name: PAR

Language: Microsoft FORTRAN 77

Compatibility: IBM PC's and compatibles

Memory Requirements: None Specified

Cost of Program: No Charge

How to obtain a copy of the program:

Send a formatted 3.5" diskette and a self-addressed, stamped mailer to:

Dr. Ronald R. Holden
Department of Psychology
Queen's University
Kingston, Ontario
K7L 3N6
Canada
holdenr@pavlov.psych.queensu.ca

PARALLEL ANALYSIS

Title: PARANAL.TOK: A Program for Developing Parallel Analysis Criteria

Author: Gary J. Lautenschlager

Source: *Applied Psychological Measurement,* 1989, *13,* 176.

Description: The program determines the number of components to keep in a principal components analysis by using parallel analysis of random data sets. The user inputs the number of cases, variables, and samples to be desired for each data set. The output file consists of the separate and cumulative eigenanalyses along with the summary statistics. The SYSTAT version handles up to 81 variables, whereas the MACRO program can handle up to 200 variables.

Program Name: PARANAL.TOK

Language: SYSTAT Version 4.0

Compatibility: IBM PC's and compatibles using MS-DOS 3.1 or higher

Memory Requirements: 640K

Cost of Program: No Charge

How to obtain a copy of the program:

Send a formatted 3.5" diskette and a self-addressed, stamped mailer to:

Dr. Gary J. Lautenschlager
Department of Psychology
University of Georgia
Athens, GA 30602
garylaut@uga.cc.uga.edu

PARALLEL ANALYSIS

Title: PAM: A Double-Precision FORTRAN Routine for the Parallel Analysis Method in Principal Components Analysis

Author: R. Stewart Longman, Albert A. Cota, Ronald R. Holden, and G. Cynthia Fekken

Source: *Behavior Research Methods, Instruments, & Computers,* 1989, *21,* 477-480.

Description: The program determines the number of components to keep in a principal components analysis by using parallel analysis. The procedure used in PAM avoids the deficiencies found in regression strategies. The output consists of mean and 95th percentile eigenvalues derived from a simulation of a certain number of correlation matrices. The analysis may be used for up to 50 subjects, 10 variables, and 100 iterations. A listing of the program is available on pages 478-480.

Program Name: PAM

Language: VS FORTRAN and IMSL subroutines

Compatibility: VMS mainframes

Memory Requirements: None Specified

Cost of Program: No Charge

How to obtain a copy of the program:

Send a formatted 3.5" diskette and a self-addressed, stamped mailer to:

Dr. Ronald R. Holden
Department of Psychology
Queen's University
Kingston, Ontario K7L 3N6
Canada
e-mail: holdenr@pavlov.psyc.queensu.ca

PART CORRELATIONS - CONTRASTS

Title: A Microsoft FORTRAN 77 Program for Contrasting Part Correlations and Related Statistics

Author: James B. Hittner, Michael S. Finger, James P. Mancuso, and N. Clayton Silver

Source: *Educational and Psychological Measurement*, 1995, *55*, 777-784.

Description: Computes the tests of significance between zero-order and semi-partial correlations, semi-partial correlations with different predictors and covariates, semi-partial correlations with the same predictor and different covariates, and semi-partial correlations with different predictors and the same covariate. These tests were based upon Malgady's (1987) applications and modifications of Hotelling's *t*, Meng, Rosenthal, and Rubin's *z* test, Olkin's *z* test, and Williams's *t* test.

Program Name: MALG.FOR

Language: Microsoft FORTRAN 77

Compatibility: IBM PC's and compatibles

Memory Requirements: Less than 100K

Cost of Program: No Charge

How to obtain a copy of the program:

Send a formatted 3.5" diskette and a self-addressed, stamped mailer to:

Dr. James B. Hittner
Department of Psychology
College of Charleston
Charleston, SC 29424
e-mail: hittnerj@cofc.edu

PARTIAL CORRELATIONS

Title: A Microsoft FORTRAN 77 Program for Testing the Differences Among Independent First-Order Partial Correlations

Author: N. Clayton Silver, Diane L. Wadiak, and Catherine J. Massey

Source: *Educational and Psychological Measurement*, 1995, *55*, 245-248.

Description: Computes the global test modified from the Rao (1970) procedure and the subsequent multiple range tests (Levy, 1976) for comparing two or more independent first-order partial correlations. The program is interactive and an output file is provided.

Program Name: INDPART.FOR

Language: FORTRAN 77

Compatibility: IBM PC's and compatibles

Memory Requirements: Less than 100K

Cost of Program: No Charge

How to obtain a copy of the program:

Send a formatted 3.5" diskette and
a self-addressed, stamped mailer to:

Dr. N. Clayton Silver
Department of Psychology
University of Nevada, Las Vegas
4505 Maryland Pkwy
Las Vegas, NV 89154-5030
e-mail: fdnsilvr@nevada.edu

PERMUTATION TESTS

Title: PERMUTE: A SAS Algorithm for Permutation Testing

Author: Jeffrey D. Kromrey, Walter Chason,
and R. Clifford Blair

Source: *Applied Psychological Measurement,* 1992,
16, 64.

Description: The program computes multivariate permutation
tests for one- and two-sample conditions.

Program Name: PERMUTE

Language: PC-SAS Version 6.04

Compatibility: None Specified

Memory Requirements: None Specified

Cost of Program: No Charge

How to obtain a copy of the program:

Send a formatted 3.5" diskette and
a self-addressed, stamped mailer to:

Dr. Walter M. Chason
Institute for Instructional Research and Practice
University of South Florida
EDU 112
Tampa, FL 33620-5650
e-mail: walter@seaweed.coedu.usf.edu

PHARMACOKINETICS

Title: An Analysis Program MULTI(ELS) Based on Extended Nonlinear Least Squares Method for Microcomputers

Author: Kiyoshi Yamaoka, Hisashi Tanaka, Katsuhiko Okumura, Masato Yasuhara, and Ryohei Hori

Source: *Journal of Pharmacobiological-Dynamics*, 1986, *9*, 161-173.

Description: This program estimates pharmacokinetic parameters as well as intra- and inter-individual variabilities for different competing user-specified pharmacokinetic models. All parameters are estimated via extended least squares analysis and Akaike's information criterion (AIC) is employed to identify the best fitting model. The program has utility for a number of applications including (1) comparing and contrasting the pharmacokinetics of a new drug preparation to a standard preparation, (2) verifying the changes in drug dispositions between children and adults, and (3) comparing the pharmacokinetic constants of a drug across different animal species.

Program Name: MULTI(ELS)

Language: FORTRAN (and BASIC on PC versions)

Compatibility: Any mainframe and IBM PC's and compatibles

Memory Requirements: A minimum of 256K

Cost of Program: No Charge

How to obtain a copy of the program:

Send a written request and a self-addressed, stamped mailer to:

Dr. Kiyoshi Yamaoka
Faculty of Pharmaceutical Sciences
Kyoto University
Sakyo-ku
Kyoto, 606
Japan
e-mail: yamaoka@pharm.kyoto-u.ac.jp

POWER ANALYSIS

Title: A Visual Approach to Statistical Power Analysis on the Microcomputer

Author: Michael Borenstein, Jacob Cohen, Hannah R. Rothstein, Simcha Pollack, and John M. Kane

Source: *Behavior Research Methods, Instruments, & Computers*, 1992, *24*, 565-572.

Description: This program uses a graphical method for displaying the power of *t* tests. That is, the user can examine how the various determinants of power (e.g., effect size, sample size, alpha) interact with each other. Hence, this program can be used for teaching the concept of power. A Monte Carlo simulation option in the program allows the user to empirically determine power. A listing of the program is provided on pages 571-572.

Program Name: None Specified

Language: None Specified

Compatibility: IBM PC's and compatibles

Memory Requirements: None Specified

Cost of Program: No Charge

How to obtain a copy of the program:

Mention what type of videocard that you have (i.e., EGA, VGA)

Send a formatted 3.5" diskette and a self-addressed, stamped mailer to:

Dr. Michael M. Borenstein
Director of Biostatistics
Hillside Hospital
Long Island Jewish Medical Center
P. O. Box 38
Glen Oaks, NY 11004

POWER ANALYSIS

Title: Topics in Research Methods: Power

Author: Tony Cook

Source: *Science Software Quarterly*, 1984, *Fall*, 39-41.

Description: This menu-driven program allows the user to conduct a series of simulated experiments for the purpose of assessing the impact of various design features on the statistical power of inferential tests. Included among the methods for increasing statistical power are increasing sample size, increasing sample homogeneity, assessing additional variables (e.g., covariates), and using matched pairs. The user has the option of manipulating multiple design features simultaneously. Written documentation is included with the program.

Program Name: None Specified

Language: None Specified

Compatibility: Runs on Apple II+ and IIe machines

Memory Requirements: None Specified

Cost of Program: $50

How to obtain a copy of the program:

Send a written request and payment to:

Marcey Levine
Marketing Department
Oxford University Press
198 Madison Avenue
New York, NY 10016

POWER ANALYSIS

Title: An Interactive FORTRAN IV Program for Calculating Power, Sample Size, or Detectable Differences in Means

Author: William P. Dunlap

Source: *Behavior Research Methods & Instrumentation,* 1981, *13,* 757-759.

Description: This interactive program calculates power and sample size for a variety of ANOVA-based designs. The user is first queried for the number of groups, the desired alpha level, and whether power or sample size should be calculated. The user then inputs either the anticipated mean square error or the estimated population standard deviation. One of the latter two pieces of information is necessary in order for the program to generate an effect size estimate. Output consists of either power or estimated sample size depending on the application selected.

Program Name: POWER

Language: FORTRAN IV

Compatibility: Although originally designed for use on DEC systems, the program can be easily modified to run on other systems.

Memory Requirements: None Specified

Cost of Program: No Charge

How to obtain a copy of the program:

Send a DOS formatted 3.5" diskette and a self-addressed, stamped mailer to:

Dr. William P. Dunlap
Department of Psychology
Tulane University
New Orleans, LA 70118
e-mail: dunlap@mailhost.tcs.tulane.edu

POWER ANALYSIS

Title: GPOWER: A General Power Analysis Program

Author: Edgar Erdfelder, Franz Faul, and Axel Buchner

Source: *Behavior Research Methods, Instruments, & Computers,*
1989, *21,* 630-635.

Description: This interactive, menu-driven program computes the power values, sample sizes, or effect sizes for the *t*, *F*, and chi-square tests. Moreover, the program graphically displays the relationship between two variables (e.g., effect size, sample size, alpha, beta).

Program Name: GPOWER (Version 2.0 for DOS) and (Version 2.1.1 for Macintosh)

Language: Turbo-Pascal, Think-Pascal for Macintosh version

Compatibility: IBM PC's and compatibles and all Macintosh versions (including Power PC)

Memory Requirements: For IBM: 640K

For Macintosh: Will run on any 68K using system 6.0.7 or higher

Cost of Program: No Charge

How to obtain a copy of the program:

Send a formatted 3.5" diskette and
a self-addressed, stamped mailer to:

Dr. Edgar Erdfelder
Psychologisches Institut
Universität Bonn
Römerstraße 164
D-53117
Bonn, Germany
e-mail:erdfelder@uni-bonn.de

You may download a copy (Macintosh and DOS versions) in which the access is via www:

http://www.psychologie.uni - trier.de:8000/projects/gpower.html

POWER ANALYSIS

Title: Sample Size Calculation, Power Analysis and
Randomization: Research Project Design in Windows

Author: Martin Hauer-Jensen

Source: *CABIOS,* 1993, *9,* 45-47.

Description: This is a windows program that calculates sample
size and statistical power for dichotomous and continuous outcome
variables, correlation coefficients, and time-to-failure outcomes
(either exponential or log-rank). The program can adjust sample
size estimates for subject noncompliance, number of participating
centers, and multiple inferential tests. Options for conducting
interim analyses and creating randomization lists are also available.

Program Name: OMNISTAT

Language: VISUAL BASIC

Compatibility: Any IBM PC or compatible computer that is
capable of supporting Microsoft Windows v.
3.0 or higher.

Memory Requirements: None Specified

Cost of Program: No Charge

How to obtain a copy of the program:

Send a formatted 3.5" diskette and
a self-addressed, stamped mailer to:

Dr. Martin Hauer-Jensen
Department of Surgery
University of Arkansas for Medical Sciences
4301 West Markham
Slot 725
Little Rock, AR 72205
e-mail: mhjensen@life.uams.edu

POWER - ANOVA

Title: BASIC Programs to Determine Sample Size and Exact Power in ANOVA Designs

Author: Richard G. Graf and Edward F. Alf, Jr.

Source: *Educational and Psychological Measurement,* 1990, *50,* 117-121.

Description: NPOWER.BAS computes the sample size needed for a particular treatment group to achieve a specified value of power for a between-subjects design. PHIPOWER.BAS provides the power (up to five decimal accuracy) given the numerator and denominator degrees of freedom, alpha, and power parameter value (phi). These programs have utility for any researcher planning a between-subjects ANOVA study.

Program Name: NPOWER.BAS, PHIPOWER.BAS

Language: BASIC

Compatibility: IBM PC's and compatibles

Memory Requirements: None Specified

Cost of Program: $15

How to obtain a copy of the program:

Send a formatted 3.5" diskette, a self-addressed stamped mailer, and payment to:

Alfagrafics
1716 Eolus
Leucadia, CA 92024

POWER - ANOVA

Title: POWERF: A Program That Computes the Power of *F* Tests in Fixed-Effects ANOVA Designs

Author: Randall Parker and Gary Borich

Source: *Behavior Research Methods & Instrumentation,* 1980, *12,* 76.

Description: Using an algorithm reported in Cohen (1977), this program computes (a) the power of *F* tests for fixed main effects, (b) *F* tests for the interactions of fixed-effects factors, and (c) effect sizes. Input for calculating power includes the critical *F* value for any desired alpha level, the degrees of freedom (df) for the *F*-ratio numerator and denominator, and the estimated effect size. When calculating effect sizes, the user enters either eta squared or the relevant sum of squares values. Output includes the cell *n*, numerator and denominator df, power, and estimated effect size.

Program Name: POWERF

Language: FORTRAN

Compatibility: Any computer that supports FORTRAN

Memory Requirements: None Specified

Cost of Program: No Charge

How to obtain a copy of the program:

The program listing may be obtained by sending a self-addressed, stamped envelope to:

Dr. Randall Parker
Department of Special Education
EDB 306
University of Texas
Austin, TX 78712

POWER - CHI-SQUARE

Title: A Program for Exact Power of the 2x2 Chi-Square

Author: William P. Dunlap

Source: *Behavior Research Methods, Instruments, & Computers,*
1989, *21,* 645-646.

Description: This program computes a power analysis for a 2 x 2
chi-square for Case 2 data (e.g., an experimental and control group
are compared on population proportions). The input consists of the
population proportions and the sample sizes.   A listing of the
program is provided in the text.

Program Name: None Specified

Language: FORTRAN

Compatibility: IBM 3081 mainframe and IBM PC's and
                    compatibles

Memory Requirements: None Specified

Cost of Program: No Charge

How to obtain a copy of the program:

Send a formatted 3.5" diskette and
a self addressed, stamped mailer to:

Dr. William P. Dunlap
Department of Psychology
Tulane University
New Orleans, LA 70118
e-mail: dunlap@mailhost.tcs.tulane.edu

POWER - CORRELATION

Title: POWCOR: A Power Analysis and Sample Size
Program for Testing Differences Between Dependent
and Independent Correlations

Author: David B. Allison and Bernard S. Gorman

Source: *Educational and Psychological Measurement,* 1993,
53, 133-137.

Description: This interactive program outputs the sample size or
power needed in order to obtain significant differences between
independent or dependent correlations . The input for estimation
of sample size includes alpha, power, and anticipated values of the
correlations for a given situation (e.g., independence or
dependence). The input for power consists of sample size, alpha,
and anticipated values of the correlations for either independent or
dependent situations. This program also accommodates unequal
sample sizes for examining independent correlations.

Program Name: POWCOR 13

Language: BASIC

Compatibility: IBM PC's and compatibles

Memory Requirements: Less than 1 MB

Cost of Program: No Charge

How to obtain a copy of the program:

Send a formatted MS-DOS 3.5" diskette
and a self-addressed, stamped mailer to:

Dr. David B. Allison
Obesity Research Center
St. Luke's-Roosevelt Hospital Center
Columbia University College of Physicians and Surgeons
1111 Amsterdam Avenue
New York, NY 10025
e-mail:dba8@columbia.edu

POWER - CORRELATION

Title: An Interactive FORTRAN IV Program for Calculating
Aspects of Power in Correlational Research

Author: William P. Dunlap and Edward R. Kemery

Source: *Behavior Research Methods, Instruments, & Computers,*
1985, *17,* 437-440.

Description: This program computes the power, prospective
sample size, or detectable correlation needed for the research. The
program also allows for correction with regard to restriction of
range. In this case, the user needs to input the standard deviation
of the population and sample. In order to correct for unreliability,
the reliability estimates for the criterion and predictor are entered.
A listing of the program is available on pages 438-440.

Program Name: POWCOR

Language: FORTRAN

Compatibility: DEC-2060, IBM PC's and compatibles

Memory Requirements: None Specified

Cost of Program: No Charge

How to obtain a copy of the program:

Send a formatted 3.5" diskette and
a self-addressed, stamped mailer to:

Dr. William P. Dunlap
Department of Psychology
Tulane University
New Orleans, LA 70118
e-mail: dunlap@mailhost.tcs.tulane.edu

POWER - DICHOTOMOUS DATA

Title: An Interactive FORTRAN IV Program for
Calculating Aspects of Power With Dichotomous Data

Author: William P. Dunlap

Source: *Behavior Research Methods & Instrumentation,*
1982, *14,* 422-424.

Description: This program uses Fleiss's (1973) formula for
calculating power and determining sample size for 2 by 2
contingency tables where the null hypothesis can be specified in
terms of the difference between two population proportions. The
program's calculations are most accurate for values near the middle
of the proportion range (around .5) and least accurate for extreme
proportions (near 0 or 1). The program is not appropriate for use
with continuity corrected data. Users indicate the alpha level to be
used and whether they wish to calculate power, sample size, or the
detectable difference in proportions. The program is interactive and
users may select multiple options.

Program Name: PROPOW

Language: FORTRAN IV

Compatibility: Any system that supports FORTRAN

Memory Requirements: None Specified

Cost of Program: No Charge

How to obtain a copy of the program:

Send a formatted 3.5" diskette and
a self-addressed, stamped mailer to:

Dr. William P. Dunlap
Department of Psychology
Tulane University
New Orleans, LA 70118
e-mail: dunlap@mailhost.tcs.tulane.edu

POWER - MODERATORS

Title: Estimating the Power to Detect Dichotomous Moderators With Moderated Multiple Regression

Author: Herman Aguinis, Charles A. Pierce, and Eugene F. Stone-Romero

Source: *Educational and Psychological Measurement*, 1994, *54*, 690-692.

Description: The program estimates the power for detecting dichotomous moderator variables in moderated multiple regression. If an individual wanted to examine the relationship between salary and performance and this relationship was different between two races, then race would be considered a moderator variable. The input consists of the sample sizes in each subgroup, and the correlations between the predictor and criterion variables for each subgroup. The output is simply the power of detecting the moderator variable.

Program Name: POWER.BAS

Language: QuickBASIC

Compatibility: IBM PC's and compatibles

Memory Requirements: None Specified

Cost of Program: No Charge

How to obtain a copy of the program:

Send either a 3.5" or 5.25" formatted diskette and a self-addressed, stamped mailer to:

Dr. Herman Aguinis
Department of Psychology
University of Colorado at Denver
Campus Box 173
P.O. Box 173364
Denver, CO 80217-3364
e-mail: haguinis@castle.cudenver.edu

POWER - MULTIPLE CORRELATION

Title: Multiple Correlation: Exact Power and Sample Size
Calculations

Author: Constantine Gatsonis and Allan R. Sampson

Source: *Psychological Bulletin*, 1989, *106*, 516-524.

Description: This program computes power and sample size
estimates for observational studies using an unconditional (versus
conditional) approach. The unconditional approach assumes that
the observations constitute a random sample drawn from an
underlying multivariate normal distribution and that the values of
the independent variables cannot be fixed in advance. In order to
obtain the power and sample size estimates, the user must specify
an expected value for the underlying population multiple
correlation coefficient (i.e., an effect size estimate).

Program Name: None Specified

Language: FORTRAN

Compatibility: Any computer that supports FORTRAN

Memory Requirements: None Specified

Cost of Program: No Charge

How to obtain a copy of the program:

Send a blank formatted 3.5" diskette and
a self-addressed, stamped mailer to:

Dr. Constantine Gatsonis
Center for Statistical Science
Brown University
Providence, RI 02912
e-mail: constantinegatsonis@brown.edu

POWER - MULTIPLE REGRESSION

Title: Statistical Power Analysis for Multiple
Regression/Correlation: A Computer Program

Author: Hannah R. Rothstein, Michael Borenstein, Jacob Cohen,
and Simcha Pollack

Source: *Educational and Psychological Measurement,* 1990,
50, 819-830.

Description: This spreadsheet-type program computes the effect
size and power of the multiple correlation coefficient. The user
inputs the number of variables in each set, the numerator and
denominator degrees of freedom, alpha, the proportion of variance
hypothetically accounted for by the set of variables, and the option
of choosing Model 1 (defined in accordance to the variables
already included in the equation) or Model 2 (with all variables
included plus others input later) error terms.

Program Name: None Specified

Language: None Specified

Compatibility: IBM PC's and compatibles

Memory Requirements: None Specified

Cost of Program: No Charge

How to obtain a copy of the program:

Specify type of monitor used.

Send a formatted 3.5" diskette and
a self-addressed, stamped mailer to:

Dr. Michael Borenstein
Hillside Hospital
Long Island Jewish Medical Center
P.O. Box 38
Glen Oaks, NY 11004

POWER - MULTIVARIATE

Title: POWER: An SPSS Matrix Program for Performing Univariate and Multivariate Power Analysis

Author: Richard F. Haase

Source: *Applied Psychological Measurement, 1993, 17*, 295.

Description: The program provides the *F* values, degrees of freedom, significance level, and power estimate for Wilks' lambda, Pillai's trace, Hotelling's trace, and univariate tests. The input includes the correlation matrix (or sums of squares and cross product matrix), sample size, alpha level, and the number of criterion and predictor variables.

Program Name: POWER

Language: SPSS

Compatibility: None Specified

Memory Requirements: None Specified

Cost of Program: No Charge

How to obtain a copy of the program:

Send a formatted 3.5" diskette and
a self-addressed, stamped mailer to:

Dr. Richard F. Haase
Department of Counseling Psychology
ED 220
State University of New York at Albany
Albany, NY 12222

POWER - PROPORTIONS

Title: Using the SAS System to Estimate Sample Size and Power for Comparing Two Binomial Proportions

Author: Hossein N. Yarandi

Source: *Nursing Research*, 1994, *43*, 124-125.

Description: Calculates the sample size per group needed to detect a particular difference between two binomial proportions at a specified level of power. Also calculates the power for detecting a specified difference between two proportions given a set of predetermined or fixed group sample sizes.

Program Name: None Specified

Language: SAS

Compatibility: Any mainframe, IBM PC's and compatibles, and Apple-based systems that support SAS

Memory Requirements: 640K for the DOS version and 4 MB for the Windows version

Cost of Program: No Charge

How to obtain a copy of the program:

The SAS code is contained within the source article. All correspondence should be addressed to:

Dr. Hossein N. Yarandi
Box 100187
H.S.C.
University of Florida
Gainesville, FL 32611-0187
e-mail:hyarandi@stat.ufl.edu

POWER - SURVIVAL ANALYSIS

Title: A Computer Program for Sample Size and Power
Calculations in the Design of Multi-Arm and Factorial
Clinical Trials With Survival Time Endpoints

Author: Ranjini Natarajan, Bruce W. Turnbull, Elizabeth H.
Slate, and Larry C. Clark

Source: *Computer Methods and Programs in Biomedicine,*
1996, *49,* 137-147.

Description: This program computes power and sample size for a
simulated clinical trial with survival time endpoints using user-
specified design characteristics. In particular, the program
calculates power and performs tests of statistical significance for
(a) the overall test of the equality of survival rates, (b) the overall
test of interaction between factors (when two or more factors are
specified), and (c) two-sided tests of the individual linear
combinations of log incidence tests. The proportion of simulated
runs, in which at least one of the linear combinations is
significant, is also reported.

Program Name: None Specified

Language: C

Compatibility: Versions are available for SUN SPARC
workstations and for IBM PC's and
compatibles.

Memory Requirements: None Specified

Cost of Program: No Charge

How to obtain a copy of the program:

Send a blank formatted 3.5" diskette and a
self-addressed, stamped mailer to:

Dr. Ranjini Natarajan
Center for Statistical Science
Box G-H
Brown University
Providence, RI 02912
e-mail: ranjini@stat.brown.edu

PREDICTION ANALYSIS

Title: BASIC Programs for Prediction Analysis of Cross Classification

Author: Alexander von Eye and Gunter Krampen

Source: *Educational and Psychological Measurement*, 1987, *47*, 141-143.

Description: Prediction analysis, which is often used in developmental studies, tests simultaneous point predictions. Five versions of the program are provided. The output consists of observed and expected frequencies, a table of hits and errors, descriptive measures of prediction success, scope, precision, and quasi-independent log-linear models to fit the data. The input consists of the size of the matrix, observed frequencies, and the predictive cells.

Program Name: PAOL.EXE (IBM version); DEL-ANALYSIS (Apple version)

Language: Microsoft BASIC, Applesoft BASIC

Compatibility: IBM PC's and compatibles, Apple IIe and Macintosh

Memory Requirements: 15KB

Cost of Program: No Charge

How to obtain a copy of the program:

Send a formatted 3.5" diskette and a self-addressed, stamped mailer to:

Dr. Alexander von Eye
Department of Psychology
Michigan State University
119 Snyder Hall
East Lansing, MI 48824-1117
e-mail: voneye@msu.edu

Dr. Gunter Krampen
Universität Trier
Fachbereich 1 - Psychologie
D-54286 Trier, Germany
e-mail: krampen@uni-trier.de

PRINCIPAL COMPONENTS

Title: Estimating Sample Properties of Principal Components Using SAS

Author: A. Narayanan

Source: *Behavior Research Methods, Instruments, & Computers*, 1994, *24*, 97-100.

Description: This program computes the standard errors in a principal components analysis which can be used in regression analysis to limit overinterpretation of the results. The program is based on the covariance matrix corrected for the mean. An example and the program listing are provided in the article.

Program Name: None Specified

Language: SAS (PROC PRINCOMP)

Compatibility: Any system that uses SAS

Memory Requirements: None Specified

Cost of Program: No Charge

How to obtain a copy of the program:

Send a written request to:

Dr. A. Narayanan
Department of Decision and Information Systems
Graduate School of Business
Indiana University
Bloomington, IN 47405

PRINCIPAL COMPONENTS

Title: SECONDOR: A Program that Computes a Second-Order Principal Components Analysis and Various Interpretation Aids

Author: Bruce Thompson

Source: *Educational and Psychological Measurement*, 1990, *50*, 575-580.

Description: Because a principal components analysis of a correlation (or variance-covariance) matrix may provide factors that when rotated obliquely may be correlated, a second-order factor solution may be appropriate. The input may consist of either raw data or a correlation matrix. Moreover, a degree of factor obliqueness is also possible in the promax rotation option. The output consists of the correlation matrix and prerotated eigenvalues, the first order factor matrices (unrotated, varimax rotated, and promax rotated) with the eigenvalues and communalities. Finally, the eigenvalues and the unrotated and orthogonally rotated second-order factor matrices along with the Schmid and Lehman (1957) solution for aid in interpretating these results is also output. An example of the output generated by the program is provided in the article.

Program Name: SECONDOR

Language: FORTRAN

Compatibility: None Specified

Memory Requirements: None Specified

Cost of Program: No Charge

How to obtain a copy of the program:

Send a written request to:

Dr. Bruce Thompson
Department of Educational Psychology
Texas A & M University
College Station, TX 77843
e-mail: e100bt@tamvm1.tamu.edu

PROBABILITY - EXACT

Title: Exact Probabilities for the General Matching Problem

Author: Gordon Rae

Source: *Educational and Psychological Measurement,* 1996,
          56, 839-842.

Description: This program computes the exact probability of x
matches given a certain number of cards with y suits. That is, it
can be thought of as an agreement (same card and suit) between
decks. Moreover, this paradigm can also be used in interrater
agreement paradigms. The input is composed of the number of
cards in each deck, the number of suits, and the number of cards in
each suit for each deck. The output consists of the exact
probability of x matches and the cumulative distribution. This
output can also be thought of as an exact significance test for
Cohen's kappa.

Program Name: MATCH

Language: FORTRAN 77

Compatibility: None Specified

Memory Requirements: None Specified

Cost of Program: No Charge

How to obtain a copy of the program:

Send a blank 3.5" diskette and a
self-addressed, stamped mailer to:

Dr. Gordon Rae
School of Behavioral and Communication Sciences
University of Ulster
Coleraine
Northern Ireland
BT52 1SA

PROFILE ANALYSIS

Title: PROF: A Computer Program for Analyzing Group Differences Based Upon Profile Data

Author: Robert I. Kabacoff and Gary K. Burger

Source: *Educational and Psychological Measurement*, 1984, *44*, 667-670.

Description: In profile analysis, groups may be compared across a number of dependent variables. This program outputs univariate and multivariate analyses of variance (including omega squared and the correlation ratio), multiple profile analysis (testing for differences in parallelness, elevation, and flatness), profile variability (i.e., differences in jaggedness), and a plot of mean profiles. The input consists of group membership and the data for each subject.

Program Name: PROF

Language: SAS (uses PROC MATRIX)

Compatibility: None Specified

Memory Requirements: None Specified

Cost of Program: No Charge

How to obtain a copy of the program:

Send a written request to:

Dr. Robert Kabacoff
Center for Psychological Studies
3301 College Avenue
Ft. Lauderdale, FL 33714-7721

PROFILE ANALYSIS

Title: Program PROFAN--A Profile Analysis Data
Converter

Author: Randall M. Parker

Source: *Behavior Research Methods & Instrumentation,*
1976, 8, 306.

Description: This program calculates the following three
measures of profile similarity: 1) Cattell's (1949) r_p which is a
function of the Mahalanobis D^2 statistic but that is scaled and
interpreted in the same manner as Pearson's product-moment
correlation; 2) Nunnally's (1962) method of analyzing the matrix of
sums of raw score cross-products; and 3) Guertin's (1971) Distance
Similarity Index (DSI). Input consists of raw or standardized
profile data. Output includes the converted data matrices and the
profile similarity measures.

Program Name: PROFAN

Language: CDC FORTRAN

Compatibility: Any computer that supports FORTRAN

Memory Requirements: None Specified

Cost of Program: No Charge

How to obtain a copy of the program:

A listing of the program may be obtained by contacting:

Dr. Randall M. Parker
Department of Special Education
EDB 306
University of Texas
Austin, TX 78712

PROFILE ANALYSIS

Title: A Computer Program to Perform a Multivariate Profile
Analysis

Author: Stephen Powers and Richard L. Lopez, Jr.

Source: *Educational and Psychological Measurement*, 1986,
46, 167-168.

Description: This program computes a profile analysis for two
independent groups by providing significance tests for parallel,
coincident, and level profiles. The input is composed of either a
sample size x number of dependent measures raw score matrix or
from DATA statements consisting of two mean vectors and a
covariance matrix.

Program Name: None Specified

Language: BASIC

Compatibility: None Specified

Memory Requirements: None Specified

Cost of Program: No Charge

How to obtain a copy of the program:

Send a written request to:

Dr. Stephen Powers
Legal and Research Services
Tucson Unified School District
P.O. Box 40400
Tucson, AZ 85717

PROFILE ANALYSIS - SUBTEST SCATTER

Title: Profile Analysis of the Wechsler Intelligence Scales:
A New Index of Subtest Scatter

Author: Adrian Burgess

Source: *British Journal of Clinical Psychology*, 1991, *30*,
257-263.

Description: This program calculates the Mahalanobis distance,
D^2, as a multivariate measure of the distance between an
individual's test score profile and the centroid of the population
from which the profile originated. A statistically significant D^2
value is taken to denote the presence of clinically significant
subtest scatter. Two versions of the program are available: one that
is designed specifically for use with the WAIS-R and a second that
can be used with any combination of test scores. The latter
program requires the means, standard deviations, and inter-subtest
correlations as user specified input.

Program Name: None Specified

Language: GWBASIC

Compatibility: IBM PC's and compatibles

Memory Requirements: None Specified

Cost of Program: No Charge

How to obtain a copy of the program:

Send a formatted 3.5" diskette and
a self-addressed, stamped mailer to:

Dr. Adrian Burgess
Psychological Medicine Unit
Mental Health Centre
1 Nightingale Place
London SW10 9NG
United Kingdom
e-mail: rnju004@s1.cxwms.ac.uk

PROPORTIONS - INDEPENDENT

Title: An Exact Unconditional Test for the 2 x 2 Comparative Trial

Author: Michael Haber

Source: *Psychological Bulletin*, 1986, *99*, 129-132.

Description: This program calculates a one-sided exact z test as a measure of the equality of two independent proportions. Monte Carlo simulations conducted by the author suggest that the exact z test is considerably more powerful than Fisher's exact test and may even be more powerful than Tocher's (1950) randomized test. The program computes the z-critical values for given sample sizes n_1 and n_2 and the user-specified alpha value.

Program Name: None Specified

Language: FORTRAN

Compatibility: VAX/VMS mainframe, IBM PC's and compatibles

Memory Requirements: None Specified

Cost of Program: No Charge

How to obtain a copy of the program:

Write to (preferably via e-mail):

Dr. Michael Haber
Department of Biostatistics
Emory University
Atlanta, GA 30322-0001
e-mail: haber@sph.emory.edu

PROXIMITY ANALYSIS

Title: A BASIC Program for Nonparametric Analyses of
Proximity Matrices

Author: Peter Van Bergem, Raymond Ditrichs,
and Seymore Simon

Source: *Behavior Research Methods, Instruments, & Computers,*
1986, *18,* 407-408.

Description: The program consists of inputting two sets of
symmetrical k x k matrices containing only the entries below the
diagonal. The output consists of the total matrices and a
correlation coefficient between these matrices. Moreover,
distributions for matched and unmatched samples can be obtained
via bootstrapping or randomization. A distribution using the
quadratic assignment technique is also available.

Program Name: None Specified

Language: Microsoft BASIC-80

Compatibility: Kaypro 10; MS-DOS environments

Memory Requirements: None Specified

Cost of Program: No Charge

How to obtain a copy of the program:

Send a formatted 3.5" diskette and
a self addressed, stamped mailer to:

Dr. Seymore Simon
Department of Psychology
Northern Illinois University
1425 W. Lincoln Hwy
DeKalb, IL 60115
e-mail:ssimon@niu.edu

PROXIMITY DATA

Title: TRIAGE: A SAS Program of Dissimilarity Data Diagnostics

Author: Tony D. Thompson and Joseph Lee Rodgers

Source: *Applied Psychological Measurement*, 1987, *11*, 160.

Description: In order to aid researchers in selecting a model for proximity data, three macro programs are presented which perform neighbor analysis (including centrality and reciprocity statistics), skewness, elongation, and triangle inequality statistics, and eigenvalues of the scalar products matrix. Documentation for interpretation and use are provided.

Program Name: TRIAGE

Language: SAS

Compatibility: Any system using SAS

Memory Requirements: None Specified

Cost of Program: No Charge

How to obtain a copy of the program:

Send a written request to:

Dr. Joseph Lee Rodgers
Department of Psychology
University of Oklahoma
Norman, OK 73019
e-mail: ab1338@uokmvsa

PROXIMITY DATA - DISSIMILARITY

Title: A SAS Macro for Calculating the Line-of-Sight Measure of Interobject Dissimilarity

Author: William G. Jacoby

Source: *Psychometrika,* 1993, *58,* 511-512.

Description: This program calculates the line-of-sight measure (LOS) of interobject dissimilarity which is based on a procedure developed by Rabinowitz (1976) for rank-ordering pairs of stimulus objects. The rank orderings can then be interpreted as proximities data which in turn can be subjected to statistical analysis (e.g., multidimensional scaling, cluster analysis). The LOS procedure is robust (produces reliable rankings) in the face of measurement error. Input consists of a rectangular n x k (SAS) data matrix. The main output consists of a symmetric matrix containing the LOS-derived ordinal dissimilarities data.

Program Name: LOS

Language: SAS

Compatibility: Any computer system that supports SAS (need base SAS and SAS/IML)

Memory Requirements: None Specified

Cost of Program: No Charge

How to obtain a copy of the program:

Send a formatted 3.5" diskette and
a self-addressed, stamped mailer to:

Dr. William G. Jacoby
Department of Government and International Studies
University of South Carolina
Columbia, SC 29208
e-mail: n350085@univscvm.csd.scarolina.edu

PROXIMITY DATA -TREE ANALYSIS

Title: Computer Programs for Fitting Ultrametric and Additive Trees to Proximity Data by Least Squares Methods

Author: Geert De Soete

Source: *Behavior Research Methods, Instruments, & Computers,* 1984, *16,* 551-552.

Description: The two programs described in this paper utilize the least squares algorithms proposed by De Soete (1983, 1984) for fitting ultrametric and additive trees to proximity data. These two types of tree fitting complement multidimensional scaling as methods for representing proximity data. The main input consists of a lower-diagonal proximity matrix comprised of either similarity or dissimilarity data. Output includes a goodness-of-fit index, a bottom-up merge list of the ultrametric or additive tree, and a matrix of residuals. Both of the programs can handle missing data.

Program Name: LSULT, LSADT

Language: A portable subset of FORTRAN IV known as PFORT

Compatibility: Runs on the VAX-11/780 system and on Cray I, Honeywell 6000, and Siemens 7551 computers. Can be modified to run on other types of systems.

Memory Requirements: None Specified

Cost of Program: No Charge

How to obtain a copy of the program:

The program listings and accompanying documentation can be obtained by contacting:

Dr. Geert De Soete
Department of Psychology
University of Ghent
Henri Dunantlaan 2
B-9000 Ghent
Belgium

PROXIMITY DATA - TREE FITTING

Title: ADDTREE/P: A PASCAL Program for Fitting
Additive Trees Based on Sattath and Tversky's
ADDTREE Algorithm

Author: James E. Corter

Source: *Behavior Research Methods & Instrumentation,*
1982, *14*, 353-354.

Description: This program fits additive trees to proximity data in
accordance with the algorithm developed by Sattath and Tversky
(1977). Input to the program consists of a matrix of proximity data
(e.g., similarity ratings, correlations). Output includes a graph of
the fitted tree structure, the obtained model distances, the residual
distances, and several measures of fit (e.g., stress, squared
monotonic and linear correlations).

Program Name: ADDTREE/P

Language: PASCAL

Compatibility: DEC, UNIX, and IBM mainframe systems,
IBM PC's and compatibles

Memory Requirements: None Specified

Cost of Program: No Charge

How to obtain a copy of the program:

From internet: http://netlib.bell-labs.com and send the message
send readme index from mds (for a list of programs available)
send addtree.pas from mds (for the source code)
send addtree_manual from mds (for the documentation)

For further information, contact:

Dr. James Corter
Department of Measurement and Statistics
Columbia University
Teachers College
525 W. 120th St.
New York, NY 10027-6696
e-mail: jec34@columbia.edu

PROXIMITY DATA - TREE FITTING

Title: Extended Similarity Trees

Author: James E. Corter

Source: *Psychometrika*, 1986, *51*, 429-451.

Description: This extended tree program for proximity data (e.g., which faces have similar characteristics) is used to pictorially demonstrate both nested and overlapping clusters from the data. Marked segments are used to represent overlapping clusters. Moreover, this program may be used for depicting nominal factorial or hierarchical structures.

Program Name: EXTREE

Language: PASCAL

Compatibility: DEC, UNIX and IBM mainframe systems, IBM PC's and compatibles

Memory Requirements: None Specified

Cost of Program: No Charge

How to obtain a copy of the program:

From internet: http://netlib.bell-labs.com and send the message
send readme index from mds (for a list of programs available)
send extree.pas from mds (for the source code)
send extree_manual from mds (for the documentation)

For further information, contact:

Dr. James Corter
Department of Measurement and Statistics
Columbia University
Teachers College
525 W. 120th St.
New York, NY 10027-6696
e-mail: jec34@columbia.edu

PROXIMITY VALUES

Title: A FORTRAN Program to Calculate Proximity Values and an Averaged Proximity Matrix

Author: Allan G. Bateson and Christy L. DeVader

Source: *Educational and Psychological Measurement,* 1990, *50,* 131-134.

Description: Proximity analysis (Friendly, 1979) is used to examine memory structure and skill differences between neophytes and experts, for example. Hence, it examines the subjective output of free recall. The output is composed of a square matrix of averaged proximity values and general diagnostics (e.g., duplication or missing values) if errors occur in the input file.

Program Name: PROXIMITY

Language: FORTRAN 77

Compatibility: VAX/VMS mainframes

Memory Requirements: None Specified

Cost of Program: No Charge

How to obtain a copy of the program:

Send a formatted 3.5" diskette and a self-addressed, stamped mailer to:

Dr. Allan G. Bateson
Department of Psychology
Towson State University
Towson, MD 21204
e-mail: e7p4bat@toe.towson.edu

PSI PHENOMENA

Title: Use of Both Sum of Ranks and Direct Hits in Free-Response Psi Experiments

Author: George P. Hansen and Jessica Utts

Source: *Journal of Parapsychology,* 1987, *51,* 321-335.

Description: This program computes two different wholistic (versus atomistic) statistical indices that are useful for evaluating the outcomes of free-response ESP or Psi Ganzfeld experiments. The two indices are the sum-of-ranks statistic (Solfvin, Kelly, & Burdick, 1978) and the frequency of direct hits (Stanford & Mayer, 1974). For both indices, exact bivariate probabilities are calculated which obviates the need for Bonferroni-type multiple comparison correction procedures. As a result, the level of statistical power for each individual test is not compromised.

Program Name: None Specified

Language: Applesoft BASIC

Compatibility: Designed to run on computers capable of supporting Applesoft BASIC. With minor modifications, the program can be adapted to run on other versions of BASIC.

Memory Requirements: None Specified

Cost of Program: No Charge

How to obtain a copy of the program:

The annotated source code is presented in the appendix of the original article. For a copy of the program, send a blank formatted diskette and a stamped, self-addressed returnable disk mailer to:

Dr. Jessica Utts
Department of Statistics
University of California
Davis, CA 95616-5270
e-mail: jmutts@ucdavis.edu

QUALITATIVE ANALYSIS

Title: Computer-Assisted Analysis of Qualitative
Gerontological Research

Author: Roger Hiemstra, Elizabeth Essman, Norbert Henry,
and Dorothea Palumbo

Source: *Educational Gerontology, 1987, 13,* 417-426.

Description: After data have been entered and coded, this
program performs a content analysis of the information (i.e., the
main codes and subcodes) which in turn results in the identification
of various themes within the dataset.   The program is capable of
listing the number of times that each code emerges (within as well
as across respondents) and the contexts in which respondents
reported information regarding each theme.   The program is useful
for organizing and synthesizing various types of qualitative data
including interviews, field notes, and direct observations.

Program Name: QUALOG

Language: None Specified

Compatibility: Two versions are available; one that runs on
IBM VM/CMS mainframe systems, and one
that runs on VAX VMS mainframes.

Memory Requirements: None Specified

Cost of Program: None Specified

How to obtain a copy of the program:

Send a blank formatted 3.5" diskette and
a self-addressed, stamped mailer to:

Dr. Elizabeth Essman
College of Nursing
Syracuse University
426 Ostrom Avenue
Syracuse, NY 13244
e-mail: eressman@syr.edu

RADIAL MAZE STATISTICS

Title: The Exact Null Distribution for Radial Maze Statistics:
A FORTRAN 77 Program

Author: Raphael Gillett

Source: *Behavior Research Methods, Instruments, & Computers,*
1994, *26,* 70-73.

Description: This program outputs the probability of making x
repetition errors and the probability of making m correct choices.
Moreover, a test of significance is available for each subject which
examines the hypothesis that the number of correct choices is
greater than chance. The input is simply the number of choices
and the number of arms in the maze. A listing of the program is
presented on pages 72-73.

Program Name: RADMAZE

Language: FORTRAN 77

Compatibility: Any mainframe, IBM PC and compatible, and
Apple-based systems that support FORTRAN 77

Memory Requirements: 640K

Cost of Program: No Charge

How to obtain a copy of the program:

Send a blank 3.5" diskette and a
self-addressed, stamped mailer to:

Dr. Raphael Gillett
Department of Psychology
University of Leicester
Leicester LE1 7RH
England
e-mail: rtg@le.ac.uk

RANDOM NUMBERS

Title: Algorithms for Randomness in the Behavioral Sciences: A Tutorial

Author: Marc Brysbaert

Source: *Behavior Research Methods, Instruments, & Computers,* 1991, *23,* 45-60.

Description: This program generates random numbers via Wichmann and Hill's (1982) method and computes standard normal random deviates via the inverse function, Box and Muller (1958), polar, ratio of uniforms, and Marsaglia-Bray (1964) methods. Additionally, the output includes exponential deviates as calculated via the inverse function, ratio of uniforms, and von-Neumann (1951) methods. Finally, algorithms concerning random sampling with the preservation of order, a geometric distribution, and generating permutations are also provided. These algorithms, written in Turbo Pascal, are contained in Appendix B of the article.

Program Name: None Specified

Language: Turbo Pascal, BASIC

Compatibility: IBM mainframes, IBM PC's and compatibles

Memory Requirements: None Specified

Cost of Program: $10

How to obtain a copy of the program:

Send a formatted 3.5" diskette and
a self-addressed returnable mailer to:

Dr. Marc Brysbaert
University of Leuven
B-3000
Leuven, Belgium
e-mail: marc.brysbaert@psy.kuleuven.ac.be

RANDOMIZATION

Title: Computer Program for Quasi-Random Stimulus Sequences With Equal Transition Frequencies

Author: Phillip L. Emerson and Randall D. Tobias

Source: *Behavior Research Methods, Instruments, & Computers,* 1995, *27,* 88-98.

Description: This program generates randomized stimulus sequences constructed from numerous presentations of stimuli in which certain sequential constraints must be satisfied. One utility of this program is in the construction of Euler paths.

Program Name: None Specified

Language: C; SAS/IML

Compatibility: IBM PC's and compatibles

Memory Requirements: None Specified

Cost of Program: No Charge

How to obtain a copy of the program:

Send a formatted 3.5" diskette and a self-addressed, stamped mailer to:

For the C Version:

Dr. Phillip L. Emerson
Department of Psychology
Cleveland State University
Cleveland, OH 44115
e-mail: r0264@vmcms.csuohio.edu

For the SAS/IML Version:

Dr. Randall D. Tobias
SAS Institute
Cary, NC 27512-8000
e-mail: sasrdt@unx.sas.com

RANDOMIZATION

Title:　RANDOMTOOLS: An Apple Pascal Unit Useful in Randomization

Author:　Burrton Woodruff

Source:　*Behavior Research Methods, Instruments, & Computers,* 1985, *17,* 133-134.

Description: Using the applications *Randomorder* and *Reorder* for generating randomized orderings, this progam has utility, for example, in sampling and assigning participants to treatment conditions. An example of the program is provided on pages 133-134.

Program Name: RANDOMTOOLS

Language:　Apple Pascal

Compatibility: Apple computers

Memory Requirements: None Specified

Cost of Program:　$5 (the source code is free of charge)

How to obtain a copy of the program:

For a 5.25" diskette and executable version of the program, send a written request and payment to:

Dr. Burrton Woodruff
Department of Psychology
Butler University
4600 Sunset Avenue
Indianapolis, IN 46208
e-mail: woodruff@butler.edu

RANDOMIZATION TEST

Title: Randomization Tests for the Macintosh

Author: Andrew F. Hayes

Source: *Behavior Research Methods, Instruments, & Computers,* 1996, *28*, 473-475.

Description: This program outputs probability values for testing that the difference between two independent (or dependent - as in repeated measures) means is zero, and testing the null hypothesis that rho (population correlation coefficient) is zero. The input consists of an ASCII data file. The program handles from 3 to 500 cases.

Program Name: PERMUSTAT (version 1.3)

Language: FUTUREBASIC

Compatibility: Macintosh (6.0.7 operating system or later)

Memory Requirements: 105K disk space and 500K RAM

Cost of Program: No Charge

How to obtain a copy of the program:

It may be downloaded using internet:

http://www.metz.une.edu/ahayes/pstat.htm

For further information, contact:

Dr. Andrew F. Hayes
Department of Psychology
University of New England
Armidale NSW 2351
Australia
e-mail: ahayes@metz.une.edu.au

RANDOMIZATION TEST - ANOVA

Title: A Computer Program for a Randomization Test for Factorial Analysis of Variance

Author: Eugene S. Edgington and Otto Haller

Source: *Behavior Research Methods & Instrumentation,* 1982, *14,* 348-349.

Description: Performs randomization tests on experimental data by calculating F-tests on the empirical data as well as on numerous random data permutations. The proportion of F-tests derived from random data that equal or exceed the F-test derived from the experimental data constitutes the probability value. The program performs main effects analyses only on a maximum of five factors, and it is incapable of accommodating repeated measures. Input includes the number of factors, the number of random permutations to be performed, and whether the data to be analyzed are ordinal, interval, or dichotomous. Output includes the between- and within- mean square terms, the F-test and its associated probability value.

Program Name: RANDIBM

Language: FORTRAN

Compatibility: IBM PC's and compatibles

Memory Requirements: None Specified

Cost of Program: No Charge

How to obtain a copy of the program:

Using anonymous ftp:

ftp.acs.ucalgary.ca
ftp> user anonymous
ftp> password: guest
ftp> cd pub/private_group_info/randibm
ftp> get readme.doc
ftp> binary
ftp> get randibm.exe

When using RANDIBM, select the "monochrome" rather than the color option

RANDOMIZATION TEST - SINGLE CASE

Title: Using Randomization Tests with Responsive Single-Case Designs

Author: John Ferron and William Ware

Source: *Behaviour Research and Therapy,* 1994, *32,* 787-791.

Description: Describes a program that performs valid randomization tests on sequential data from single-case designs in which the design incorporates both a responsive element and a randomized element. Given user-defined phase change criteria, the program calculates a probability value for the randomization test which indicates the probability that the observed between-phase difference is truly greater than all other possible treatment sequences.

Program Name: None Specified

Language: SAS

Compatibility: Any system capable of supporting SAS

Memory Requirements: None Specified

Cost of Program: No Charge

How to obtain a copy of the program:

The program listing is contained in the appendix of the original article. For additional information, please contact:

Dr. John Ferron
School of Education
University of North Carolina
Chapel Hill, NC 27599-3500

RASCH MODEL

Title: PRASCH: A FORTRAN Program for Latent Class Polytomous Response Rasch Models

Author: John M. Grego

Source: *Applied Psychological Measurement,* 1993, *17,* 238.

Description: The program computes the conditional maximum likelihood estimates and a covariance matrix for a polytomous response Rasch model, tests a moment condition on a sequence of ratio statistics, fits latent class polytomous response Rasch models, and computes the likelihood gradient function for a latent class model.

Program Name: PRASCH

Language: FORTRAN (VAX and 77)

Compatibility: Any mainframe or PC that can compile FORTRAN 77

Memory Requirements: None Specified

Cost of Program: No Charge

How to obtain a copy of the program:

Send a formatted 3.5" diskette and a self-addressed, stamped mailer to:

Dr. John M. Grego
Department of Statistics
University of South Carolina
Columbia, SC 29208
e-mail: grego@stat.sc.edu

RASCH MODEL

Title: Exact and Best Confidence Intervals for the Ability Parameter of the Rasch Model

Author: Karl Christoph Klauer

Source: *Psychometrika*, 1991, *56*, 535-547.

Description: In response to user-supplied item difficulty parameters, this program calculates ability parameters and provides for those parameters confidence intervals (CI's) that do not rely on asymptotic approximations. The first type of CI calculated is referred to as the optimal randomized confidence interval, whereas the second type of CI is known as the Clopper-Pearson interval and represents the best nonrandomized approximation of the optimal randomized CI. Use of these CI's, rather than asymptotic approximations, are most appropriate with tests of moderate length.

Program Name: CONF-INT.EXE

Language: Turbo Pascal 4.0

Compatibility: IBM PC's and compatibles

Memory Requirements: 100K

Cost of Program: No Charge

How to obtain a copy of the program:

Send a formatted 3.5" diskette and
a self-addressed, stamped mailer to:

Dr. Karl Christoph Klauer
Psychologisches Institut
Römerstraße 164
53117 Bonn
Germany
e-mail: christoph.klauer@uni-bonn.de

RASCH MODEL

Title: DICOT: Analyzing Classroom Tests with the Rasch Model

Author: Geofferey N. Masters

Source: *Educational and Psychological Measurement,* 1984, *44,* 145-150.

Description: This program outputs a classroom data matrix, score distribution, and item analysis (includes item difficulty and consistency orders). This program, using the Rasch Model, will aid in providing teachers with the strengths and weaknesses of individuals and to determine which items are inconsistent.

Program Name: DICOT

Language: FORTRAN IV

Compatibility: None Specified

Memory Requirements: None Specified

Cost of Program: No Charge

How to obtain a copy of the program:

Send a formatted MS-DOS 3.5" diskette and a self-addressed, stamped mailer to:

Dr. Geofferey N. Masters
Educational Testing Service
Rosedale Rd.
Princeton, NJ 08544

RASCH MODEL - DOMAIN SCORES

Title: DOMAIN: Estimation of Domain Scores Using the Rasch Model

Author: Gary W. Phillips and Sandra S. Gedeik

Source: *Applied Psychological Measurement,* 1983, 7, 56.

Description: This program computes domain score estimates from a one-parameter (Rasch) model. A summary of the item group coupled with the standard errors and plot of the test characteristic curve are also outputted. The input consists of up to 500 Rasch calibrated items from which up to 10 item sets can be used to estimate domain scores.

Program Name: DOMAIN

Language: FORTRAN IV

Compatibility: HP3000 (however, minor modifications may be needed to accommodate various mainframes and PC's)

Memory Requirements: None Specified

Cost of Program: No Charge

How to obtain a copy of the program:

Send a formatted MS-DOS 3.5" diskette and a self-addressed, stamped mailer to:

Dr. Gary W. Phillips
U.S. Department of Education
555 New Jersey Avenue
Washington, DC 20208

RASCH MODEL - RELIABILITY

Title: RKAPPA: Reliability of Mastery Tests -- An Application of the Rasch Model

Author: Gary W. Phillips and Sandra S. Gedeik

Source: *Applied Psychological Measurement,* 1984, *8*, 286.

Description: In order to examine the reliability of a mastery test, the program outputs means and standard deviations of the logit distribution, a linear transformation of the logit scale and the standard error of measurement, the probability that (and number of) examinees with a certain ability will pass or fail the test and will be consistently classified, the probability of chance consistent classification, the average probability of consistent classification, and Kuder-Richardson 20 and 21 estimates. The input consists of ability estimates, standard errors of measurement, and frequencies associated with the maximum likelihood difficulty estimates.

Program Name: RKAPPA

Language: FORTRAN IV

Compatibility: HP3000-68 (however, minor modifications may be needed to accommodate various mainframes and PC's)

Memory Requirements: None Specified

Cost of Program: No Charge

How to obtain a copy of the program:

Send a formatted MS-DOS 3.5" diskette and a self-addressed, stamped mailer to:

Dr. Gary W. Phillips
U.S. Department of Education
555 New Jersey Avenue
Washington, DC 20208

RATINGS - COMPARING

Title: An Exact Probability Program for Comparing Ratings in Several Samples

Author: Lewis R. Aiken

Source: *Educational and Psychological Measurement*, 1989, *49*, 137-139.

Description: This program computes the difference and similarity indices and the statistical significance values of each for independent or dependent samples. The input consists of the number of sets of ratings, the number of categories on the scale, whether these ratings are independent or dependent, the sample size, and the ratings themselves.

Program Name: DIFSIM

Language: FORTRAN, BASIC

Compatibility: IBM PC's and compatibles

Memory Requirements: None Specified

Cost of Program: No Charge

How to obtain a copy of the program:

Send a formatted 3.5" double-density diskette and a self-addressed, stamped mailer to:

Dr. Lewis R. Aiken
12449 Mountain Trail Court
Moorpark, CA 93021
Phone: (805) 523-8165

RATINGS - ERRORS

Title: A Program for Computing Rating Errors

Author: Lewis R. Aiken

Source: *Educational and Psychological Measurement*, 1989, *49*, 145-146.

Description: This program allows the individual to judge the validity of ratings. The output consists of the overall rating score, severity or leniency of ratings, central tendency, homogeneity of ratings, contrast with ratings of adjacent items, and chance mean and standard deviations (for each rater to all items in total or for each item to all raters in total). Moreover, these indices are compared with the frequency distributions of all items or raters and the proportions of the left and right tail of the distribution are computed for each index value. The input consists of a rater x item matrix of ratings, and the number of rating categories.

Program Name: RATINGS

Language: FORTRAN, BASIC

Compatibility: IBM PC's and compatibles

Memory Requirements: None Specified

Cost of Program: No Charge

How to obtain a copy of the program:

Send a formatted 3.5" double-density diskette and a self-addressed, stamped mailer to:

Dr. Lewis R. Aiken
12449 Mountain Trail Court
Moorpark, CA 93021
Phone: (805) 523-2165

RATINGS - SCORING

Title: A Program for Constructing and Scoring Several Types of Rating Scales and Checklists

Author: Lewis R. Aiken

Source: *Educational and Psychological Measurement*, 1996, *56*, 1048-1051.

Description: A group of 11 menu-driven subprograms are presented that construct the following: bipolar, forced-choice, graphic, numerical, standard, semantic differential, and Likert-type rating scales. Moreover, questionnaires using the paired-comparison procedure (ranking each individual against each other) or ranking individuals on various behaviors, and checklists for evaluating one individual on various behaviors at different times, individuals on one behavior across various conditions or times, and individuals on various behaviors for one condition or time are provided. Finally, the total score, mean, standard deviation, frequency distribution of answers and composite frequency distribution of answers are given.

Program Name: 11 separate subprograms

Language: BASICA

Compatibility: IBM PC's and compatibles (need BASICA to run the programs)

Memory Requirements: None Specified

Cost of Program: No Charge

How to obtain a copy of the program:

Send either a formatted 3.5" or 5.25" double-density diskette and a self-addressed, stamped mailer to:

Dr. Lewis R. Aiken
12449 Mountain Trail Court
Moorpark, CA 93021
Phone: (805) 523-2165

RATINGS - VALIDITY

Title: VRH: A Program for Computing and Evaluating Three Rating Coefficients

Author: Lewis R. Aiken

Source: *Applied Psychological Measurement,* 1988, *12,* 438.

Description: The program outputs the statistical significance of a validity, repeatability, or homogeneity coefficient (see Aiken, 1985) and the significance level between two validity, repeatability, or homogeneity coefficients computed over a number of ratings. The input consists of determining the type of coefficient, the number of samples, the number of raters, and the number of rating categories.

Program Name: VRH

Language: BASIC, FORTRAN

Compatibility: IBM PC's and compatibles

Memory Requirements: None Specified

Cost of Program: No Charge

How to obtain a copy of the program:

Send a formatted 3.5" diskette and
a self-addressed, stamped mailer to:

Dr. Lewis R. Aiken
12449 Mountain Trail Court
Moorpark, CA 93021
Phone (805) 523-8165

RATINGS - VALIDITY

Title: LEQUATE: Linear Equating for the Common-Item Nonequivalent-Populations Design

Author: William J. Waldron

Source: *Applied Psychological Measurement,* 1988, *12*, 323.

Description: This interactive program allows the user to examine two groups taking a particular form of a test combined with a common set of target items. These items may contribute or not contribute to the overall test score. The output consists of the estimated test form statistics for the synthetic population (user defines weights for each population to be combined into one population), the slope and intercept, and a score conversion table with the range and interval defined by the user.

Program Name: LEQUATE

Language: BASIC

Compatibility: IBM PC's and compatibles (should have a color monitor)

Memory Requirements: 100K disk space and 220K free memory

Cost of Program: No Charge

How to obtain a copy of the program:

Send a 5.25" MS-DOS formatted diskette and a self-addressed, stamped mailer to:

Dr. William J. Waldron
Tampa Electric Company
Administration of Employee Testing and Assessment
P.O. Box 111
Tampa, FL 33601
e-mail: bill@bwaldron.com

REACTION TIMES

Title: DORF2R.BAS: Analyzing Signal-Detection Theory Rating Data in the BASIC Programming Language

Author: Edward F. Alf, Jr., and John M. Grossberg

Source: *Behavior Research Methods, Instruments, & Computers,* 1987, *19,* 475-482.

Description: This program provides an estimate of various signal-detection parameters and confidence intervals using a maximum likelihood solution. The output includes observed frequencies and proportions from the noise and signal, the estimate of parameters (and variances) of A, B, DELTA M, D(E), A(Z), and D(A) as defined by Dorfman (1982) along with the standard deviation of the signal-plus-noise distribution, the ratio of the differences in means to the difference in variances for the noise and signal-plus-noise distributions, the standard normal score in which A(Z) lies, the variance-covariance matrix, and chi-square and log-likelihood statistics. A listing of the program and output is given on pages 476-482.

Program Name: DORF2R.BAS

Language: BASIC

Compatibility: IBM PC's and compatibles

Memory Requirements: None Specified

Cost of Program: None Specified

How to obtain a copy of the program:

Send a written request to:

Dr. Edward F. Alf, Jr.
RGI, Inc.
3111 Camino Del Rio North
Suite 802
San Diego, CA 92108

REACTION TIMES

Title: MEANCOMP: A Pascal Program for Computing Mean Reaction Times With Outlier Selection

Author: Paul Whitney

Source: *Behavior Research Methods, Instruments, & Computers,* 1986, *18,* 53.

Description: This program provides mean reaction times for each subject along with the total number of scores entered, counts of outliers, and missing data. The input consists of up to 200 reaction times per subject and may detect outliers using a critical value determined by the Dixon (1951) ratio, a user-supplied cutoff score, or a specified number of standard deviations beyond the mean. A source file is built that could be used for the major statistical packages (e.g., SPSS).

Program Name: MEANCOMP

Language: Pascal

Compatibility: VAX 11, VAX/VMS (Version 4.2)

Memory Requirements: None Specified

Cost of Program: No Charge

How to obtain a copy of the program:

Send a written request to:

Dr. Paul Whitney
Department of Psychology
Washington State University
1 SE Stadium Way
Pullman, WA 99164

RECALL TESTS

Title: Scoring Options for Recall Tests (SORT): A BASIC Program for Entry and Analysis of Recall Test Data

Author: Claude J. Elie, Jason M. Blackwell, and David G. Payne

Source: *Behavior Research Methods, Instruments, & Computers,* 1996, *28,* 479-482.

Description: In order to analyze data from recall tests in a more thorough manner, the program outputs net recall, net recall by minute, number of categories, number of items recalled per category, and the adjusted ratio of clustering score (Roenker, Thompson, & Brown, 1971) for individual test analyses, whereas for repeated testing, item loss, item gain, item gain by minute, cumulative recall, and pair frequency (Sternberg & Tulving, 1977) are provided. The program can be used for both categorized and uncategorized lists.

Program Name: SORT

Language: Microsoft QuickBASIC 4.5

Compatibility: IBM PC's and compatibles (need to have Microsoft QuickBASIC 4.5 to examine the source code)

Memory Requirements: None Specified

Cost of Program: $10 (reproduction and handling costs)

How to obtain a copy of the program:

Send a written request and payment to:

Dr. David G. Payne
Department of Psychology
Binghamton University
Binghamton, NY 13902
e-mail: dpayne@bingvmb.cc.binghamton.edu

REGRESSION COMPONENT ANALYSIS

Title: RCA: A Program for Regression Component Analysis

Author: Rolf Langeheine and Holger Sonnichsen

Source: *Behavior Research Methods & Instrumentation,*
1981, 13, 761-762.

Description: This program performs regression component analysis (RCA; Schonemann & Steiger, 1976) as a means of extracting principal components from either a regression pattern matrix or a matrix of defining weights. The advantage of RCA over the conventional factor model is that the matrices produced by RCA are completely determinate (i.e., the factor indeterminacy problem is avoided). Users of the RCA program have the option of performing orthogonal, oblique, and procrustes rotations. The program can handle up to 35 variables.

Program Name: RCA

Language: FORTRAN IV

Compatibility: Any system that supports FORTRAN

Memory Requirements: At least 35K

Cost of Program: No Charge

How to obtain a copy of the program:

Send a formatted 3.5" diskette and
a self-addressed, stamped mailer to:

Dr. Rolf Langeheine
IPN
Olshausenstraße
D-24098
Kiel
Germany
e-mail: langeheine@ipn.uni-kiel.de

REGRESSION - MIXED EFFECTS

Title: MIXOR: A Computer Program for Mixed-Effects
Ordinal Regression Analysis

Author: Donald Hedeker and Robert D. Gibbons

Source: *Computer Methods and Programs in Biomedicine,*
1996, 49, 157-176.

Description: This program performs a mixed-effects regression
analysis on data containing dichotomous or ordinal outcomes from
either a clustered or longitudinal design. In addition to evaluating
change at both the group and individual levels, the program also
estimates (and adjusts for) the degree of dependency present in the
data. The user specifies an input file containing the multilevel data
and indicates whether a probit, logistic, or complementary log-log
response is to be utilized. Output includes the log-likelihood value
for the final model, the number and proportion of level-1
observations for each category, the number and proportion of level-
2 units with non-varying level-1 responses on the dependent
variable and for each model parameter, maximum marginal
likelihood estimates, standard errors, z-values, and p-values.

Program Name: MIXOR

Language: FORTRAN 77

Compatibility: IBM PC's and compatibles, Macintosh (a math
coprocessor is necessary)

Memory Requirements: None Specified

Cost of Program: No Charge

How to obtain a copy of the program:

Contact Dr. Hedeker via e-mail:
e-mail: hedeker@uic.edu

Or send a formatted 3.5" diskette and
a self-addressed, stamped mailer to:

Dr. Ann Hohmann
NIMH Services Research Branch
5800 Fishers Lane, Room #10C-06
Rockville, MD 20857

REGRESSION - MIXED EFFECTS

Title: MIXREGF: A Computer Program for Mixed-Effects Regression Analysis With Autocorrelated Errors

Author: Donald Hedeker and Robert D. Gibbons

Source: *Computer Methods and Programs in Biomedicine, 1996, 49, 229-252.*

Description: When observations contain both fixed effects and random effects (e.g., longitudinal data where measurements are nested within individuals or multilevel clustered data), then this program may be utilized to perform a mixed-effects regression analysis. In addition to calculating average change in a sample, the program estimates individual change for each subject and estimates (and adjusts for) the degree of autocorrelation present in the data. The user specifies an input file containing the hierarchically structured data. Output includes the log-likelihood value for the final model and for each model parameter, maximum marginal likelihood estimates, standard errors, z-values, and p-values. Empirical Bayes estimates of the R random effects may also be obtained.

Program Name: MIXREG

Language: FORTRAN 77

Compatibility: IBM PC's and compatibles, Macintosh (a math coprocessor is necessary)

Memory Requirements: None Specified

Cost of Program: No Charge

How to obtain a copy of the program:

Contact Dr. Hedeker via e-mail:
e-mail: hedeker@uic.edu

Or send a formatted 3.5" diskette and
a self-addressed, stamped mailer to:

Dr. Ann Hohmann
NIMH Services Research Branch
5800 Fishers Lane, Room #10C-06
Rockville, MD 20857

RELIABILITY

Title: Program for Computing and Evaluating Reliability Coefficients for Criterion-Referenced Tests

Author: Lewis R. Aiken

Source: *Educational and Psychological Measurement*, 1988, *48*, 697-700.

Description: This program computes the coefficient of agreement, kappa, and three linear transformations of these coefficients, the ranges for all five coefficients, and the hypergeometric or approximate probabilities for these coefficients. The input consists of the number of examinees above the criterion on both tests, the number of examinees below the criterion on both tests, the number of examinees above the criterion on test 1 but below the criterion on test 2, and the number of examinees falling below the criterion on test 1 and above the criterion on test 2. In the BASIC and PASCAL versions, data are entered via the keyboard and the output is provided on the screen. In the FORTRAN version, however, a data file is required as input and the results are presented in an output file.

Program Name: CRITREL

Language: FORTRAN, BASIC, PASCAL

Compatibility: IBM PC's and compatibles

Memory Requirements: None Specified

Cost of Program: No Charge

How to obtain a copy of the program:

Send a formatted 3.5" double-density diskette and a self-addressed, stamped mailer to:

Dr. Lewis R. Aiken
12449 Mountain Trail Court
Moorpark, CA 93021
Phone: (805) 523-8165

RELIABILITY

Title: RELIA: A PASCAL Program to Examine the
Reliability of a Set of Items

Author: Johannes Kingma and Johan Reuvekamp

Source: *Educational and Psychological Measurement,* 1987,
47, 131-133.

Description: This program computes the Kuder-Richardson 20,
inter-item variance-covariance and correlation matrices, proportion
of correct responses for each item in order to establish a difficulty
level, item-corrected total correlations, sample size, and a listing of
the input. The input consists of a file containing the number of
variables, a positive alternative, and all variables used in the
analysis. Moreover, a second data file is needed. The maximum
number of items is 50 and the program can accommodate only one
record per individual.

Program Name: RELIA

Language: Pascal

Compatibility: Apple II+

Memory Requirements: 64K

Cost of Program: None Specified

How to obtain a copy of the program:

Send a formatted 5.25" diskette and
a self-addressed, stamped mailer to:

Dr. Johannes Kingma
University Hospital at Groningen
Department of Traumatology
Groningen
Netherlands

RELIABILITY - COMPARISONS

Title: A Computer Program for Feldt's Test of the Equality of
Two Reliability Coefficients

Author: Ricardo Duran and Stephen Powers

Source: *Educational and Psychological Measurement*, 1994,
54, 92-93.

Description: Computes Feldt's test for examining the equality of
two independent Cronbach's alphas or Kuder-Richardson
reliability coefficients. The user provides the sample sizes of the
two groups, the number of items, and the data. The output
consists of item variances and total variances for each group,
sample sizes, Cronbach's alphas , Feldt's *F* test, and its probability.

Program Name: None Specified

Language: BASIC

Compatibility: IBM PC's and compatibles

Memory Requirements: 640 KB of RAM using DOS 3.0

Cost of Program: No Charge

How to obtain a copy of the program:

To receive a listing and sample output, send a written request to:

Dr. Ricardo Duran
Creative Research Associates
241 South Atlanta Drive
Tucson, AZ 85747

RELIABILITY - SCALED DATA

Title: A Computer Program for Determining the Reliability of Dimensionally Scaled Data When the Numbers and Specific Sets of Examiners May Vary at Each Assessment

Author: Domenic V. Cicchetti and Donald Showalter

Source: *Educational and Psychological Measurement*, 1988, *48*, 717-720.

Description: This program is used for continuous data when there are two or more raters per object assessed and the number of raters may vary from object to object. Hence, this program computes the intraclass correlation coefficient and its test of statistical significance. Additionally, summary information such as the number of subjects, raters, and variables is also provided. The input consists of various parameter lines followed by the data.

Program Name: None Specified

Language: FORTRAN 77

Compatibility: IBM compatible computers, VA370/CMS, OS/MVS TSO and batch

Memory Requirements: None Specified

Cost of Program: No Charge

How to obtain a copy of the program:

Send a formatted 3.5" double-density diskette and a self-addressed, stamped mailer to:

Dr. Domenic V. Cicchetti
Senior Research Psychologist and Biostatistician
VA Medical Center
West Haven, CT 06516
e-mail: domenic.cicchetti@yale.edu

RELIABILITY - STUDY OUTCOME

Title: Demonstrating the Influence of Sample Size and
Reliability on Study Outcome

Author: Michael J. Strube

Source: *Teaching of Psychology,* 1991, *18,* 113-115.

Description: This program contains two options for examining
the impact of sample size and reliability on study outcome. The
first option allows the user to examine the influence of different
sample sizes and estimates of reliability (for variables X and Y) on
sample statistics and correlation coefficients. The second option
demonstrates the association of reliability to validity by showing
how the sample correlation is affected by changes in the
reliabilities of variables X and Y.

Program Name: None Specified

Language: GW-BASIC

Compatibility: IBM PC's and compatibles

Memory Requirements: A minimum of 14K. The actual
memory required can be approximated
by the following formula: $16N + 450$,
where N = sample size.

Cost of Program: No Charge

How to obtain a copy of the program:

Send a blank formatted 3.5" diskette
and a self-addressed, stamped mailer to:

Dr. Michael J. Strube
Department of Psychology
Washington University
St. Louis, MO 63130
e-mail: mjstrube@artsci.wustl.edu

RELIABILITY - WEIGHTED COMPOSITE

Title: A Program for Computing the Reliability and Maximum Reliability of a Weighted Composite

Author: Lewis R. Aiken

Source: *Educational and Psychological Measurement*, 1988, *48*, 703-706.

Description: This program computes the composite and maximum reliabilities and the standard errors of measurement for each. A summary of the intercorrelations and weights for up to eight variables are also provided. The input consists of the number of variables needed to weight (and the weights if the user opts to compute the reliability coefficient, or maximum reliability, given specified variable weights), the reliability coefficient and standard deviation for each variable, and the correlation for each pair of variables entered.

Program Name: RELWATE

Language: BASIC, PASCAL

Compatibility: IBM PC's and compatibles

Memory Requirements: None Specified

Cost of Program: No Charge

How to obtain a copy of the program:

Send a formatted 3.5" double-density diskette and a self-addressed, stamped mailer to:

Dr. Lewis R. Aiken
12449 Mountain Trail Court
Moorpark, CA 93021
Phone (805) 523-8165

REPERTORY GRID

Title: COMPU-GRID: A Program for Computing, Sorting,
Categorizing, and Graphing Multiple Bieri Grid
Measurements of Cognitive Complexity

Author: Joel N. Greene, Richard E. Plank,
and Donald G. Fowler

Source: *Educational and Psychological Measurement*, 1989,
49, 623-626.

Description: This program outputs the scores and sorts,
categorizes, and graphs Bieri grids, which are measures of
cognitive complexity. Matrices of any dimension are accepted and
the researcher may set the number of divisions of categorized Bieri
scores. The input is composed of an ASCII file of scale scores.

Program Name: COMPU-GRID

Language: BASIC (runs in BASICA)

Compatibility: IBM PC's and compatibles

Memory Requirements: None Specified

Cost of Program: No Charge

How to obtain a copy of the program:

Send a formatted 5.25" double-sided double-density
floppy diskette and a self-addressed, stamped mailer to:

Dr. Joel N. Greene
Department of Marketing
Hofstra University
1000 Fulton Ave.
Hempstead, NY 11550-1030
e-mail: 72163.3042@compuserve.com

REPERTORY GRID

Title: OMNIGRID: A General Repertory Grid Design, Administration, and Analysis Program

Author: John Mitterer and Jack Adams-Webber

Source: *Behavior Research Methods, Instruments, & Computers,* 1988, *20,* 359-360.

Description: This program constructs and analyzes data from a repertory grid (a numeric representation of an individual's construct system - such as ranking a set of people on intelligence). For the dichotomous classification grid: matching scores, self-esteem, self-other differentiation, positivity bias, uncertainty, salience, and interelement distances are given. For rank-order grids: Kendall's tau, the average correlation between the constructs, Kendall's coefficient of concordance, intensity, common variance, and interelement distances are provided. For the rating grids: the correlation coefficient, angular distances between the constructs, extremity measures, common variance, variability of intensity, interelement distances, observed-expected distances, and self-other distances are output. The input is composed of a set of answers to 10-30 questions in order to form the grid.

Program Name: OMNIGRID 3.0

Language: Hypercard 2.1

Compatibility: Macintosh System 7 or later

Memory Requirements: 4 MB

Cost of Program: No Charge

How to obtain a copy of the program:

Send a formatted 3.5" diskette and
a self-addressed, stamped mailer to:

Dr. Jack Adams-Webber
Department of Psychology
Brock University
St. Catharines, Ontario
L2S 3A1
CANADA
e-mail: jadams@spartan.ac.brocku.ca

RESPONSE ANALYSIS

Title: ISRA: An SAS Macro Program for Item and Subject
Response Analysis

Author: Mao-Neng Fred Li, Stephen Olejnik, and
Louis Bashaw

Source: *Applied Psychological Measurement,* 1991,
15, 94.

Description: The program computes the item and respondent
caution indices of Harnisch and Linn (1981) and Sato (1975).
Moreover, the output also includes various item analysis measures
(e.g., internal consistency, item difficulty). If the indices have
values greater than .3, then the veracity of the item or respondent is
questioned.

Program Name: ISRA

Language: SAS

Compatibility: None Specified

Memory Requirements: None Specified

Cost of Program: No Charge

How to obtain a copy of the program:

Send a formatted 3.5" diskette and
a self-addressed, stamped mailer to:

Dr. Mao-Neng Fred Li
Department of Educational Psychology
University of Georgia
Athens, GA 30602

RESPONSE SEQUENCE ANALYSIS

Title: ERROR: A BASIC Program for Response Sequence Analysis of Two-Choice Learning Data

Author: John P. Capitanio and James E. King

Source: *Behavior Research Methods, Instruments, & Computers,* 1993, *25,* 419-421.

Description: This menu driven program provides an error analysis on data from a dichotomous-choice learning task. The error analyses consist of a number of descriptive measures (e.g., single- and two-trial measures) across a 4 (rewarded sequences) x 4 (outcome sequences) matrix and a more formal procedure using sequential state theory (King & Michels, 1989). The input is composed of an ASCII file with multiple records containing the side rewarded for each trial and whether the responses were correct or not.

Program Name: ERROR

Language: BASIC (uncompiled) - will work for BASICA, GWBASIC, or QuickBASIC but not for VISUAL BASIC.

Compatibility: IBM PC's and compatibles

Memory Requirements: 512K RAM

Cost of Program: No Charge

How to obtain a copy of the program:

Send a formatted 3.5" diskette and a self-addressed, stamped mailer to:

Dr. John P. Capitanio
Department of Psychology
University of California
Davis, CA 95616
email: jpcapitanio@ucdavis.edu

RESTRICTION OF RANGE

Title: Correcting for Multivariate Range Restriction: Two Computer Programs

Author: George M. Alliger and Ralph A. Alexander

Source: *Educational and Psychological Measurement*, 1984, *44*, 677-678.

Description: These programs compute corrections for multivariate range restriction which may reduce correlations, the multiple correlation, and intercorrelations between the predictors. The input consists of the variance-covariance matrices.

Program Name: None Specified

Language: SAS, FORTRAN

Compatibility: IBM PC's and compatibles (386 or 486)

Memory Requirements: None Specified

Cost of Program: No Charge

How to obtain a copy of the program:

Send a formatted 3.5" diskette and a self-addressed, stamped mailer to:

Dr. George M. Alliger
Department of Psychology
SUNY at Albany
1400 Washington Avenue
Albany, NY 12222-1080
e-mail: gmago@cnsibm.albany.edu

RESTRICTION OF RANGE

Title: RANGEJ: A Pascal Program to Compute the Multivariate Correction for Range Restriction

Author: James T. Johnson and Malcolm J. Ree

Source: *Educational and Psychological Measurement*, 1994, *54*, 693-695.

Description: The program computes the Lawley (1943) multivariate correction for range restriction for correlations. An input file is needed which consists of various keywords (title, names, means, standard deviations, and correlations) for both the restricted and unrestricted samples. The output consists of an input summary, an estimate of the corrected means and standard deviations for each variable, and a corrected correlation matrix. The program will allow up to 100 variables, whereas the 286 version (RANGEJS), allows up to 30 variables. The methodology will not work if there are linear dependencies in the data. The newer version of the program includes regression analysis and eigenvalue analysis.

Program Name: RANGEJ for Windows

Language: Pascal

Compatibility: IBM PC's and compatibles. Runs on a 386 or later version with Windows 3.11 or later version.

RANGEJS (works on 286 machine or without math co-processor)

Memory Requirements: 4MB

Cost of Program: No Charge

How to obtain a copy of the program:

Send a formatted 3.5" diskette and a self-addressed, stamped mailer to:

Dr. Malcolm J. Ree
AL/HRMA
7909 Lindbergh Drive
Brooks AFB, TX 78235-5352
e-mail: ree@alhrm.brook.af.mil

RIDGE REGRESSION - STEPWISE

Title: Calculating a Stepwise Ridge Regression

Author: John D. Morris

Source: *Educational and Psychological Measurement,* 1986, *46,* 151-155.

Description: This program computes a stepwise ridge regression that produces predictor weights that might be more accurate in cross-validation than traditional methods. The output consists of the weights and multiple correlations for both the stepwise ridge regression and traditional least squares approaches. Moreover, eigenvalues of the predictor correlation matrix and validities are also given.   The input is composed of either a raw data or a correlation matrix. Moreover, the user selects either a forward, backward, or all combinations regression approach and provides a value of the biasing parameter (between 0 and 1).

Program Name: None Specified

Language: FORTRAN

Compatibility: CYBER 170

Memory Requirements: None Specified

Cost of Program: No Charge

How to obtain a copy of the program:

Send an MS-DOS formatted 3.5" diskette and a self-addressed, stamped mailer to:

Dr. John D. Morris
Department of Education
Florida Atlantic University
Boca Raton, FL 33431

RIDGE REGRESSION - STEPWISE

Title: Stepwise Ridge Regression: A Computational
Clarification

Author: John D. Morris

Source: *Psychological Bulletin,* 1983, *94,* 363-366.

Description: This program performs ridge regression
(Darlington, 1978) using an algorithm that allows not only for the
correct calculation of regression coefficients but also for the correct
calculation of the multiple correlation coefficient (i.e., the
correlation of ridge predicted scores with actual criterion scores).
Calculation of the correct multiple correlation should help
researchers to avoid selecting inappropriate predictor variable
subsets when conducting stepwise ridge regression analysis. The
user has the option of determining the entry and/or exit criterion, in
terms of percentage levels of explained outcome variance, for each
predictor variable in the model.

Program Name: None Specified

Language: None Specified

Compatibility: None Specified

Memory Requirements: None Specified

Cost of Program: No Charge

How to obtain a copy of the program:

Send a blank formatted 3.5" diskette and
a self-addressed, stamped mailer to:

Dr. John D. Morris
Department of Education
Florida Atlantic University
Boca Raton, FL 33431

ROC CURVES

Title: ROC: Estimation of the Area Under a Receiver
Operating Characteristic Curve

Author: Ron D. Hays

Source: *Applied Psychological Measurement,* 1990,
14, 208.

Description: The program estimates the area under a receiver
operating characteristic curve for a 2 x n contingency table and
computes the z test for examining the significance of the difference
between receiver operating characteristic curves from the same
sample. The input consists of the contingency table and standard
error(s), and correlations (for comparing the two curves).

Program Name: ROC.EXE

Language: BASIC

Compatibility: IBM PC's and compatibles

Memory Requirements: Minimal

Cost of Program: No Charge

How to obtain a copy of the program:

Send a formatted 3.5" diskette and
a self-addressed, stamped mailer to:

Dr. Ron D. Hays
The RAND Corporation
1700 Main Street
P.O. Box 2138
Santa Monica, CA 90407-2138
Internet: Ronald_Hays@rand.org

ROY'S LARGEST ROOT CRITERION

Title: A Turbo Pascal Unit for Approximating the Cumulative Distribution Function of Roy's Largest Root Criterion

Author: J. Gary Lutz

Source: *Educational and Psychological Measurement,* 1992, *52,* 899-904.

Description: The program approximates the Roy's largest root criterion cumulative distribution for allowing the researcher to make significance decisions or forming confidence intervals. The demonstration program's input entails a value of Roy's criterion or the level of significance. Next, the distribution parameters (or problem parameters such as sample size and degrees of freedom) are input.

Program Name: ROY.PAS

Language: Turbo Pascal 5.0

Compatibility: IBM PC's and compatibles

Memory Requirements: 4 MB

Cost of Program: $10 (check or money order to Lehigh University)

How to obtain a copy of the program:

Send either a 3.5" or 5.25" diskette, a self-addressed, stamped mailer and payment to:

Dr. J. Gary Lutz
Lehigh University
Iacocca Hall
Bethlehem, PA 18015
e-mail: jgl3@lehigh.edu

RUNS TEST

Title: A FORTRAN 77 Program for the Runs Test

Author: Edward F. Krieg, Jr.

Source: *Behavior Research Methods, Instruments, & Computers,* 1988, *20,* 361.

Description: In order to determine whether a regression model is appropriate by examining the residuals, this program provides the exact and normal approximations of probabilities for the runs (of the residuals). The input consists of the number of positive and negative residuals and the number of runs.

Program Name: RUNS

Language: FORTRAN 77

Compatibility: IBM PC's and compatibles

Memory Requirements: 64K memory and a math coprocessor

Cost of Program: No Charge

How to obtain a copy of the program:

Send either a formatted 3.5" or 5.25"diskette
and a self addressed, stamped mailer to:

Dr. Edward F. Krieg, Jr.
NIOSH
4676 Columbia Pkwy
MS C-22
Cincinnati, OH 45226
e-mail: erk3@niobbs1.em.cdc.gov

SAMPLE SIZE - REPLICATION

Title: A FORTRAN 77 Program for Sample-Size Determination in Replication Attempts When Effect Size is Uncertain

Author: Raphael Gillett

Source: *Behavior Research Methods, Instruments, & Computers,* 1991, *23*, 442-446.

Description: This program computes the sample size for a replication study concerning means, proportions, or correlations. The techniques for performing these computations are found in Gillett (1986). The input includes the statistic (e.g., z value), the sample size, and the variance from the previous study, the power needed in the replication, and the critical value of the z statistic with the appropriate significance level. A listing of the program may be found on pages 444-446.

Program Name: ZREPSAM

Language: FORTRAN 77

Compatibility: Any mainframe, IBM PC and compatible, and Apple-based systems that support FORTRAN 77.

Memory Requirements: 640K

Cost of Program: No Charge

How to obtain a copy of the program:

Send a blank 3.5" diskette and a self-addressed, stamped mailer to:

Dr. Raphael Gillett
Department of Psychology
University of Leicester
Leicester LE1 7RH
England
email: rtg@le.ac.uk

SAMPLING

Title: Sixteen Computer Programs for Selecting, Assigning, and Evaluating Samples

Author: Lewis R. Aiken

Source: *Educational and Psychological Measurement*, 1994, *54*, 699-704.

Description:

a) selects x random numbers from a population of y numbers
b) randomly places x elements to y groups
c) randomly selects from or places into m strata (equals y groups)
d) multistage cluster sampling
e) sample size needed for the z test on population proportions
f) computes power and sample sizes for binomial tests
g) power and sample sizes for one- and two-sample z tests (means)
h) minimum proportion of respondents acceptable in a survey
i) minimum sample sizes for groups in randomized block designs
j) minimum and maximum values of population proportions
k) provides confidence intervals for proportions
l) matches two or more groups on a particular variable
m) matches subjects at random to a given number of groups
n) determines dependence or independence of paired samples
o) provides Latin square designs
p) confidence intervals for proportions and means for z tests

Program Name: None Specified

Language: BASICA

Compatibility: None Specified

Memory Requirements: None Specified

Cost of Program: No Charge

How to obtain a copy of the program:

Send a formatted 3.5" diskette and
a self-addressed, stamped mailer to:

Dr. Lewis R. Aiken
12449 Mountain Trail Court
Moorpark, CA 93021
Phone: (805) 523-8165

SAMPLING

Title: Using and Evaluating ISEE, A New Computer Program for Teaching Sampling and Statistical Inference

Author: Ganka Dimitrova, Caroline Hodges Persell, and Richard Maisel

Source: *Teaching Sociology,* 1993, *21,* 341-351.

Description: This program allows users to examine the effects that type of sampling distribution and sampling design strategy have upon sampling statistics and sampling errors. Users have the option of selecting from among simple random, systematic, replicated, stratified, and thin zone (stratified replicated) sampling designs. The sample size selected, and the numbers of samples drawn (from 1 to 9,999), can also be varied.

Program Name: ISEE

Language: None Specified

Compatibility: IBM PC's and compatibles (386 or higher) with VGA graphics capability. The presence of a math coprocessor will enhance performance.

Memory Requirements: At least 8MG RAM

Cost of Program: About $15 - contact Pine Ridge

How to obtain a copy of the program:

For further information, contact:

Dr. Caroline Hodges Persell
Department of Sociology
New York University
269 Mercer Street
New York, NY 10003
e-mail: persell@is.nyu.edu

Pine Ridge - e-mail: sales@pfp.sagepub.com

SCALE ANALYSIS

Title: NSCALE II: A Program to Analyze and Score
Multiscale Surveys and Test Batteries

Author: J. J. Ray and R. S. Bozek

Source: *Behavior Research Methods & Instrumentation,*
1978, 11, 402.

Description: This program performs various types of scale
analyses. In addition to examining each scale's internal consistency
and calculating interscale associations, the program is capable of
analyzing a single scale as if it were both a Likert and a Thurstone
scale. The program can also perform subscale analyses and can
execute a user-specified reverse scoring routine. Standard output
includes each subject's total scale and subscale scores, item
analyses and item level statistics, interscale correlations, and
correlations between the scales and demographic variables. The
user may also cluster analyze the matrix of interscale correlations.
The program can accommodate a maximum of 220 scale items
distributed among up to 23 scales.

Program Name: NSCALE II

Language: FORTRAN

Compatibility: IBM PC's and compatibles

Memory Requirements: 1 MG

Cost of Program: $5 (mailing costs)

How to obtain a copy of the program:

The source code and executable may be obtained by sending
a written request and payment to:

Dr. J. J. Ray
16 Gonzales St.
Macgregor 4109
Queensland
Australia

SCALE UNIDIMENSIONALITY

Title: A Program for Computing an Index of Scale
Unidimensionality

Author: John K. Butler, Jr.

Source: *Educational and Psychological Measurement,* 1983,
43, 845-847.

Description: This program computes an index of scale
unidimensionality (Green, Lissitz, & Mulaik, 1977) using either
raw data or the interitem correlation matrix. To the extent that the
first factor explains all of the scale variance, then the value of the
unidimensionality coefficient will be 1.00.

Program Name: None Specified

Language: SAS

Compatibility: Any computer with SAS capability

Memory Requirements: 240K

Cost of Program: No Charge

How to obtain a copy of the program:

Send a blank 3.5" diskette and a
self-addressed, stamped mailer to:

Dr. John K. Butler, Jr.
Management Department
College of Commerce and Industry
Clemson University
Clemson, SC 29634

SCALING - UNIDIMENSIONAL

Title: A BASIC Program for Calculating Scale Values Using Four Unidimensional Scaling Methods in Random Subsamples

Author: Jesús G. Molina, Jose L. Meliá, and Jaime Sanmartín

Source: *Educational and Psychological Measurement*, 1993, *53*, 103-105.

Description: This program computes scalar values from random subsamples or the entire data set using Thurstone's Case V, Thurstone-Chave's IAI, Green's successive categories, and Dunn-Rankin's variance stable rank sums. The input file consists of the number of items, number of cases needed in the subsample, and total number of cases. According to Dr. Molina, UniEscal is an improved version of this program. This reference may be found in *Psicologica* (1992), *13*, 89-93.

Program Name: UniEscal

Language: QuickBASIC

Compatibility: Macintosh

Memory Requirements: 246K

Cost of Program: No Charge

How to obtain a copy of the program:

Send a formatted 3.5" diskette and
a self-addressed, stamped mailer to:

Dr. Jesús Gabriel Molina
Facultad de Psicología
Area de Metodología
Av. Blasco Ibañez 21
46010-Valencia
Spain
e-mail: gabriel.molina@uv.es

SCALOGRAM ANALYSIS

Title: An Improvement Over Guttman Scalogram Analysis: A Computer Program for Evaluating Cumulative, Nonparametric Scales of Dichotomous Items

Author: Gary A. Cziko

Source: *Educational and Psychological Measurement,* 1984, *44,* 159-163.

Description: Because Guttman's (1944) coefficient of reproducibility is influenced by unidimensionality, cumulativeness, and the extremeness of items and subjects, a SAS program is provided (page 162) that performs Loevinger's H (cumulativeness of a set of items) and Mokken's H_i (degree of scalability of each item) which supposedly avoid the problems of Guttman's procedure. The data input consists of the 0,1 dichotomy.

Program Name: None Specified

Language: SAS (using the MATRIX procedure)

Compatibility: Any computer with SAS capabilities

Memory Requirements: None Specified

Cost of Program: No Charge

How to obtain a copy of the program:

Send a written request to:

Dr. Gary A. Cziko
Department of Educational Psychology
University of Illinois
1310 S. Sixth Street
Champaign, IL 61820

SCALOGRAM ANALYSIS

Title: GSCALE: Scalogram Analysis for Dichotomously
Scored Items

Author: Marilyn D. Wang

Source: *Behavior Research Methods & Instrumentation,*
1976, 8, 460-461.

Description: This program performs a unidimensional scalogram
(Guttman) analysis on a set of dichotomously scored items that
have been ranked in terms of either difficulty or popularity. Input
includes the number of subjects and items, and a subjects by items
data matrix. Output includes a rank ordering of the items with the
number of subjects passing each item, the coefficient of
reproducibility (R), tests of significance on R, and the value of R_I
which represents an index of item independence.

Program Name: GSCALE

Language: FORTRAN IV

Compatibility: VMS mainframes

Memory Requirements: None Specified

Cost of Program: No Charge

How to obtain a copy of the program:

Send a blank 3.5" diskette and a
self-addressed, stamped mailer to:

Dr. Marilyn Demorest
Department of Psychology
University of Maryland Baltimore County
1000 Hilltop Circle
Baltimore, MD 21250
e-mail: demorest@umbc2.umbc.edu

SCORE ABILITY ESTIMATES

Title: ABIL: An Interactive Microcomputer Program for Calculating Score Ability Estimates From Item Difficulty Statistics

Author: David E. W. Mott and Thomas O. Hall III

Source: *Educational and Psychological Measurement,* 1983, *43,* 159-162.

Description: This interactive program provides a table of ability estimates with standard errors and item difficulties derived from the Rasch model. Descriptive statistics such as the mean, variance, skewness, and kurtosis are also given. Finally, the ability estimate and item difficulty information is also plotted.

Program Name: ABIL

Language: FORTRAN

Compatibility: Macintosh

Memory Requirements: 512K

Cost of Program: No Charge

How to obtain a copy of the program:

Send a blank 3.5" diskette and a self-addressed, stamped mailer to:

Dr. David E. W. Mott
2821 Ellwood Avenue
Richmond, VA 23221
e-mail:demott@aol.com

SCREENING INDICES

Title: A BASIC Program to Compute the Sensitivity, Specificity, and Predictive Values of Screening Tests

Author: Herman R. Green and Jerrold H. Zar

Source: *Educational and Psychological Measurement*, 1989, *49*, 147-150.

Description: The program computes sensitivity, specificity, and positive and negative predictive values of a diagnostic test. The input consists of the number of true positive, true negative, false positive, and false negative results, and the population proportion. A listing of the program is provided on pages 149-150 of the article.

Program Name: None Specified

Language: BASIC

Compatibility: None Specified

Memory Requirements: None Specified

Cost of Program: No Charge

How to obtain a copy of the program:

Send a written request to:

Dr. Jerrold H. Zar
c/o Graduate School
205A Provost
Northern Illinois University
DeKalb, IL 60115
e-mail: t80jhz1@wpo.cso.niu.edu

SCREENING INDICES - QROC

Title: CUTOFF: A FORTRAN Program for Establishing
Thresholds for Screening Indices

Author: Dean P. McKenzie and David M. Clarke

Source: *Educational and Psychological Measurement,* 1992,
52, 891-893.

Description: The program can be used for establishing certain
cutoffs for separating individuals into two classes. The output
consists of sensitivity (making a correct positive diagnosis),
specificity (making a correct negative diagnosis), positive and
negative predictive power, and kappa statistics using a quality
receiver operating characteristic analysis. The input consists of a
standard ASCII data file.

Program Name: CUTOFF

Language: FORTRAN 77

Compatibility: IBM PC's and compatibles

Memory Requirements: None Specified

Cost of Program: No Charge

How to obtain a copy of the program:

Send a formatted 5.25" diskette and
a self-addressed, stamped mailer to:

Dr. Dean McKenzie
Biostatistics and Psychometrics Unit
Mental Health Research Institute
Royal Park Hospital
Private Bag 3
P.O. Parkville
Victoria, Australia 3052

SEGMENTED-CURVE MODELS

Title: A Program for Fitting Two-Phase Segmented Curve Models With an Unknown Change Point, With an Application to the Analysis of Strategy Shifts in a Cognitive Task

Author: A. Leo Beem

Source: *Behavior Research Methods, Instruments, & Computers,* 1995, *27,* 392-399.

Description: In order to examine strategy shifts in a cognitive task (e.g., mental rotation), a regression model in which there are two distinct equations (one for each of two mutually exclusive ranges of the independent variable) is provided. Moreover, estimated asymptotic variances, covariances, and correlations of the parameter estimates are given. The program can create the data file interactively or read from a specified data file.

Program Name: SEGCURVE

Language: Turbo Pascal

Compatibility: IBM PC's and compatibles

Memory Requirements: 60K. However, it depends on the size of the problem and the memory is allocated dynamically

Cost of Program: No Charge. However, $20 which includes distribution costs and a manual would be appreciated by Dr. Beem.

How to obtain a copy of the program:

Send a written request to:

Dr. A. Leo Beem
Centre for the Study of Education and Instruction
Leiden University
Wassenaarseweg 52
P.O. Box 9555
2300 RB Leiden
The Netherlands
e-mail: beem@rulfsw.leidenuniv.nl

SELECTING PREDICTORS

Title: Selecting Predictor Variables in Two-Group
Classification Problems

Author: John D. Morris and Alice Meshbane

Source: *Educational and Psychological Measurement*, 1995,
55, 438-441.

Description: For a two-group classification function (i.e.,
discriminant analysis), the program compares the cross-validated
classification accuracies of all possible subsets of predictor
variables and identifies the specified number of best subsets in toto
and for each subset size. The user inputs the file name (where raw
data are stored), sample size, number of predictor variables,
number of best subsets (and the size of each subset), group indices,
and codes for missing data. The output consists of group means,
the within-group covariance matrix, and estimates of the number of
correct classifications for the specified number of subsets (and for
each specified subset size).

Program Name: CLASSVSP

Language: Microsoft FORTRAN 5.0

Compatibility: IBM PC's and compatibles

Memory Requirements: 23,600 bytes

Cost of Program: No Charge

How to obtain a copy of the program:

Send a formatted 3.5" diskette and
a self-addressed, stamped mailer to:

Dr. Alice Meshbane
P.O. Box 2847
Boca Raton, FL 33427-2847
e-mail: meshbane@acc.fau.edu

SELECTION PROCEDURES

Title:　EVAL: A FORTRAN Program for the Evaluation of Selection Procedures

Author:　Eckhard Klieme and Heinrich Stumpf

Source:　*Educational and Psychological Measurement*, 1990, *50*, 127-130.

Description:　In order to examine questions such as predicting the proportion of successful employees selected for a specific job, this program provides success rates for a specific validity coefficient and certain selection ratios and base rates in accordance with the Taylor-Russell (1939) paradigm. The program also outputs hoist effects, which is the proportion of individuals of those persons selected by a second method but rejected in the first method. The tetrachoric coefficient and the probability values are also given.

Program Name:　EVAL

Language:　FORTRAN 77

Compatibility:　IBM PC's and compatibles

Memory Requirements:　None Specified

Cost of Program:　No Charge

How to obtain a copy of the program:

Send a formatted 3.5" diskette and
a self-addressed, stamped mailer to:

Dr. Eckhard Klieme
Institute for Educational Research
Koblenzer Strasse 77
D-53777
Bonn
Germany
e-mail: team@ibf.bn.evnet.de

SELECTION PROCEDURES

Title: SELECT3: A BASIC Program for Determining the Consequences of Using a Selection Procedure

Author: Brian Mullen

Source: *Behavior Research Methods, Instruments, & Computers*, 1985, *17*, 579.

Description: This program computes the mean criterion score for selected job applicants using the Naylor-Shine (1965) table. Moreover, an estimate of the number of dollars saved per year for each individual hired is also provided. The input consists of the mean and standard deviation of the criterion, the average yearly salary for individuals who were just hired, validity coefficient, and either the selection ratio or cutoff score of the predictor. This program may also have utility in teaching these basic concepts in an industrial/organizational psychology class.

Program Name: SELECT3

Language: BASIC

Compatibility: None Specified

Memory Requirements: 4000 bytes

Cost of Program: No Charge

How to obtain a copy of the program:

Send an MS-DOS formatted 3.5" diskette and a self-addressed, stamped mailer to:

Dr. Brian Mullen
Department of Psychology
Syracuse University
Syracuse, NY 13210
e-mail: bmullen@syr.edu

SEQUENTIAL ANALYSIS

Title: Testing Sequential Association: Estimating Exact *p* Values Using Sampled Permutations

Author: Roger Bakeman, Byron F. Robinson, and Vicenc Quera

Source: *Psychological Methods,* 1996, *1,* 4-15.

Description: This program utilizes permutation tests to analyze event sequences that arise in the context of sequential analysis studies. Like nonparametric tests, permutation tests can accommodate data that derive from nonnormal distributions. Furthermore, unlike asymptotic estimates (e.g., z, F, chi-square) that provide approximate probability levels, permutation tests yield exact *p* values. Input to the program consists of event sequential data files written in SDIS format (Bakeman & Quera, 1992, 1995). Standard output includes exact *p* values, mean *p* values, and confidence intervals for every cell in lags 1 through 10 (if so desired) in two-way contingency tables. By default, the program shuffles (permutes) the observed data sequences 10,000 times.

Program Name: PSEQ

Language: Borland C

Compatibility: IBM PC's and compatibles

Memory Requirements: None Specified

Cost of Program: No Charge

How to obtain a copy of the program:

May download from Internet: www.gsu.edu and search for Dr. Bakeman's website. For further information, contact:

Dr. Roger Bakeman
Department of Psychology
Georgia State University
University Plaza
Atlanta, GA 30303-3044
e-mail: bakeman@gsu.edu

SEQUENTIAL ANALYSIS

Title: Analyzing Sequential Categorical Data on Dyadic Interaction: A Latent Structure Approach

Author: William R. Dillon, Thomas J. Madden, and Ajith Kumar

Source: *Psychological Bulletin*, 1983, *94*, 564-583.

Description: In the course of discussing latent structure analysis as a Markov-type method for analyzing categorical sequential data, the authors make note of the Maximum Likelihood Latent Structure Analysis (MLLSA) computer program developed by C.C. Clogg. MLLSA can be used to test a number of different unrestricted and restricted latent structure models. The degree to which transitional probabilities and/or group membership are dependent upon latent class membership can also be examined. An additional feature of the program is that it calculates the rank of the full information matrix which allows the user to check the identifiability of the specified latent class model. This is an important feature given that poorly specified (or nonidentified) models typically yield erroneous parameter estimates.

Program Name: MLLSA

Language: None Specified

Compatibility: None Specified

Memory Requirements: None Specified

Cost of Program: None Specified

How to obtain a copy of the program:

To request possible payment information and obtain a copy of the program, contact:

Dr. Brian Jessup
Computer Core
Pennsylvania State University
University Park, PA 16802

SEQUENTIAL ANALYSIS

Title: Two PASCAL Programs for Managing Observational
Data Bases and for Performing Multivariate
Information Analysis and Log-Linear Contingency
Table Analysis of Sequential and Nonsequential Data

Author: David G. Schlundt

Source: *Behavior Research Methods & Instrumentation,*
1982, *14*, 351-352.

Description: The main program performs multivariate
information analysis and log-linear analysis of contingency tables
that contain either sequential or nonsequential data. In addition to
producing statistics relevant for assessing model fit, measures of
uncertainty and proportional reduction in uncertainty are also
calculated. Lagged analyses incorporating pairs of sequential
variables (if-then relationships) can also be evaluated. The second
program is a preprocessor program that allows the user to set up a
data base of behavioral observations that can then be analyzed by
the main program.

Program Name: SBA and SBA PREPROCESSOR

Language: PASCAL

Compatibility: Should run on any computer with a compiler
capable of reading standard PASCAL

Memory Requirements: At least 60K

Cost of Program: No Charge

How to obtain a copy of the program:

The program listings and user's manuals may be obtained by
contacting:

Dr. David G. Schlundt
Department of Psychology
301 Wilson Hall
Vanderbilt University
Nashville, TN 37240-0001

SEQUENTIAL DEPENDENCIES

Title: Identification of Sequential Dependencies in Conversations: A Pascal Program

Author: Portia E. File and John Todman

Source: *Behavior Research Methods, Instruments, & Computers,* 1994, *26,* 65-69.

Description: This program performs verbal protocol analysis (conversational events) using lag sequential analysis which measures how likely one type of event is likely to be immediately (or more distantly, given other extraneous events - called lags) followed by another type of event. The program outputs the 95% and 99% confidence intervals, chi-square statistic, and the binomial z statistic. Moreover, estimated conditional and unconditional probabilities of valid (selected) events, and the observed and expected frequencies of these events are also provided. Autocorrelated adjustment results are also available. An example of the output is provided on pages 68 and 69.

Program Name: CONSEQ

Language: PASCAL

Compatibility: VAX/VMS, IBM PC's and compatibles

Memory Requirements: 1.5 MB memory and 40K disk space for the VAX/VMS version, 20K for the IBM compatible version

Cost of Program: No Charge

How to obtain a copy of the program:

Send a formatted 3.5" high-density diskette and a self-addressed, stamped mailer to:

Dr. Portia E. File
School of Informatics
University of Abertay Dundee
Bell Street
Dundee
DD1 1HG
Scotland, U.K.
e-mail: p.file@tay.ac.uk

SET CORRELATION

Title: CORSET: A FORTRAN IV Program for Set
Correlation Analysis

Author: Jacob Cohen and John Nee

Source: *Educational and Psychological Measurement,* 1983,
43, 817-820.

Description: This program performs set correlation, which is a
multivariate extension of multiple regression analysis, in which
relationships are examined between sets of variables and other sets
of variables can be partialled out. By partialling, this allows
interpretable components of sets to be identified. The input
consists of either correlation or variance-covariance matrices. The
output consists of Rao's F, Bartlett's chi-square, Pillai's F,
canonical roots, R^2, Hotelling's T^2, and regression coefficients for
each variable. Up to 500 variables may be used.

Program Name: CORSET

Language: FORTRAN

Compatibility: IBM PC's and compatibles

Memory Requirements: 64K

Cost of Program: $100 (manual is free of charge)

How to obtain a copy of the program:

Send a written request and payment to:

Dr. John Nee
Department of Math and Computer Science
Bridgewater State College
131 Summer St.
Bridgewater, MA 02324

SIGNAL DETECTION ANALYSIS

Title: A Computer Program to Generate Parametric and Nonparametric Signal-Detection Parameters

Author: Russel Boice and Rick M. Gardner

Source: *Bulletin of the Psychonomic Society*, 1988, *26*, 365-367.

Description: This program computes several signal-detection parameters that are of utility in psychophysical research including parametric and nonparametric measures of both sensory sensitivity and response bias. The only user input required is the proportion of hits and false alarms.

Program Name: None Specified

Language: Turbo Pascal

Compatibility: Any computer that supports Turbo Pascal.

Memory Requirements: None Specified

Cost of Program: No Charge

How to obtain a copy of the program:

The source code is contained in the appendix of the article. Send either a 3.5" or 5.25" diskette and a self-addressed, stamped mailer to:

Dr. Rick M. Gardner
Department of Psychology
University of Colorado at Denver
Campus Box 173
P.O. Box 173364
Denver, CO 80217-3364
e-mail:rgardner@carbon.cudenver.edu

SIGNAL DETECTION ANALYSIS

Title: Alternatives to a Table of Criterion Values in Signal Detection Theory

Author: Alfred L. Brophy

Source: *Behavior Research Methods, Instruments, & Computers*, 1986, *18*, 285-286.

Description: This program computes beta (magnitude of the stringency of the criterion that the individual uses when supposedly detecting that a signal was present) and d', the sensitivity index (measure of stimulus detectability). The short BASIC program is shown on page 286.

Program Name: None Specified

Language: BASIC

Compatibility: None Specified

Memory Requirements: None Specified

Cost of Program: No Charge

How to obtain a copy of the program:

Send a written request to:

Dr. Alfred L. Brophy
Behavioral Sciences Associates
P.O. Box 748
West Chester, PA 19381

SIGNAL DETECTION ANALYSIS

Title: SDT_SP, a Program in Pascal for Computing Parameters and Significance Tests from Several Detection Theory Designs

Author: Jose M. Reales and Soledad Ballesteros

Source: *Behavior Research Methods, Instruments, & Computers*, 1994, *26*, 151-155.

Description: This menu-driven program (available in both English and Spanish) computes parameters from one-interval designs, rating experiments, and two-alternative (and modified alternative) forced-choice designs. Receiver operating characteristic curves and group d's are output. Significance tests for the one-parameter model and nonparametric analysis (e.g., A' - index of sensitivity for only one data point), and Hodos, Grier, and Donaldson's indices of bias are also output.

Program Name: SDT_SP

Language: Turbo Pascal (Version 7.0)

Compatibility: IBM PC's and compatibles

Memory Requirements: 300K

Cost of Program: No Charge

How to obtain a copy of the program:

Send a formatted 3.5" diskette and
a self-addressed, stamped mailer to:

Dr. Soledad Ballesteros
Departamento de Psicologia Basica II
P.B. Apartado 50487
Madrid
Spain
e-mail: sballest@cu.umed.es

SINGLE CASE DESIGNS

Title: SCRT 1.1: Single-Case Randomization Tests

Author: Patrick Onghena and Geert Van Damme

Source: *Behavior Research Methods, Instruments, & Computers,* 1993, *25*, 369.

Description: This program analyzes and graphs data from alternating treatment designs, multiple baseline designs, and AB designs. These analyses are based on randomization tests. Additionally, descriptive statistics and an option for data transformation is also provided. The program can be operated either by keyboard or via a mouse. The input data can either come from an ASCII file or via the program's data editor.

Program Name: SCRT (version 1.1)

Language: None Specified

Compatibility: IBM PC's and compatibles (with at least DOS 2.0)

Memory Requirements: 640K RAM

Cost of Program: $20

How to obtain a copy of the program:

For the program, manual, and file with examples, send a written request and payment to:

Dr. Patrick Onghena
Katholieke Universiteit Leuven
Department of Psychology
Tiensestraat 102
B-3000
Leuven, Belgium
e-mail: patrick.onghena@psy.kuleuven.ac.be

SMOOTHING DATA

Title: SMOOTH: A BASIC Program for Smoothing a Data Series

Author: Michael J. Strube

Source: *Behavior Research Methods, Instruments, & Computers,* 1986, *18,* 475.

Description: This program uses the 53R'H method (Hartwig & Dearing, 1979), which runs medians across five, three, and two data points, for softening the influence of outliers in a data set. This procedure aids in determining trends in the data. The data may be either directly entered into the program or provided on disk.

Program Name: SMOOTH

Language: BASIC

Compatibility: IBM PC's and compatibles

Memory Requirements: None Specified

Cost of Program: No Charge

How to obtain a copy of the program:

Send a written request to:

Dr. Michael J. Strube
Department of Psychology
Washington University
St. Louis, MO 63130
e-mail: mjstrube@artsci.wustl.edu

SOCIOMETRIC ANALYSIS

Title: SHED: A FORTRAN IV Program for the Analysis of Small Group Sociometric Structure

Author: Elliot Noma and D. Randall Smith

Source: *Behavior Research Methods & Instrumentation,* 1978, *10,* 60-62.

Description: This program breaks down an N by N sociomatrix by sorting, counting and analyzing the dyad and triad types. When defining the triad types (or trichotomized sociometric data), either (a) a positive-nonpositive affect dichotomous coding scheme can be used, in which case there would be 16 triad types, or (b) a positive-negative-indifferent trichotomous coding scheme can be used which would give rise to 138 triad types. Regardless of the coding scheme employed, the program attempts to model the data in an effort to uncover the best underlying sociometric structure. Output includes the observed and expected values for each dyad and triad type, the variance of each expected value, and a *z*-score and significance level for each dyad and triad type. The tau and tau-split statistics are also computed for each group of critical triads. The program will analyze any number of groups containing 40 or fewer individuals.

Program Name: Version 2

Language: FORTRAN IV

Compatibility: Any computer that supports FORTRAN

Memory Requirements: About 1 MB

Cost of Program: No Charge

How to obtain a copy of the program:

Send a blank formatted 3.5" diskette and a self-addressed, stamped mailer to:

Dr. D. Randall Smith
Department of Sociology
Lucy Stone Hall
Rutgers University
New Brunswick, NJ 08903
e-mail: drasmith@rci.rutgers.edu

SORTING DATA

Title: Ranking Data with BASIC

Author: Jerrold H. Zar

Source: *Behavior Research Methods, Instruments, & Computers,* 1985, *17,* 142.

Description: This program provides a procedure for sorting data. This algorithm can be used, for example, for assigning ranks to data for use in various nonparametric procedures or for testing individual correlations in a matrix using the rank adjusted method (Stavig & Acock, 1976) or a modification of that procedure (Silver, 1989).

Program Name: None Specified

Language: BASIC

Compatibility: None Specified

Memory Requirements: None Specified

Cost of Program: No Charge

How to obtain a copy of the program:

Send a written request to:

Dr. Jerrold H. Zar
c/o Graduate School
205A Provost
Northern Illinois University
DeKalb, IL 60115
e-mail: t80jhz1@wpo.cso.niu.edu

STANDARDIZING

Title: EQUATE: Linear and Equipercentile Equating

Author: Gary W. Phillips and Sandra S. Gedeik

Source: *Applied Psychological Measurement*, 1984,
             8, 306.

Description: The program provides a table of equated scores using the linear and equipercentile methods, percentile ranks, z-scores, means, standard deviations, and the Kuder-Richardson 20. This program can be used when either one or more tests are administered to each group. The Tukey-Cureton 7-point rolling average smoothing procedure is an option on the inputted frequency distributions.

Program Name: EQUATE

Language: FORTRAN IV

Compatibility: HP3000-68 (however, minor modifications may be needed to accommodate various mainframes and PC's)

Memory Requirements: None Specified

Cost of Program: No Charge

How to obtain a copy of the program:

Send a formatted MS-DOS 3.5" diskette and a self-addressed, stamped mailer to:

Dr. Gary W. Phillips
U.S. Department of Education
555 New Jersey Avenue
Washington, DC 20208

STATISTICAL ANALYSIS

Title: PSYCHO-STATS 80: A Basic Statistical Package for the TRS-80

Author: David E. Anderson

Source: *Behavior Research Methods & Instrumentation*, 1980, *12*, 565.

Description: This statistical package represents a translation of most of Gilbert's (1979) "PSYCHOSTATS" programs to TRS-80 BASIC. Several additional programs that were not contained in the original PSYCHOSTATS package have also been included. Among the statistical procedures performed are repeated measures ANOVA, correlation, linear regression, analysis of covariance, chi-square analysis, and nonparametrics. The program is also capable of analyzing Latin square designs and of generating bivariate scatterplots. A new version (not for the TRS-80) is presented.

Program Name: PSYC-STATS (new version)

Language: BASIC

Compatibility: IBM PC's and compatibles

Memory Requirements: 500K

Cost of Program: $12 (unless you send two double-density diskettes and mailer - then there is no charge).

How to obtain a copy of the program:

Send two formatted 3.5" diskettes and a self-addressed, stamped mailer to:

Dr. David E. Anderson
Director of Academic Computing
Allegheny College
520 Main St.
Meadville, PA 16335
e-mail:danders@alleg.edu

STATISTICAL ANALYSIS

Title: An Intelligent Computer Based Learning Program

Author: George A. Marcoulides

Source: *Collegiate Microcomputer, 1988, 6, 123-126.*

Description: An interactive expert system designed to provide statistical consultation is discussed. The program prompts the user for all relevant information and, using a rule-based system, assists the user in choosing the correct statistical procedure. In response to the data prompt, the user may input either raw data or intermediate values (e.g., means and standard deviations). The program is capable of performing hypothesis tests via independent and dependent samples z-tests and t-tests, as well as independent groups and repeated measures analysis of variance.

Program Name: ZEERA

Language: PASCAL

Compatibility: IBM PC's and compatibles

Memory Requirements: 640K

Cost of Program: No Charge

How to obtain a copy of the program:

Send either a 3.5" or 5.25" diskette and a self-addressed, stamped mailer to:

Dr. George A. Marcoulides
Langsdorf Hall 540
California State University
Fullerton, CA 92634
e-mail: gmarcoulides@fullerton.edu

STATISTICAL TECHNIQUES - TUTORIAL

Title: A Guide to Statistical Techniques in Psychology and Education

Author: Gordon Rae

Source: *Behavior Research Methods & Instrumentation,* 1980, *12,* 469-470.

Description: This interactive program advises students as to the most appropriate statistical technique to use for a variety of univariate procedures. The assumptions associated with each procedure are also noted. The program is designed to tutor students on three separate categories of statistical procedures: (1) measures of the association between two variables, (2) multiple comparison tests, and (3) parametric and nonparametric tests that assess whether a given sample could have been derived from a specified population. For each statistical technique, references to relevant textbooks and journal articles are provided.

Program Name: None Specified

Language: BASIC

Compatibility: Any computer that supports BASIC

Memory Requirements: None Specified

Cost of Program: No Charge

How to obtain a copy of the program:

The program listing and sample output may be obtained by contacting:

Dr. Gordon Rae
School of Behavioral and Communication Sciences
University of Ulster
Coleraine
Northern Ireland
BT52 1SA

STEPWISE REGRESSION - BINARY

Title: A SAS Macro for Stepwise Correlated Binary Regression

Author: Isaac F. Nuamah, Yinsheng Qu, and Saeid B. Amini

Source: *Computer Methods and Programs in Biomedicine, 1996, 49,* 199-210.

Description: This program performs stepwise regression analysis for correlated binary response variables. In evaluating predictors for model inclusion, the stepwise procedure employs a score test for forward selection as well as Wald's test for backward elimination. The primary purpose of the program is to select, from an initial set of correlated covariates, a reduced set of statistically significant covariates. The statistical significance of the final model is tested using the generalized score test for model adequacy.

Program Name: STEPGEE

Language: SAS

Compatibility: Any system capable of supporting SAS

Memory Requirements: None Specified

Cost of Program: No Charge

How to obtain a copy of the program:

Send a formatted 3.5" diskette and a self-addressed, stamped mailer to:

Dr. Isaac F. Nuamah
University of Pennsylvania Cancer Center
528 Blockley Hall
Philadelphia, PA 19101-6021
e-mail: nuamah@mail.med.upenn.edu

STRUCTURAL EQUATION MODELING

Title: Computing Reproduced Correlations in Structural
Equation Models

Author: Richard F. Haase and Harlen R. Juster

Source: *Educational and Psychological Measurement,* 1986,
46, 157-161.

Description: This program provides reproduced correlation
matrices from computed path coefficients from the algorithm
found in Heise (1969). This aids in determining the goodness-of-
fit of the model. The input consists of a matrix containing the path
coefficients of the endogenous and exogenous variables. An
example of the input and output are given in the article.

Program Name: None Specified

Language: BASIC

Compatibility: Any computer that supports BASIC

Memory Requirements: None Specified

Cost of Program: No Charge

How to obtain a copy of the program:

Send an MS-DOS formatted 3.5" diskette
and a self-addressed, stamped mailer to:

Dr. Richard F. Haase
Department of Counseling Psychology
State University of New York at albany
ED 220
1400 Washington Avenue
Albany, NY 12222

STRUCTURAL EQUATION MODELING

Title: X.EXE: A Program for Simplifying EQS Input

Author: Ron D. Hays

Source: *Applied Psychological Measurement,* 1988,
12, 322.

Description: The program input consists of the title, number of cases, type of analysis, latent variables, and relationships among the variables and converts this information into EQS language for prospective analysis. EQS is a program developed by Bentler (1985) for performing structural equation modeling. This program aids those researchers who think more conceptually rather than algebraically.

Program Name: X.EXE

Language: BASIC

Compatibility: IBM PC's and compatibles

Memory Requirements: Minimal

Cost of Program: No Charge

How to obtain a copy of the program:

Send a formatted 3.5" diskette and
a self-addressed, stamped mailer to:

Dr. Ron D. Hays
The RAND Corporation
1700 Main Street
P.O. Box 2138
Santa Monica, CA 90407-2138
Internet: Ronald_Hays@rand.org

STRUCTURAL EQUATION MODELING

Title: LISPATH: A Program for Generating Structural Equation Path Diagrams

Author: George A. Marcoulides and Dimos Papadopoulos

Source: *Educational and Psychological Measurement*, 1993, *53*, 675-678.

Description: This program outputs and prints a structural equation path diagram using the model structure input from a LISREL command file. The program accommodates up to 80 observed and 35 latent variables.

Program Name: LISPATH

Language: Turbo Pascal 5.5

Compatibility: IBM PC's and compatibles

Memory Requirements: 640K

Cost of Program: No Charge

How to obtain a copy of the program:

Send either a formatted 3.5" or 5.25" diskette and a self-addressed, stamped mailer to:

Dr. George A. Marcoulides
Langdorf Hall 540
California State University
Fullerton, CA 92634
e-mail: gmarcoulides@fullerton.edu

STRUCTURAL EQUATION MODELING

Title: GEMINI: Program for Analysis of Structural Equations
With Standard Errors of Indirect Effects

Author: Lee M. Wolfle and Corinna A. Ethington

Source: *Behavior Research Methods, Instruments, & Computers,*
1985, 17, 581-584.

Description: This program provides matrices of direct effects,
unstandardized indirect effects and standard errors, and *t* statistics
and their probabilities. Furthermore, for each equation in the
model, the multiple correlation, the coefficient of determination,
standard error of estimate, unstandardized and standardized
regression coefficients, *t* statistics and their probabilities are
output. Summary statistics from the input (e.g., means, standard
deviations, correlation matrix, and sample size) are also included.
The input consists of the number of variables to be analyzed,
number of endogenous variables, sample size, correlation matrix,
means and standard deviations, dependent variable, number of
independent variables, and order of the causal model.

Program Name: GEMINI

Language: FORTRAN 77

Compatibility: IBM mainframes

Memory Requirements: None Specified

Cost of Program: No Charge

How to obtain a copy of the program:

Send either a formatted 3.5" or 5.25" diskette
and a self-addressed, stamped mailer to:

Dr. Lee M. Wolfle
College of Human Resources and Education
311 E. Eggleston
Virginia Polytechnic Institute and State University
Blacksburg, VA 24060-0302
wolfle@vtvm1.ec.vt.edu

SUBJECTIVE ORGANIZATION

Title: An SPSS Program to Compute Subjective Organization

Author: Joseph K. Kazen and Hajime Otani

Source: *Behavior Research Methods, Instruments, & Computers,*
1996, 28, 476-478.

Description: This program computes a number of measures of
subjective organization (clustering) of free recall data, for example.
These measures include Pellegrino's ARC' for bidirectional pairs
and unordered triplets, Tulving's (1962) subjective organization
measure, and Bousfield and Bousfield's (1966) deviation measure
for bidirectional pairs. The input consists of a set of SPSS
statements. An example of how to create a data file is presented on
page 477 of the article.

Program Name: None Specified

Language: SPSS

Compatibility: Any computer system that supports SPSS

Memory Requirements: None Specified

Cost of Program: No Charge

How to obtain a copy of the program:

Send a formatted 3.5" diskette and
a self-addressed, stamped mailer to:

Dr. Hajimi Otani
Department of Psychology
Central Michigan University
Mount Pleasant, MI 48859
e-mail: hajime.otani@cmich.edu

SUMMARY STATISTICS

Title: A_STAT: Statistical Hypotheses and Utilities (Version 2.0)

Author: John R. Reddon

Source: *Applied Psychological Measurement,* 1992, *16,* 86.

Description:

a) Means
b) Variances
c) Correlations
d) Bernoulli trials
e) Skewness and kurtosis
f) Cumulative percent for normal, t, chi-square, or F distributions
g) Percentiles for normal, t, chi-square, or F distributions
h) Testing procedures (e.g., coefficient alpha)

Information on these procedures and output files are also available.

Program Name: A_STAT (Statistical Hypotheses and Utilities - Version 2.1)

Language: FORTRAN 77

Compatibility: IBM PC's and compatibles

Memory Requirements: 533KB

Cost of Program: No Charge

How to obtain a copy of the program:

Send either a formatted 3.5" or 5.25" diskette and a self-addressed, stamped mailer to:

Dr. John R. Reddon
Research Centre
Alberta Hospital Edmonton
Box 307
Edmonton, Alberta
T5J 2J7
Canada
e-mail: jreddon@pmhab.ab.ca

SURFACE MAPPING

Title: Reconciling Data From Different Geographic
Databases

Author: Kenneth E. Hinze

Source: *Social Science Computer Review, 1989, 7, 285-295.*

Description: Discusses and provides examples of the data
reconciliation routine contained in PC DATAGRAPHICS AND
MAPPING (PCDM; Hinze, 1989). The purpose of the
reconciliation routine is to combine, for purposes of data analysis,
information that was collected on different geographic sampling
units. PCDM accomplishes this goal by comparing continuous
spatial surfaces or statistical density functions across geographic
databases (known as geobases). This procedure allows for
variables from different geobases or statistical surfaces to be
combined as if they originated from the same geographic structure.

Program Name: PC DATAGRAPHICS AND MAPPING

Language: None Specified

Compatibility: IBM PC's and compatibles

Memory Requirements: 256K

Cost of Program: None Specified

How to obtain a copy of the program:

For ordering and price information, please contact:

Technical Support
West Publishing Company
610 Opperman Drive
Eagan, MN 55123

SURVIVAL ANALYSIS

Title: SURVIVAL - An Integrated Software Package for Survival Curve Estimation and Statistical Comparison of Survival Rates of Two Groups of Patients or Experimental Animals

Author: Mária Durišová and Ladislav Dedík

Source: *Methods and Findings in Experimental and Clinical Pharmacology*, 1993, *15*, 535-540.

Description: This program estimates survival curves via the Kaplan-Meier approach and utilizes the Mantel-Haenszel and/or Fisher's test to compare the survival rates between two censored or uncensored groups of subjects (patients or animals). The program's data handling capacity allows for a maximum of 600 subjects. The user may input data in the form of either dates (e.g., the date of diagnosis; the date of the patient's death) or survival times. In addition to the executable file, a help file is included that explains the program's capabilities and discusses the principles underlying the Mantel-Haenszel and Fisher's tests.

Program Name: SURVIVAL

Language: TURBO PASCAL

Compatibility: IBM PC's and compatibles (VGA monitor)

Memory Requirements: 240KB

Cost of Program: $80

How to obtain a copy of the program:

Send either a formatted 3.5" or 5.25" diskette, a self-addressed, stamped mailer, and payment to:

Mária Durišová
Institute of Experimental Pharmacology
Slovak Academy of Sciences
84216 Bratislava
Slovak Republic
e-mail: exfamadu@savba.sk

t DISTRIBUTION

Title: Efficient Estimation of Probabilities in the *t* Distribution

Author: Alfred L. Brophy

Source: *Behavior Research Methods, Instruments, & Computers,* 1987, *19,* 462-466.

Description: This program provides a list of a number of approximations of the probabilities of *t*. The author concluded that the Hill (1970) asymptotic approximation is recommended for being reasonably accurate given the short subroutine. A listing of the approximations is provided on page 463.

Program Name: None Specified

Language: GW-BASIC

Compatibility: IBM PC's and compatibles

Memory Requirements: None Specified

Cost of Program: No Charge

How to obtain a copy of the program:

Send a written request to:

Dr. Alfred L. Brophy
Behavioral Science Associates
P. O. Box 748
West Chester, PA 19381

t PROBABILITY

Title: TINT: A Microsoft BASIC *t* Integration Program

Author: D. Louis Wood and Dianne Wood

Source: *Behavior Research Methods, Instruments, & Computers,* 1984, *16*, 479-480.

Description: This program numerically integrates the density function of the *t* distribution via Simpson's rule. Input consists of the number of degrees of freedom for the problem and the value of *t*. The program outputs the "area within" (i.e., the chance probability of a *t* having a smaller absolute value than the *t* entered) and the "area beyond" (i.e., the two-tailed probability). The author is willing to furnish a copy of GWBASICA upon request.

Program Name: TINT

Language: GWBASICA

Compatibility: IBM PC's and compatibles

Memory Requirements: None Specified

Cost of Program: No Charge

How to obtain a copy of the program:

Send either a 3.5" or 5.25" formatted diskette and a self-addressed, stamped mailer to:

Dr. D. Louis Wood
University of Arkansas at Little Rock
2801 South University
Little Rock, AR 72204

t TEST

Title: A SAS Macro for Producing SAS *t* Test Output When Raw Data are Not Available

Author: Kevin P. Weinfurt

Source: *Applied Psychological Measurement*, 1996, *20*, 99.

Description: This macro program produces a two-sample independent *t*-test by inputting sample sizes, means, and standard deviations. The *F*-max test is also included.

Program Name: TTEST.BAS

Language: SAS

Compatibility: Any system that implements SAS

Memory Requirements: None Specified

Cost of Program: No Charge

How to obtain a copy of the program:

Send a formatted 3.5" diskette and a self-addressed, stamped mailer to:

Dr. Kevin P. Weinfurt
Department of Psychiatry
Georgetown University Medical Center
3750 Reservoir Road, NW
Washington, DC 20007
e-mail: kweinf@gumedlib.dml.georgetown.edu

TAXOMETRICS

Title: Simple Regression-Based Procedures for Taxometric
Investigations

Author: William M. Grove and Paul E. Meehl

Source: *Psychological Reports,* 1993, *73,* 707-737.

Description: Examines whether a sample is derived from the
mixing of different latent populations or taxa. The procedure
entails fitting a quadratic regression function to the section of the
data where a maximum slope appears to occur. The resultant
regression slope is then smoothed and its maximum is examined.
The latter maximum is interpreted as the most probable point of
intersection between latent taxa.

Program Name: MAXSLOPE

Language: S-Plus

Compatibility: IBM PC's and compatibles (iAPX386
machines or higher)

Memory Requirements: None Specified

Cost of Program: $7.75 for photocopy of code or $4.00 for
microfiche

How to obtain a copy of the program:

Send a written request and payment (specifying whether photocopy
or fiche is desired) to:

National Auxiliary Publications Service
c/o Microfiche Publications
Re: Document NAPS-05050
POB 3513
Grand Central Station
New York, NY 10163

TEACHING MEASUREMENT THEORY

Title: Illustration of the Theory of True and Error Scores:
Computer Based Method of Idealized Data Sets

Author: David J. Krus and Ellen A. Fuller

Source: *Educational and Psychological Measurement,* 1982,
42, 837-841.

Description: This program permits students to construct idealized
data matrices (either via the terminal or in a separate data file) that
should conform to classical test theory assumptions. The
hypothetical data for two test halves are examined in terms of
means and variances and intercorrelations are provided between
obtained, true, and error scores. Finally, a degree of congruence
between the hypothetical data structure and the structure that
would be postulated by classical test theory (true and error scores)
provides students with performance feedback.

Program Name: None Specified

Language: FORTRAN

Compatibility: None Specified

Memory Requirements: None Specified

Cost of Program: No Charge

How to obtain a copy of the program:

Send a blank 3.5" diskette and a
self-addressed, stamped mailer to:

Dr. David J. Krus
Educational Psychology Department
Arizona State University
Tempe, AZ 85287-0611

TEACHING STATISTICS

Title: A Simulation Laboratory for Statistics

Author: Drake R. Bradley, Robert L. Hemstreet, and
Susan T. Ziegenhausen

Source: *Behavior Research Methods, Instruments, & Computers,*
1992, *24,* 190-204.

Description: This program simulates sampling distributions,
central limit theorem, Type I and Type II errors, power, orthogonal
and nonorthogonal comparisons, partial correlation, regression
toward the mean, and the effects of violating normality and
homoscedasticity assumptions (among other statistical concepts)
for the purposes of statistics instruction. The program, which also
allows for various plots, is menu driven (similar to windows).

Program Name: DATASIM 1.1 (IBM); DATASIM 1.2
(Macintosh)

Language: TrueBASIC 2.62

Compatibility: IBM PC's and compatibles, Apple Mac II and
newer

Memory Requirements: 640 K for IBM, 2 MB for Macintosh

Cost of Program: $35 for IBM version; $55 for Macintosh

How to obtain a copy of the program:

Send a written request and payment to:

Dr. Drake Bradley
Desktop Press
90 Bardwell Street
Lewiston, ME 04240
e-mail: dbradley@abacus.bates.edu

TEACHING STATISTICS

Title: Data Generation and Analysis Using Spreadsheets

Author: Douglas B. Eamon

Source: *Behavior Research Methods, Instruments, & Computers,*
      1992, *24,* 174-179.

Description: General instructions (templates) for macroprograms
are provided for between- and within-groups *t*-tests and analysis of
variance. These programs have utility for teaching these basic
concepts using various spreadsheet programs (e.g., Lotus 1-2-3).
These listings are provided in the text.

Program Name: None Specified

Language: None Specified

Compatibility: None Specified

Memory Requirements: None Specified

Cost of Program: No Charge

How to obtain a copy of the program:

Send an MS-DOS formatted 3.5" diskette
and a self-addressed, stamped mailer to:

Dr. Douglas B. Eamon
Department of Psychology
University of Wisconsin
Whitewater, WI 53190
e-mail: eamond@uwwvax.uww.edu

TEST BIAS

Title: Assessing Predictive Test Bias With the Microcomputer

Author: Leon D. Larimer and Marley W. Watkins

Source: *Behavior Research Methods & Instrumentation,* 1980, *12,* 568.

Description: For cases in which a single independent variable is used to predict a single dependent variable, this program calculates both simultaneous and separate tests of regression slopes and intercepts in order to examine data for the presence of test bias. A statistically significant F-test indicates predictive test bias. User input consists of the number of groups and the predictor and criterion scores for each group member. The output includes three F ratios (the simultaneous test of slopes and intercepts, the separate test of slopes, and the separate test of intercepts) as well as the probability values associated with each F ratio.

Program Name: None Specified

Language: Applesoft BASIC

Compatibility: Designed for the Apple II microcomputer. The code can be modified to accommodate other versions of BASIC.

Memory Requirements: A minimum of 6K

Cost of Program: No Charge

How to obtain a copy of the program:

Send a written request to:

Dr. Marley W. Watkins
Penn State University
227 Cedar Bldg
University Park, PA 16802
e-mail:mww10@psu.edu

TEST BIAS

Title: A Microcomputer BASIC Program to Calculate
Univariable Regression Model Analysis of Test Bias

Author: Marley W. Watkins and Leon D. Larimer

Source: *Educational and Psychological Measurement*, 1981,
41, 219-221.

Description: This interactive program evaluates bias using the
regression algorithm of Potthoff (1966) in which a significant F
test from the omnibus test would indicate that test bias exists.
Subsequent tests then indicate whether this bias is constant or
differs as a function of the distance of the scores from the mean.
The input consists of the number of groups and the raw data of the
independent and dependent variables.

Program Name: None Specified

Language: Applesoft BASIC

Compatibility: Apple IIe microcomputers

Memory Requirements: 48K

Cost of Program: No Charge

How to obtain a copy of the program:

Send a written request to:

Dr. Marley W. Watkins
Penn State University
227 Cedar Bldg
University Park, PA 16802
e-mail:mww10@psu.edu

TETRACHORIC CORRELATION

Title: TETRA: A FORTRAN IV Program for Computing the Cosine-Pi Approximation to the Tetrachoric Correlation Coefficient

Author: Gilbert Becker and John Hilton

Source: *Educational and Psychological Measurement*, 1992, *52*, 81-85.

Description: When arbitararily dichotomizing variables, a loss of power may ensue relative to the product-moment correlation used on continuous data. To obtain a more accurate estimate of the relationship, a tetrachoric correlation is used. Because the actual formula for the tetrachoric correlation is incredibly complex, a cosine-pi approximation (Pearson, 1901) is offered. The input consists of the number of variables (up to 150), the format specification and the data. Output consists of a square matrix of cosine-pi approximations to the tetrachoric correlation and the number of cases for each 2 x 2 binomial combination is provided as output.

Program Name: TETRA

Language: FORTRAN IV

Compatibility: Amdahl-5870

Memory Requirements: None Specified

Cost of Program: No Charge

How to obtain a copy of the program:

For a listing, send a written request to:

Dr. Gilbert Becker
Department of Psychology
University of Winnipeg
Winnipeg, MB
Canada R3B 2E9

TIME SERIES ANALYSIS

Title: Algorithm for Autocorrelation Analysis of Secular
Trends

Author: David J. Krus and Hyon O. Ko

Source: *Educational and Psychological Measurement*, 1983,
43, 821-828.

Description: Autocorrelation analysis is important in determining
whether components in the series are cyclic or of random origin.
This subroutine (shown on page 825) computes the true product-
moment autocorrelation coefficients throughout a lagged time
series.

Program Name: None Specified

Language: FORTRAN

Compatibility: None Specified

Memory Requirements: None Specified

Cost of Program: No Charge

How to obtain a copy of the program:

Send an MS-DOS 5.25" formatted diskette
and a self-addressed, stamped mailer to:

Dr. David J. Krus
Educational Psychology Department
Arizona State University
Tempe, AZ 85287-0611

TIME SERIES - AUTOCORRELATION

Title: Confidence Intervals for Statistical Inference in
Single-Subject Research: A BASIC Program

Author: Greg Hilliker and Bruce A. Thyer

Source: *Behavioral Engineering*, 1985, *9*, 88-93.

Description: Tests each phase of sequentially collected data from
a single-subject experiment for lag-1 autocorrelation and then
calculates the difference between the means of any two phases
(adjacent or nonadjacent). A confidence interval for the mean
difference is then computed which, when interpreted in
conjunction with *p*-values, minimizes the probability of Type I
errors and aids in the evaluation of treatment effects.

Program Name: CONFICALC

Language: BASIC

Compatibility: Any computer that supports BASIC

Memory Requirements: None Specified

Cost of Program: No Charge

How to obtain a copy of the program:

The complete BASIC code is contained in the appendix of the
source article. For further information contact:

Dr. Bruce A. Thyer
School of Social Work
University of Georgia
Athens, GA 30602
e-mail: bthyer@uga.cc.uga.edu

TIME SERIES - KALMAN FILTER

Title: Detection of Change in Physiological Measures Using an Adaptive Kalman Filter Algorithm

Author: Richard A. Heath

Source: *Psychological Bulletin,* 1984, *96,* 581-588.

Description: This program analyzes a time series of observations using an optimal linear prediction method known as the Kalman filter (Gregson, 1983). The Kalman filter is a powerful procedure for handling nonstationarities and, during the change-detection or parameter estimation/updating process, the autocorrelation coefficients are adjusted automatically. In this regard, the Kalman filter procedure is advantageous over traditional autoregressive models. The manner by which parameter changes are detected is through accumulation of the residuals generated by the Kalman filter and then testing whether the residual pattern deviates from a white noise series of residuals.

Program Name: KALMAN

Language: FORTRAN 77

Compatibility: VMS/VAX and UNIX mainframes, IBM PC's and compatibles. The program code can be modified for use with Macintosh computers.

Memory Requirements: None Specified

Cost of Program: No Charge

How to obtain a copy of the program:

Send a blank formatted 3.5" diskette and a self-addressed, stamped mailer to:

Dr.Richard A. Heath
Department of Psychology
The University of Newcastle
University Drive
Callaghan New South Wales, 2308
Australia
e-mail: rheath@hiplab.newcastle.edu.au

TIME SERIES - TREND

Title: TMSGN: A Program for Testing Trend Against a Nonrandom Alternative

Author: Ronald L. Ray, Henry H. Emurian, and Richard M. Wurster

Source: *Behavior Research Methods & Instrumentation,* 1982, *14,* 355-356.

Description: Performs a modification of Cox's sign test (Cox & Stuart, 1955) for detecting trend in time series data. In particular, the Cox algorithm has been modified based on the results of Goodman (1963) and Sen (1965) so that it can accommodate dependent (i.e., serially correlated) data points. The modified time-series sign test, which is approximately distributed as z, is most useful when the presence of trend is questionable. In the case of severe trend or a very strong treatment effect, the test may yield inaccurate results.

Program Name: TMSGN

Language: BASIC and FORTRAN IV versions are available

Compatibility: Should run on any system containing the appropriate language compiler (i.e., BASIC or FORTRAN).

Memory Requirements: None Specified

Cost of Program: No Charge

How to obtain a copy of the program:

The program listing, user's instructions, and sample input may be obtained by contacting:

Dr. Henry H. Emurian
Information Systems Department
University of Maryland Baltimore County
1000 Hilltop Circle
Baltimore, MD 21250
e-mail: emurian@umbc.edu

TRANSFORMATIONS - DATA

Title: Sixteen Computer Programs for Statistical and Psychometric Transformations

Author: Lewis R. Aiken

Source: *Educational and Psychological Measurement*, 1994, *54*, 98-100.

Description:

a) linear transformations of raw data for slope and intercepts
b) square root of raw data
c) power transformations of raw data
d) logarithmic transformation of raw data
e) reciprocals of raw data
f) sine transformations of proportions
g) z scores and normal curve percentages
h) three types of corrected for guessing scores for objective tests
i) transformation used when ranking test items
j) changes raw data to ranks
k) changes raw data to percentile ranks, deciles, and quartiles
l) transforms ratings to a different rating scale
m) changes a frequency distribution into relative frequency and cumulative relative distributions
n) changes raw data to standard scores
o) changes raw data to normalized z and T scores
p) assigns letter grades to scores using the modified Cajori method

Program Name: None Specified

Language: BASICA

Compatibility: IBM PC's and compatibles

Memory Requirements: None Specified

Cost of Program: No Charge

How to obtain a copy of the program:

Send a formatted 3.5" double-density diskette and a self-addressed, stamped mailer to:

Dr. Lewis R. Aiken
12449 Mountain Trail Court
Moorpark, CA 93021

TRANSFORMATION - NONNORMAL

Title: A FORTRAN Solution for Evaluating the Coefficients of the Power Method for Nonnormal Transformation

Author: Kijong Rhee

Source: *Educational and Psychological Measurement*, 1993, *53*, 107-109.

Description: This program performs nonnormal transformations using coefficients from the power method (Fleishman, 1978) in which specified skewness and kurtosis values from a standard normal variable may be obtained. This program is valuable to researchers performing Monte Carlo simulations that involve nonnormal variables.

Program Name: None Specified

Language: FORTRAN

Compatibility: The computer needs IMSL capabilities

Memory Requirements: None Specified

Cost of Program: No Charge

How to obtain a copy of the program:

Send a formatted MS-DOS 3.5" diskette and a self-addressed, stamped mailer to:

Dr. Kijong Rhee
208 Bong-Yang
Whoi-Cheon
Yang-ju
Kyung Ki-Do
482-850
Seoul, Korea

TRANSFORMATION - NORMAL

Title: UNICORN: A Program for Transforming Data to Approximate Normality

Author: David B. Allison, Bernard S. Gorman, and Elizabeth M. Kucera

Source: *Educational and Psychological Measurement*, 1995, *55*, 625-629.

Description: Computes the first four moments, the third and fourth L-moments, the Kolmogorov-Smirnov test, and the D'Agostino, Belanger, and D'Agostino (1990) tests of normality of the data for a particular variable. The output consists of an ASCII file with the transformed data..

Program Name: UNICORN

Language: BASIC

Compatibility: IBM PC's and compatibles

Memory Requirements: Less than 1 MB

Cost of Program: No Charge

How to obtain a copy of the program:

Send a formatted 3.5" diskette and a self-addressed, stamped mailer to:

Dr. David B. Allison
Obesity Research Center
Columbia University College of Physicians and Surgeons
St. Luke's-Roosevelt Hospital Center
1111 Amsterdam Avenue
New York, NY 10025
e-mail:dba8@columbia.edu

TRANSFORMATION - PROBITS

Title: A BASIC Program That Computes Probits to Suggest Optimal Data Transformations

Author: Yvette Hester

Source: *Educational and Psychological Measurement*, 1993, *53*, 689-698.

Description: This program plots the expected normal distribution values on the x axis (probits) and rank order of observations on the y axis. If the data are normally distributed, then the plot is linear. Otherwise, a transformation is in order. By examining the plot, the user can find an inverse to the plot and include it in the program (e.g., a parabolic function might need a square root transformation). The BASIC program and examples for using the program are provided in the article.

Program Name: None Specified

Language: BASIC

Compatibility: Macintosh or IBM PC's and compatibles with spreadsheet and plotting software. Any system that uses BASIC.

Memory Requirements: None Specified

Cost of Program: No Charge

How to obtain a copy of the program:

For further information, send a written request to:

Dr. Yvette Hester
Department of Mathematics
Texas A&M University
College Station, TX 77843
e-mail: hester@math.tamu.edu

TRANSFORMATION - RANDOM VARIATE

Title: A Random Variable Transformation Process

Author: Larry Scheuermann

Source: *Journal of Computers in Mathematics and Science Teaching, 1988/89, Winter, 65-68.*

Description: Discusses the program RANVAR (Moore, 1970), which transforms uniform random fractions into random variates, for the purpose of conducting Monte Carlo simulation research. Random variates may be calculated for any one of the following seven types of distributions: uniform, exponential, normal, binomial, Poisson, Pascal, and triangular.

Program Name: RANVAR

Language: BASIC

Compatibility: Any computer that supports BASIC

Memory Requirements: None Specified

Cost of Program: No Charge

How to obtain a copy of the program:

The BASIC subprograms are contained in the appendix of the article. Send a formatted 3.5" diskette and a self-addressed, stamped mailer to:

Dr. Larry Scheuermann
Department of Business Systems, Analysis, and Technology
University of Southwestern Louisiana
P.O. Box 43930
Lafayette, LA 70504-3930
e-mail: les2097@usl.edu

TRANSFORMATION - REGRESSION

Title: A Program to Determine Data Transformations
Maximizing Linear Regression

Author: William P. Dunlap and Jeffrey L. Rasmussen

Source: *Behavior Research Methods & Instrumentation,*
1982, 14, 357-358.

Description: This program utilizes the data transformation
technique proposed by Box and Cox (1964) for producing linear
relations in nonlinear paired data. Considering each of the two
variables in turn, the program iteratively solves for the best value
of lambda which is a parameter that, when optimized, maximizes
the linear regression between the two variables. User input consists
of the sample size and the relevant pairs of data points. The
transformed data may be either printed or written to an output file
for later use.

Program Name: None Specified

Language: FORTRAN IV

Compatibility: Any computer that supports FORTRAN

Memory Requirements: None Specified

Cost of Program: No Charge

How to obtain a copy of the program:

Send a blank 3.5" diskette and a
self-addressed, stamped mailer to:

Dr. William P. Dunlap
Department of Psychology
Tulane University
New Orleans, LA 70118
e-mail: dunlap@mailhost.tcs.tulane.edu

TREND ANALYSIS

Title: Orthogonal Polynomials for the Analysis of Trend

Author: Kenneth J. Berry

Source: *Educational and Psychological Measurement,* 1993,
             53, 139-141.

Description: This interactive program generates orthogonal
polynomials for equal and unequal sample sizes (or treatment
intervals) for the purpose of performing trend analysis. The input
consists of the number of treatments, specific levels of treatment,
and sample size. Examples of program usage are provided in the
article.

Program Name: TREND

Language: FORTRAN 77

Compatibility: IBM and UNIX mainframes, IBM PC's and
                    compatibles

Memory Requirements: None Specified

Cost of Program: No Charge

How to obtain a copy of the program:

The author prefers to e-mail the program,
however, you may send a formatted 3.5" diskette
and a self-addressed, stamped mailer to:

Dr. Kenneth J. Berry
Department of Sociology
Colorado State University
Fort Collins, CO 80523
e-mail: berry@lamar.colo.state.edu

TREND ANALYSIS

Title: A Computer Program for Analyzing Ordinal Trends With Dichotomous Outcomes: Application to Neuropsychological Research

Author: Domenic V. Cicchetti, Donald Showalter, Byron P. Rourke, and Darren Fuerst

Source: *The Clinical Neuropsychologist,* 1992, *6,* 458-463.

Description: Calculates Jonckheere's (1970) Z test of linear trend which is appropriate in situations where the classification or independent variable is ordinally scaled and the dependent variable is dichotomous. The user inputs the variable names and the cell frequencies for a given k x 2 contingency table. Output includes the labeled k x 2 contingency table, Jonckheere's Z test, and the corresponding p value for a two-tailed test of significance.

Program Name: None Specified

Language: C

Compatibility: IBM PC's and compatibles

Memory Requirements: None Specified

Cost of Program: No Charge

How to obtain a copy of the program:

For the C source code, a program listing and complete documentation, contact:

Dr. Domenic V. Cicchetti
Senior Research Psychologist and Biostatistician
VA Medical Center and Yale University
950 Campbell Avenue
West Haven, CT 06516
e-mail: domenic.cicchetti@yale.edu

TREND ANALYSIS

Title: TRENDMEAS: A Program for Measuring and
Correlating Trend Scores

Author: Robert J. Jannarone, James R. Lindley, and
James S. Roberts

Source: *Applied Psychological Measurement,* 1986,
10, 105.

Description: This program provides trend scores for each
individual over repeated trials on one variable and correlates these
trend scores with scores from other variables with the appropriate
significance probabilities.

Program Name: TRENDMEAS

Language: SAS, FORTRAN

Compatibility: Any system that supports SAS or
FORTRAN and IMSL

Memory Requirements: None Specified

Cost of Program: No Charge

How to obtain a copy of the program:

Specify whether you want the SAS or FORTRAN version
(or both).

Send a written request to:

Dr. James S. Roberts
Social and Behavioral Sciences Laboratory
University of South Carolina
Columbia, SC 29208
e-mail: jimbob@phar2.pharm.scar.olina.edu

UNCERTAINTY ANALYSIS

Title: SINFA: Multivariate Uncertainty Analysis for
Confusion Matrices

Author: Marilyn D. Wang

Source: *Behavior Research Methods & Instrumentation,*
1976, 8, 471-472.

Description: This program was designed for use in perceptual
experiments in which subjects identify which stimuli from a closed
set of stimuli have been presented. The amount of stimulus
information transmitted is assessed via contingent uncertainty
analysis where the contingency is between stimuli and responses.
For each stimulus dimension or feature transmitted, the program
calculates a single contingent uncertainty. Input includes the
number of stimuli, the number of features, and the stimulus-
response confusion matrix. Output consists of the uncertainty
analysis results including the partial contingent uncertainties for
each feature.

Program Name: SINFA

Language: FORTRAN IV

Compatibility: VMS mainframes

Memory Requirements: None Specified

Cost of Program: No Charge

How to obtain a copy of the program:

Send a blank 3.5" diskette and a
self-addressed, stamped mailer to:

Dr. Marilyn Demorest
Department of Psychology
University of Maryland Baltimore County
1000 Hilltop Circle
Baltimore, MD 21250
e-mail: demorest@umbc2.umbc.edu

UNIDIMENSIONAL SCALING

Title: Psychology of Computer Use: VIII. Utilizing a Nonparametric Item Response Model to Develop Unidimensional Scales: MOKSCAL

Author: Elisabeth Tenvergert, Johannes Kingma, and Terry Taerum

Source: *Perceptual and Motor Skills*, 1989, *68*, 987-1000.

Description: Analyzes dichotomous items in which one alternative is a positive marker of the underlying latent construct of interest (e.g., attitudes or ability). The scaling analyses proceed according to Mokken's model (Mokken, 1971) in which, for any unidimensional set of items, a person parameter (the number of items a person correctly responds to) and item parameters (the proportion of individuals responding correctly to each item) are calculated. Unlike the Rasch model, the (nonparametric) Mokken model does not require that the item characteristic curves be parallel. Input consists of the number of subjects, the number of items, the item data, and which items are to be included in the Mokken analysis. Output consists of four different scale reliability coefficients, the phi inverse coefficient (z) for the best start pair, the scale coefficient H, and the T statistic for scale robustness.

Program Name: MOKSCAL

Language: FORTRAN 77

Compatibility: IBM PC's and compatibles

Memory Requirements: 268K

Cost of Program: No Charge

How to obtain a copy of the program:

Send a formatted 5.25" diskette and a self-addressed, stamped mailer to:

Dr. Johannes Kingma
University Hospital at Groningen
Department of Traumatology
Groningen
Netherlands

UNIVARIATE LINEAR MODELING

Title: UGLM: A PASCAL Program for Univariate Linear Modeling

Author: J. Gary Lutz and Leigh A. Cundari

Source: *Educational and Psychological Measurement,* 1990, *50,* 113-115.

Description: This interactive program computes:

1. goodness-of-fit
2. interval and least squares point estimates of the model parameters
3. tests of specific hypotheses (repeated measures and other parametric functions)
4. most significant parametric function for each hypothesis

The user inputs the observation and fixed design matrices. The program works for up to nine parameter models. This can be used as a tool for teaching univariate modeling.

Program Name: UGLM

Language: Turbo Pascal 5.0

Compatibility: IBM PC's and compatibles

Memory Requirements: 4 MB

Cost of Program: $10 (check or money order to Lehigh University)

How to obtain a copy of the program:

Send either a 3.5" or 5.25"diskette, a self-addressed, stamped mailer, and payment to:

Dr. J. Gary Lutz
Lehigh University
Iacocca Hall
Bethlehem, PA 18015
e-mail:jgl3@lehigh.edu

UNIVARIATE STATISTICS

Title: An Elementary Statistical Package for 6502-based Microcomputers

Author: Michael David Coovert

Source: *Behavior Research Methods & Instrumentation,* 1980, *12,* 562.

Description: This statistical package computes numerous univariate procedures including (1) descriptives (with calculation of the geometric and harmonic means), (2) independent and dependent samples *t*-tests, (3) correlations, (4) chi-square analyses (with Yates correction when needed), (5) the phi statistic, and (6) one-way analysis of variance. The program is completely interactive.

Program Name: None Specified

Language: BASIC

Compatibility: IBM PC's and compatibles, Apple-based systems

Memory Requirements: A minimum of 4K

Cost of Program: No Charge

How to obtain a copy of the program:

Send a formatted 3.5" diskette and a self-addressed, stamped mailer to:

Dr. Michael D. Coovert
Department of Psychology
BEH 339
University of South Florida
Tampa, FL 33620-8200
e-mail: coovert@luna.cas.udf.edu

UTILITY ANALYSIS

Title: A Taylor-Russell/Naylor-Shine Utility Calculator

Author: Brett Myors

Source: *Behavior Research Methods, Instruments, & Computers,*
1993, *25*, 483-484.

Description: This program provides estimates of utility via the
Taylor-Russell method (in which utility is expressed as the percent
increase in performance using the new selection procedure rather
than the current procedure) and the Naylor-Shine method (in which
utility is explained by an increase in standardized criterion scores).
The input consists of the validity coefficient, selection ratio, and
base rate. The output includes both utility estimates and the
Taylor-Russell table for various values of the selection ratio and
validity coefficient given the inputted base rate.

Program Name: None Specified

Language: Microsoft C

Compatibility: IBM PC's and compatibles

Memory Requirements: None Specified

Cost of Program: No Charge

How to obtain a copy of the program:

To obtain copies of the program listings, contact:

Dr. Brett Myors
School of Psychology
University of New South Wales
P.O. Box 1
Kensington, NSW
2033
Australia
e-mail: b.hesketh@unsw.edu.au

VALIDITY COEFFICIENTS

Title: SIGVALID: Testing for Differences in Values of Validity Coefficients

Author: Michael S. Trevisan and F. Leon Paulson

Source: *Applied Psychological Measurement,* 1990, *14,* 106.

Description: The program provides multiple comparisons of validity coefficients using Marascuilo's (1966) technique. If the omnibus test is significant, then subsequent pairwise comparisons are provided. The input consists of the number of validity coefficients (up to five), sample size, and the magnitude of each coefficient.

Program Name: SIGVALID

Language: C

Compatibility: IBM PC's and compatibles

Memory Requirements: None Specified

Cost of Program: No Charge

How to obtain a copy of the program:

Send a formatted 3.5" diskette and a self-addressed, stamped mailer to:

Dr. Michael S. Trevisan
ELCP
P.O. Box 642136
Washington State University
Pullman, WA 99164-2136
e-mail: trevisan@mail.wsu.edu

VALIDITY GENERALIZATION

Title: VGBOOT: A Computer Program for Generating Bootstrap Validity Generalization Estimates, Standard Errors, and Confidence Intervals

Author: Fred S. Switzer, III

Source: *Applied Psychological Measurement,* 1991, *15,* 360.

Description: The program bootstraps the Schmidt, Gast-Rosenberg, and Hunter (1980) validity generalization procedure for estimation of standard errors and confidence intervals. Three input files are needed consisting of data and specific sampling distributions. Moreover, the number of iterations and random number generator seed may be manipulated.

Program Name: VGBOOT2

Language: Turbo Pascal 6.0

Compatibility: IBM PC's and compatibles

Memory Requirements: About 1 MB

Cost of Program: No Charge

How to obtain a copy of the program:

Send a formatted 3.5" diskette and a self-addressed, stamped mailer to:

Dr. Fred Switzer
Department of Psychology
410F Brackett Hall
Clemson University
Clemson, SC 29634-1511
e-mail: switzef@clemson.edu

VECTOR SUMS

Title: A Program for Computing the Vector Sum of Scores in a Multidimensional Test

Author: John K. Butler, Jr.

Source: *Educational and Psychological Measurement,* 1983, *43,* 849-851.

Description: This program computes the vector sums of scores for an individual and these vector sums are compared among individuals. The assumptions of unidimensionality among scales is relaxed with this procedure. The input consists of either the raw data or correlation matrix.

Program Name: None Specified

Language: SAS

Compatibility: Any computer with SAS capability

Memory Requirements: None Specified

Cost of Program: No Charge

How to obtain a copy of the program:

Send a blank 3.5" diskette and a self-addressed, stamped mailer to:

Dr. John K. Butler, Jr.
Management Department
College of Commerce and Industry
Clemson University
Clemson, SC 29631

VERBAL PROTOCOL ANALYSIS

Title: Heuristic and Statistical Support for Protocol Analysis With SHAPA Version 2.01

Author: Jeffrey M. James and Penelope M. Sanderson

Source: *Behavior Research Methods, Instruments, & Computers,* 1991, *23,* 449-460.

Description: This menu-driven program performs verbal protocol analysis in which it aids researchers in examining different possible coding schemes. Moreover, lag sequential analysis, transition matrices, and frequency of cycles are used for pattern analytic reports. Cross-reliability (kappa), value lists, and predicate instances are also provided. Examples for the utility of the program are given in the article.

Program Name: SHAPA (Version 2.01)

Language: Turbo C

Compatibility: IBM PC's and compatibles

Memory Requirements: 512K RAM

Cost of Program: $10

How to obtain a copy of the program:

Send a written request and payment to:

Dr. Penelope. M. Sanderson
Department of Mechanical and Industrial Engineering
University of Illinois at Urbana-Champaign
Urbana, IL 61801
e-mail: psanders@psych.uiuc.edu

WAVEFORM ANALYSIS

Title: Waveform Moment Analysis in Psychophysiological Research

Author: John T. Cacioppo and Donald D. Dorfman

Source: *Psychological Bulletin*, 1987, *102*, 421-438.

Description: This program computes a number of moment-based indicants (e.g., mean, variance, skewness, kurtosis) that are useful for distinguishing between psychophysiological response patterns that occur over time and that are both nonnegative (N) and bounded (B) within the amplitude and frequency domains. Such response patterns are known as NB Waveforms and the general data analytic procedure is referred to as Waveform Moments Analysis or WAMA.

Program Name: None Specified

Language: Versions are available in BASIC and ASYST

Compatibility: Apple II Plus, Apple IIe, or Apple Macintosh (BASIC version); IBM PC's and compatibles (ASYST version)

Memory Requirements: None Specified

Cost of Program: No Charge

How to obtain a copy of the program:

Send a blank formatted 3.5" diskette and a self-addressed, stamped mailer to:

Dr. John T. Cacioppo
Department of Psychology
Ohio State University
1885 Neil Avenue
Columbus, OH 43210-1222
e-mail: cacioppo.1@osu.edu

WITHIN-GROUP AGREEMENT

Title: Estimation of Quantiles for the Sampling Distribution of the r_{WG} Within-Group Agreement Index

Author: John M. Charnes and Chester A. Schriesheim

Source: *Educational and Psychological Measurement*, 1995, *55*, 435-437.

Description: This program simulates the sampling distribution of r_{WG}, the James, Demaree, and Wolf (1984) within-group agreement index (when two or more judges provide ratings for one or more targets). The output consists of 95% confidence intervals for quantiles of this sampling distribution for the purpose of significance testing. The program allows up to 30 judges and targets in which the scaling may range from 1 to 9.

Program Name: AGREESIM.FOR

Language: FORTRAN

Compatibility: Any mainframe, IBM PC and compatible, and Apple-based systems that support FORTRAN

Memory Requirements: 640K

Cost of Program: None

How to obtain a copy of the program:

Send a formatted 3.5" diskette and a self-addressed, stamped mailer to:

Dr. John M. Charnes
School of Business
University of Kansas
345 Summerfield Hall
Lawrence, KS 66045-2003
e-mail: jcharnes@ukans.edu

AUTHOR INDEX

KEY WORD INDEX